Authentic™

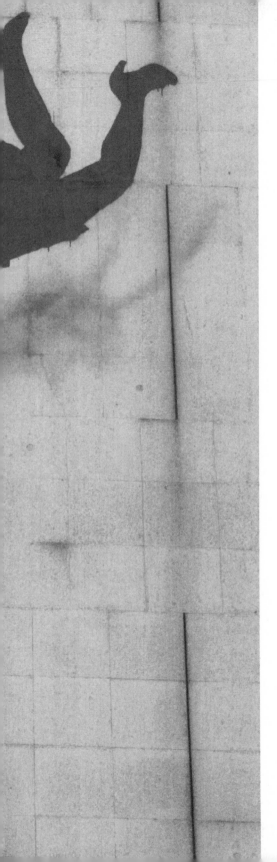

Authentic™

The Politics of
Ambivalence in a
Brand Culture

Sarah Banet-Weiser

NEW YORK UNIVERSITY PRESS
New York and London

CRITICAL CULTURAL COMMUNICATION
General Editors: Sarah Banet-Weiser and Kent A. Ono

Dangerous Curves: Latina
Bodies in the Media
Isabel Molina-Guzmán

The Net Effect: Technology,
Romanticism, Capitalism
Thomas Streeter

Our Biometric Future: The Pursuit
of Automated Facial Perception
Kelly A. Gates

Critical Rhetorics of Race
Edited by Michael G. Lacy and Kent A. Ono

Circuits of Visibility: Gender and
Transnational Media Cultures
Edited by Radha S. Hegde

Commodity Activism: Cultural
Resistance in Neoliberal Times
Edited by Roopali Mukherjee
and Sarah Banet-Weiser

Arabs and Muslims in the Media:
Race and Representation after 9/11
Evelyn Alsultany

Visualizing Atrocity: Arendt, Evil,
and the Optics of Thoughtlessness
Valerie Hartouni

The Makeover: Reality Television
and Reflexive Audiences
Katherine Sender

Authentic™: The Politics of
Ambivalence in a Brand Culture
Sarah Banet-Weiser

NEW YORK UNIVERSITY PRESS
New York and London
www.nyupress.org

References to Internet Websites (URLs) were accurate at the time of writing.
Neither the author nor New York University Press is responsible for URLs that
may have expired or changed since the manuscript was prepared.

LIBRARY OF CONGRESS CATALOGING-IN-PUBLICATION DATA
Banet-Weiser, Sarah, 1966-
Authentic TM : The politics of ambivalence in a brand culture / Sarah Banet-Weiser.
p. cm. — (Critical cultural communication)
ncludes bibliographical references and index.
ISBN 978-0-8147-8713-7 (cl : alk. paper) — ISBN 978-0-8147-8714-4 (pb   ) — ISBN 978-0-8147-
8715-1 (ebook) — ISBN 978-0-8147-3937-2 (ebook)
1. Brand name products. I. Title.
HD69.B7B256 2012
306.3—dc23
2012024949

New York University Press books

Manufactured in the United States of America
c 10 9 8 7 6 5 4 3 2 1
p 10 9 8 7 6 5 4 3 2 1

Frontispiece: *Shop Til You Drop* (detail), Banksy. Photograph by Patrick Mayon.

For my daughter,
Lily Banet Weiser,
whose irrepressible spirit
has never failed
to inspire me.

CONTENTS

ACKNOWLEDGMENTS

When you decide to write a book about contemporary branding, it inevitably ends up being a collaborative effort. As I argue throughout this book, everyone has some relationship with branding, and almost everyone has something to say about this relationship. I am grateful for the opportunity here to offer my thanks and appreciation to the many friends and colleagues who have directed me toward branding references, sent me links and examples, challenged my thinking about branding, and listened patiently while I tested out ideas.

A few folks deserve special mention for their crucial role in supporting and encouraging me to take on this admittedly huge project. I am immensely grateful to my cherished friend and colleague Josh Kun. From the moment I began thinking of branding and culture, he encouraged me, supported me, heard me out, connected me with sources, read drafts, gave me helpful and honest feedback. To quote one of his favorite pop stars: my life would suck without you. I have also had the singular pleasure of establishing a profound friendship with Inna Arzumanova over the course of the past five years. She is truly one of the most intellectually and emotionally generous people I know. She read every word of this book—many times over!—and offered brilliant feedback. As the kids say, 4LYFE, sister. Daniela Baroffio is a wonderful friend, and I am so grateful she is in my life. I simply could not have completed this project if not for our time together, solving our problems, and those of the world. I deeply appreciate her love and friendship. Eric Zinner, my editor at NYU Press, encouraged me from the beginnings of this project. He was instrumental in my thinking through this book, from his initial "Well, it's not quite there, keep working on it" to the editing of the final chapters. He is not only an extraordinary editor but also a cherished friend. Of course, I have other lives outside of the academy and beyond this project, and the maintenance of these other lives and roles made completing this book possible. My mother was quite ill at both the beginning and the end of this project. I was only able to finish this book because of the tireless energy and generosity of my sister Suzannah Collins, who stepped in and took care of literally everything. I am forever grateful to her.

There are some friends and colleagues who read entire earlier drafts of this book; their feedback has immeasurably improved the final version. Larry Gross offered helpful comments and histories to consider, and his support and intellectual generosity over the past ten years have been invaluable to me; not for nothing, I asked Dana Polan for his feedback, and as always, he provided helpful critiques and insights (particularly on the word "particular"); Steve Duncombe has had the unfortunate luck of being asked to read practically everything I have written in the past five years—I, on the other hand, have had the incredible good fortune of benefiting from his sharp insight and inspirational politics; Laurie Oullette, who continually offered brilliant feedback and whose own creative work on branding has been key to this project; and Nitin Govil, with whom I became friends later in the project, generously gave his unique insight and suggestions. Others read portions of the book and generously offered their expertise and feedback. Manuel Castells has been part of this project since the beginning; our brainstorming sessions about branding and possibility shaped the direction of this book. His generosity and kindness toward me, from inviting me to be a part of the Aftermath group in Portugal to title suggestions to his gentle pushing me to think through ideas, have been invaluable to me, as a scholar and a friend. I thank Henry Jenkins for his insightful and tough read of several chapters, which helped so much in honing my argument. Diane Winston and Jane Iwamura were key readers of chapter 5, offering crucial critique of my take on the branding of religion. Marita Sturken has been, as always, a wonderful friend and confidante, and her work on consumer culture continues to be an inspiration to me. Aniko Imre read an early draft of the introduction and gave helpful feedback (along with supportive reassurance about parenting and academic life!), and Macarena Gomez-Barris gave insightful critique of chapter 3 as well as the introduction. Cynthia Chris read a version of the introduction and gave valuable feedback on many ideas in the book. She is my touchstone; I cherish her friendship and her sharp insight, as well as her willingness to entertain me whenever I am in New York. Another New York friend, Roopali Mukherjee, inspires me with her work on commodity culture and greatly improved chapter 1 with her suggestions; working with her on *Commodity Activism* while also completing this book was a true intellectual gift. I have shared many important conversations about neoliberalism and consumerism with Nick Couldry, and I am grateful for his insights. Melissa Brough and Cara Wallis both read portions of several chapters and always offered valuable advice and generous support. Kent Ono has also been incredibly supportive, and I appreciate his willingness to offer comments and include the book in our series at NYU Press. Ciara McLaughlin at NYU Press has been patient and encouraging; it has been a delight to work with her on this project, as well as on the book series.

Susan Ecklund was a careful and skilled copyeditor for the book. I also thank Alexia Traganas from the NYU Press production department for her assistance.

I have benefited greatly from conversations and other exchanges with my good friends and colleagues over the past several years; these relationships continually sustain me. I am immensely grateful to Alison Trope, Kara Keeling, Karen Tongson, Taj Frazier, Stacy Smith, Ruthie Gilmore, Val Hartouni, Angela McRobbie, George Sanchez, Barbie Zelizer, James Hay, Alison Hearn, Anne Balsamo, Tom Streeter, Herman Gray, Susan Douglas, Toby Miller, Jo Littler, and Ellen Seiter for their unflagging support. Alison Trope was an especially important friend throughout this process. My dear friend Joyce Campion lent me her ear whenever I asked, counseled me, and basically kept me (relatively) sane in my nonacademic world. Julie Main is a sheer gift in my life; laughing, talking, and commiserating with her over the past five years has been amazingly nourishing.

More than any other project I have worked on, my students have been instrumental to the research and writing of this book. At the very beginning of this project, Jade Miller and Deborah Hanan kept me up-to-date and organized on all sorts of branding companies and practices. My first effort into the world of branding culminated in an article I coauthored with Charlotte Lapsansky, "RED Is the New Black"; it was a joy to work with her. D. Travers Scott provided professional copyediting and was a willing participant in lots of brainstorming sessions, as were Cara Wallis, Melissa Brough, Anjali Nath, Russ Newman, Joyee Chatterjee, Lana Schwartz, and John Cheney. Laura Portwood-Stacer helped me immensely with chapter 2, and lent a willing ear when I needed it. Garret Broad offered sharp insight and feedback for chapter 4; Lori Lopez, Jess Butler, and Brittany Farr provided crucial help with references and copyediting. Dayna Chatman helped out at the very end of this project, with research assistance and thoughtful ideas. Evan Brody helped out tremendously with last-minute copyediting and the index. Finally, Kevin Driscoll was a model research assistant, pushing me to think in more expansive ways about this project and always coming up with new and important examples. Other students, including undergraduates, in classes I have taught over the past five years have been a willing and supportive audience for my work and have generously indulged me when I assigned them drafts of chapters.

At the University of Southern California, my colleagues at the Annenberg School have been incredibly encouraging. My thanks go in particular to Dean Ernie Wilson, Larry Gross, Sandra Ball-Rokeach, François Bar, Peter Monge, Sheila Murphy, Peggy McLaughlin, Manuel Castells, Henry Jenkins,

Abby Kaun, Jonathan Aronson, Taj Frazier, and Michael Cody. The Annenberg staff, especially Carol Kretzer, Christine Lloreda, and Billie Shotlow, were patient and accomodating. I am grateful to the Norman Lear Center for the Study of Entertainment for generously supporting my faculty research group, BrandSpace, especially Johanna Blakely and Marty Kaplan. The members of that group, Josh Kun, Karen Tongson, Tara McPherson, Chris Smith, Alison Trope, Steve Ross, Jay Wang, Diane Winston, Andrea Hollingshead, and Henry Jenkins, provided provocative conversations and insights about the world of branding and were important to my thinking through different stages of this material. I am also grateful to the University of California Vision and Voices program, which gave me funding to hold an event with Shepard Fairey in 2009. The University of Southern California Advancing Scholarship in the Humanities and Social Sciences initiative provided a generous grant for me at the early stages of this project and made possible numerous trips to interview brand managers and marketers. The Advertising Educational Foundation awarded me a visiting professor fellowship, which allowed me to conduct a mini-ethnography of a major advertising firm in Los Angeles. I am grateful to all employees at that firm, from new hires to leadership, for generously giving me their time and guidance about the world of marketing and social media. Indeed, I am grateful to all the marketers and brand consultants whom I interviewed for this book. Those conversations were more often than not a welcome surprise, and my interviews confirmed my feeling that one should always talk to the producers of media and culture before coming to conclusions about their motivations.

During the time I was writing this book, I had the great pleasure of working with a wonderful group of people on *American Quarterly*. I have learned so much through my conversations with Claire Kim, Rosa-Linda Fregoso, George Lipsitz, Kara Keeling, Josh Kun, Macarena Gomez-Barris, Jack Halberstam, Shelley Streeby, Danny Widener, Natalia Molina, Julie Sze, Kelly Lytle Hernandez, and our beloved Clyde Woods. My time at *AQ* was, and continues to be, made possible by the tireless energy and impressive work of Jih-Fei Cheng. The Aftermath group, organized by Manuel Castells, met for the past three years of this project in beautiful Lisbon, Portugal, and I was able to try out many of these ideas with the wonderful participants of that group. I am especially grateful to Tehri Rentanen and Rosalind Williams for their insight and sisterhood.

Throughout the past six years, I have given many talks on this material that have provided me with helpful feedback, incisive critiques that have made me think, and stimulated provocative conversations: the Annenberg School for Communication and Journalism, USC; the Annenberg School at the University of Pennsylvania; University of California, Santa Cruz; University of California, San Diego; the Society of Cinema and Media Studies; the American Studies Association; the International Communication Association; Goldsmiths University, UK; the Institute for Communication Research, University of Lisbon, Portugal; Pennsylvania State University; the School of Cinematic Arts, USC; and the Department of Communication at the University of Washington.

I am also grateful to the anonymous readers of the manuscript—their comments and critiques made this a better book to be sure. And, David Lobenstine, who carefully edited and made suggestions on the final version of this manuscript, was immeasurably helpful. He was a true gift at the end of a long journey.

Parts of chapter 3 are derived from my essay "Convergence on the Street: Rethinking the Authentic/Commercial Divide," published in *Cultural Studies,* September/October 2011; as well as an essay coauthored with Marita Sturken, "The Politics of Commerce: Shepard Fairey and the New Cultural Entrepreneur," in *Blowing Up the Brand,* edited by Melissa Aroncyzk and Devon Powers (Peter Lang, 2011). Part of chapter 2 was published as an essay, "Branding the Post-feminist Self: Girls' Video Production and YouTube," in *Mediated Girlhoods,* edited by Mary Celeste Kearney (Peter Lang, 2010).

Finally, but most important, I am grateful to my family for all their patience, love, and support. My mother, Anne Banet, is unfaltering in her support and pride in me; I hope she knows how much I appreciate it. My siblings, Angela, Matt, Suzannah, Genevieve, and Joey, have always been there for me; they are so important to my life. Kathy and Les Weiser encouraged me and supported me throughout this entire endeavor. During the past five years, I have watched—often with anxiety!—my son Sam develop into a thoughtful and interesting adult. His forceful personality and self-confidence have been an inspiration. My son Lucas makes parenting look easy (which it is not)—his sense of personal responsibility, sharp intelligence, and sheer generosity are a steadfast joy in my life. My husband, Bill Weiser, has been patient and loving throughout, listening to my talks, giving feedback to my ideas, and picking up on all the daily life things I have ignored; I am forever grateful to him. And I remember my promise. Finally, my daughter, Lily Banet Weiser, is a light in my life, a sheer delight to be around, a beautiful spirit. She personifies the most excellent kind of girl power, and this book is dedicated to her.

INTRODUCTION

BRANDING THE AUTHENTIC

If there is, among all words, one that is inauthentic, then surely it is
the word "authentic."
Maurice Blanchot[1]

Welcome to the future of Los Angeles. It is a city made up entirely of brands, logos, and trademarked characters. Every visual landmark in the city has been stamped with a brand. Every resident is a branded or licensed character: Ronald MacDonald wreaks havoc on the city, the cops are the rounded, treaded lumps of the Michelin tire logo, crowds of people are depicted as the America On-Line instant message logo, Bob's Big Boy is taken hostage and finds a love match in the Esso girl. Anonymous individuals walk around the city with the trademark symbol ™ hovering about their heads. Scanning the skyline, we see the U-Haul building, the Eveready skyscraper, the MTV apartment building.

Corporate logos—Microsoft, BP, Enron, Visa, and countless others— blanket the city's infrastructure, including the roads, cars, and even the city zoo. The animals in the zoo are also brands: the lion of Metro-Goldwyn-Mayer film corporation, the alligator from Lacoste clothing company, and Microsoft Window's butterflies, with the zoo tour bus driven by the iconic Mr. Clean.

Logorama's brand landscape.

Ronald McDonald holding Bob's Big Boy hostage.

This is the world of *Logorama*, a sixteen-minute animated short film written and directed in 2009 by the French creative collective H5, composed of François Alaux, Hervé de Crécy, and Ludovic Houplain.[2] The film's simple and familiar narrative—which replicates an age-old trope of good versus evil—takes place in a futuristic, stylized, war-zone Los Angeles, where a homicidal psychopath armed with a gun takes people hostage, wreaks havoc on the city, and leads the police in a prolonged, violent chase. After the hostages escape, a natural apocalypse ensues: an earthquake destroys LA, and what is left is immediately drowned with a tidal wave of oil. *Logorama*, in its own quirky, campy way, is a warning about the future.

What are we warned about? Brands. The motivation behind *Logorama*, according to the filmmakers, is to demonstrate the extent to which brands are ubiquitous, embedded in every aspect of our lives and relationships. The violent film, crafted entirely out of brands (more than 2,500 are used in the film), is an indictment of their ubiquity. The filmmakers intend the film as a critique of how a rabid consumerism is now taken for granted in Western culture. In their "alarming universe," they collapse the distinction between (and thus reinforce the connection between) brands and individuals, brands and violence, and brands and natural disasters.[3]

In some ways, the subject matter of *Logorama* is also the subject matter of this book. The critique of consumer culture that is the heart of *Logorama* is also a critique of something else, equally important but perhaps even harder to define: the loss of a kind of authenticity. In the US, the 21st century is an age that hungers for anything that *feels* authentic, just as we lament more and more that it is a world of inauthenticity, that we are governed by superficiality. People pay exorbitant rents to live in the part of town that is edgy and "real," that has not yet sold out to bland suburbia; we go to extraordinary lengths to prove we are not "sellouts"; we defensively define ourselves as "authentic." Throughout, there is the looming sense that we are not real enough, that our world is becoming more and more inauthentic, despite our endless efforts to the contrary. *Logorama* fulfills our dark fears, epitomizes our great laments: it is a world where brands are everywhere, where even culture has been branded, where even authenticity has been trademarked.

I became interested in brand cultures because I was thinking about what consumer citizenship means within contemporary capitalism. In my previous work, I examined consumer citizenship from a variety of vantage points, such as postfeminist culture and the television industry, but the current moment felt different to me. Business models were now being used as structuring frameworks for cultural institutions such as the university, as well as for social change movements. My own students, eager for career advice, were now asking me about how to build a "self-brand." I was struck by the use of market language in US politics, from the "Obama brand" to endless press accounts of how Democrats and Republicans have succeeded in trademarking their message, or protecting their brand. Perhaps most urgently, I was interested in, and dismayed by, the endless ways that people use the logic, strategies, and language of brands as a dominant way to express our politics, our creativity, our religious practices—indeed, our very selves.

This book is my attempt to define the processes that create the world of contemporary branding. Branding in our era has extended beyond a business model; branding is now both reliant on, and reflective of, our most basic social and cultural relations. First, then, a few definitions. I use the term "brand" to refer to the intersecting relationship between marketing, a product, and consumers. "Brand cultures" refers to the way in which these types of brand relationships have increasingly become cultural contexts for everyday living, individual identity, and affective relationships. There are different brand cultures that at times overlap and compete with each other: the brand culture of street art in urban spaces, religious brand cultures such as "New Age spirituality" and "Prosperity Christianity," the culture of green branding with its focus on the environment. The practice of branding is typically understood as a complex economic tool, a method of attaching social or cultural meaning to a commodity as a means to make the commodity more personally resonant with an individual consumer. But it is my argument that in the contemporary era, brands are about *culture* as much as they are about economics. As marketers have continually relayed to me, brands are meant to invoke the experience associated with a company or product; far from the cynical view of academics, or beleaguered parents, brands are actually a story told to the consumer.[4] When that story is successful, it surpasses simple identification with just a tangible product; it becomes a story that is familiar, intimate, personal, a story with a unique history. Brands become the setting around which individuals weave their own stories, where individuals position themselves as the central character in the narrative of the brand: "I'm a Mac user," many of us say smugly, or, "I drink Coke, not Pepsi." While brands are visible and often audible, through symbols and logos, through jingles and mottoes, through all means of visual and auditory design—and occasionally, even through a smell!—the definition of a brand exceeds its materiality. More than just the object itself, a brand is the perception—the series of images, themes, morals, values, feelings, and sense of authenticity conjured by the product itself. The brand is the essence of what will be experienced; the brand is a promise as much as a practicality.

Because a brand's value extends beyond a tangible product, the process of branding—if successful—is different from commodification: it is a cultural phenomenon more than an economic strategy. Commodification implies the literal transformation of things into commodities; branding is a much more deeply interrelated and diffused set of dynamics. To commodify something means to turn it into, or treat it as, a commodity; it means to make commercial something that was not previously thought of as a product, such as a melody or racial identity. Commodification is a marketing strategy, a monetization of different spheres of life, a transformation of social and cultural life into something that can be bought and sold. In contrast, the process of branding impacts the way we understand who we are, how we organize ourselves in the world, what stories we tell ourselves about ourselves. While commodities are certainly part of branding—indeed, commodities are a crucial part of these stories about ourselves—the process of branding is broader, situated within culture. It is this cultural process of branding—that marks the transformation of everyday, lived culture to brand culture—with which this book is concerned.

Even if we discard as false a simple opposition between the authentic and the inauthentic, we still must reckon with the power of authenticity—of the self, of experience, of relationships. It is a symbolic construct that, even in a cynical age, continues to have cultural value in how we understand our moral frameworks and ourselves, and more generally how we make decisions about how to live our lives. We want to believe—indeed, I argue that we *need* to believe—that there are spaces in our lives driven by genuine affect and emotions, something outside of mere consumer culture, something above the reductiveness of profit margins, the crassness of capital exchange.

In the following chapters, then, I examine cultural spaces that we like to think of as "authentic"—self-identity, creativity, politics, and religion—and the ways these spaces are increasingly formed as branded spaces, structured by brand logic and strategies, and understood and expressed through the language of branding. This transformation of culture of everyday living into brand culture signals a broader shift, from "authentic" culture to the branding of authenticity. Contemporary brand cultures are so thoroughly imbricated with culture at large that they become indistinguishable from it.

So I ask, in the ensuing pages: What happens to authenticity in a brand culture? What are the stakes for living in a world that resembles *Logorama*? While I resist the causal relationship implied by the film—brand culture unequivocally leads to global disaster—I do have grave concerns about the increasing presence in the West of brands as symbolic structures for crafting selves, creativity, politics, and spirituality. At the same time, I try to avoid the simple assumption that situates branding and consumer culture as oppositional to "real" politics and culture. Not all brand cultures are the same, nor do they contain the same pitfalls (or promises). Rather than generalize all branding strategies as egregious effects of today's market, and think wistfully of a bygone world that was truly authentic, it is more productive to situate brand cultures in terms of their ambivalence, where both economic imperatives and "authenticity" are expressed and experienced simultaneously. Thus, this book looks at key cultural contexts where we craft our individual identities—the realms of creativity, religion, politics, history—to see how brand cultures operate within them, and analyzes these contexts for their productive contradictions.

The Culture of the Brand

Everyone who lives in the US in the 21st century has a relationship with brands: the products that we recognize from an image or even just a font; the numerous items that we buy (or try to avoid buying) because they are made by a particular company. Coca-Cola, Apple, Starbucks, Levi's, Visa, MTV, and thousands of others inundate the cultural, economic, and political landscape of everyday life.

The legitimacy of the brand is now established, regularized, and surveyed in a way that is unique to contemporary culture. But precisely because of the uniqueness of our branded landscape, it can be understood by looking at its connections to earlier histories of the market and culture. In the US of the 18th century, branding was the very literal process of creating and distributing a brand name that was protected by a trademark. This was signified, for instance, by the branding of cattle so that ranchers could differentiate their herds. The emergence of mass production as part of the industrialization of the 19th century, alongside changes in technologies (including printing and design), transportation, and labor practices, ushered in a new era of branding.[5] As branding became more of a normative practice, commodities began to take on cultural "value" because of the way in which they were imaged, packaged, and distributed in an increasingly competitive commercial landscape.[6] The attention (and money) paid to the way a product was branded and distributed only increased in the 20th century. By the mid-20th century, as I develop in chapter 1, companies recognized what Liz Moor signals as the heightened "necessity of cultural value for economic value" and leveraged branding as a way to market to a mass culture, a strategy that took shape in an America marked by immigration, persistent social and cultural conflict, and two world wars. Moor notes that after World War II, "People were encouraged to buy these brand-name products as a sign of their own loyalty to this new version of America, but the success of such injunctions appears to have depended in large part upon the fact that brand-name commodities would have fulfilled a pressing social need for common bonds, and for a common vernacular language, among socially disparate groups during a time of immense upheaval."[7]

My focus here is on the later 20th and early 21st centuries, when branding seems to be fulfilling an even more "pressing social need" in the US: arguably all areas of social relations and cultural life are commercialized, and common bonds and common language are articulated and experienced, as corporations have longed dreamed, through consumption.[8] Given the reliance of Fordist and post-Fordist capitalism on marketing and advertising, the eventual emergence of branding as a primary marketing strategy and cultural form makes sense. The connection between marketing, commercialization, and cultural values, however, is neither direct nor deterministic. The relationship between commerce and culture is formed obliquely, through a multilayered set of dynamic historical discourses. As Viviana Zelizer argues, historically there has been a general aversion to monetizing the relationships between individuals and culture; in law, social arrangements, and individual relations there has been a "resistance to evaluating human beings in monetary terms."[9] But changes in Western political economies, from industrialization to liberal capitalism to post-Fordist capitalism to neoliberalism, mark shifts not only in how culture itself is valued but also in how individuals themselves are given particular value.

As Zelizer reminds us, economic exchange is organized in and by cultural meanings.[10] But contemporary brand culture also comes at this dynamic from the opposite direction: *cultural meanings are organized by economic exchange.* The process of branding is created and validated in these interrelated dynamics. As I discuss throughout this book, a number of entangled discourses and practices are involved in the complex process of branding: it entails the making and selling of immaterial things—feelings and affects, personalities and values—rather than actual goods. It engages the labor of consumers so that there is not a clear demarcation between marketer and consumer, between seller and buyer. The engagement of consumers as part of building brands, through such practices as consumer-generated content online and the coproduction of brands by consumers through customization, potentially engenders new relationships between the buyer and the bought, the latest in an ever-expanding catalog of branding logic and language.

Celia Lury points out that the invention of "social marketing" and the increasing reliance of contemporary marketers on nonbusiness approaches (such as anthropology and sociology) have encouraged a shift in perception on the part of both consumers and marketers as to what it means to "brand" a product.[11] Indeed, Lury notes that one of the key stages in late 20th-century branding practices is "a changed view of the producer-consumer relationship: no longer viewed in terms of stimulus-response, the relation was increasingly conceived of as an exchange."[12] This changed relationship requires labor on the part of both consumers and marketers. This is perhaps most starkly demonstrated in the increasing corporate use of social media, such as when a corporation has a "personal" Facebook page; or uses of YouTube to promote commercial endeavors, where consumers and marketers engage in "authentic" exchanges that help to build corporate brands. Through the use of such social media, marketers increasingly assume (and exploit) the existence of consumers' dialogic relationship with cultural products and emphasize an affective exchange between corporations and consumers. As a relationship based on exchange (even if this is an unequal exchange), branding cannot be explained as commodification or as the mere incorporation of cultural spheres of life by advanced capitalism. As Tiziana Terranova has pointed out, explaining the labor of consumers as commodification or corporate appropriation usually presumes the co-optation of an "authentic" element of a consumer's life by a marketer: the creation of street art, for instance, when sponsored by a corporation is understood as "selling out"; a similar "crime" against authenticity is the manufacturing of T-shirts featuring the words "Jesus is my homeboy," which are then sold at chain retail stores.[13] Explaining brand culture as a sophisticated form of corporate appropriation, then, keeps intact the idea that corporate culture exists outside—indeed, in opposition to—"authentic" culture. Rather than thinking of incorporation by capital from some "authentic" place outside of consumerism, brand culture requires a more complex frame of analysis, where incorporation, as Terranova points out, is not about capital encroaching on authentic culture but rather is a process of transforming and shifting cultural labor into capitalist business practices.[14] This channeling of labor into business practices is precisely what mobilizes the building of brand cultures by individual consumers and what distinguishes brand culture in the contemporary moment. It is also a hallmark of contemporary social media and consumer participation, which in turn distinguishes branding from more conventional marketing.

In a broad sense, one of the initial motivating factors for me in writing this book involved thinking through these kinds of politics within advanced capitalism. While I recognize how commodification works as a powerful corporate tool in advanced capitalism, it also seemed that the ubiquity of brand culture signaled something else. Brand cultures are not the same across all contexts. Commodities and money do not circulate in the same way in different spheres of life. I discuss these different modes of circulation in the chapters in this book and think about the ways brand cultures also authorize consumption as praxis—the act of buying goods that have a politics attached to them or critiquing consumer culture through corporate-sponsored street art.[15]

In the contemporary US, building a brand is about building an affective, authentic *relationship* with a consumer, one based—just like a relationship between two people—on the accumulation of memories, emotions, personal narratives, and expectations. Brands create what Raymond Williams called a structure of feeling, an ethos of intangible qualities that resonate in different ways with varied communities.[16] We cannot productively think about brand culture, or what brands mean for culture, without accounting for the affective relational quality—the *experience*—of brands. These affective relationships with brands are slippery, mobile, and often ambivalent, which makes them as powerful and profitable as they are difficult to predict and discuss. It is through these affective relationships that our very selves are created, expressed, and validated. Far more than an economic strategy of capitalism, brands are the cultural spaces in which individuals feel safe, secure, relevant, and authentic.

Culture, in this sense, indicates the values and affect, the hopes and anxieties, the material artifacts and the power dynamics upon which we construct our individual lives, our communities, our histories. Williams, when writing about the "ordinariness" of culture in 1958, perhaps could not have predicted the ways in which capitalism would come to define global networks of production, consumption, and distribution.[17] He situated culture and capitalism as related but not determined by each other; he opposed the idea that relations of production could somehow direct culture because culture is something made "by living." And yet in a moment of global advanced capitalism, the making—and selling, and using—of things is often impossible to separate from the ways that we make our own lives. Brand strategies and logics are not only the backdrop but also become the tools for "living" in culture. Culture is some thing, some place, that is made and remade, and therefore depends on individuals in relation to a system of production. In the contemporary moment, branding is part of this making and remaking, and is part of culture that is produced and given meaning by consumers. There is of course much that is left out of culture if we rely on a static definition of capitalism as its central frame.[18] Yet as brand logic and strategies become normative contexts for the forming of individual and social relations of affect and emotion, the relationship between culture and economic logic grows deeper and more entangled. Connecting brand to culture thus challenges a historical aversion to defining culture in economic terms, but not because brand culture simply "seeks to bring all human action into the domain of the market."[19] Rather than positioning the market as my entry point in this analysis, following Williams I center *culture*, focusing on the ways in which it is continually reimagined and reshaped, a process inherently ambivalent and contradictory. US culture is predicated not on the separate domains of individual experience, everyday life, and the market but rather on their deep interrelation.

The interpenetration of brands and culture is not simply another logical stop on a capitalist continuum. Rather, a great deal is at stake in a life lived through the culture of brands. When individuals invest in brands as "authentic" culture, it privileges individual relationships over collective ones and helps to locate the individual, rather than the social, as a site for political action (or inaction) and cultural change (or merely exchange).

Clamoring for Authenticity

The authentic is tricky to define. Its definition has been the subject of passionate debates involving far-ranging thinkers, from Plato to Marx, from Andy Warhol to Lady Gaga. I am not offering a new definition of authenticity. Nor am I arguing for a return to a "pure," unbranded authenticity. I am, however, thinking about how, and in what ways, the concept of authenticity remains central to how individuals organize their everyday activities and craft their very selves. Moreover, in a culture that is increasingly understood and experienced through the logic and strategies of commercial branding, and in a culture characterized by the postmodern styles of irony, parody, and the superficial, the concept of authenticity seems to carry even *more* weight, not less. In the following pages, I explore the ways in which the "authentic" is brought to bear in brand culture. More specifically, I discuss the maintenance of authenticity in two, interrelated ways: as a cultural space defined by branding, and as a relationship between consumers and branders.

Many scholars of consumer culture, both historical and contemporary, have argued that in the face of brands and commodities we risk a loss of "authentic" humanity. The branded spaces I examine in *Authentic*™—the self, creativity, politics, religion—are precisely those spaces that have been historically understood as "authentic," positioned and understood as outside the crass realm of the market. What is understood (and experienced) as authentic is considered such precisely because it is perceived as *not* commercial. Even when history bears out the fallacy of this binary, as it inevitably does, individuals continue to invest in the notion that authentic spaces exist—the space of the self, of creativity, of spirituality. Social theorists and commentators from Rousseau to Marx to Thoreau have contemplated the space of the authentic as a space that is not material.[20] This arrangement is mirrored within individuals: the authentic resides in the inner self (or, for Marx, the unalienated self); the outer self is merely an expression, a performance, and is often corrupted by material things (and more specifically, as Marx points out so eloquently, by capitalism). Thoreau and Rousseau saw a clear distinction between the authentic inner self and the performative outer self and saw social and cultural relations as a potential threat to individual authenticity. For these thinkers, as well as Marx, this threat was not empty but had serious consequences, leading individuals to invert values and fetishize commodities as if they were living things. The inauthentic, commercial world alienates us from social interaction and constructs such interactions as spurious and dehumanizing.[21]

The binary link between commercial and inauthentic, and noncommercial and authentic, is no doubt too simple. But at the same time, it seems that even the theorizing of Marx and others is no longer adequate to describe the penetration of the material world into our inner lives. It is becoming more and more clear that brand culture shapes not only consumer habits but also political, cultural, and civic practices, so that, in the contemporary era, brands have become what Lury calls a "logos" that structures, rationalizes, and cultivates everyday life.[22] The concept of brands as logos, and the idea that branding is a primary context for identity construction and creative production, indicates a shift in focus from our persistent frame of reference: instead of debating whether or not we fetishize the commodities we buy, and whether or not those commodities oppress the people who make them, I am now thinking through what it means that authenticity *itself* is a brand, and that "authentic" spaces are branded.

Some contemporary scholars use this perilous state of authenticity as a central focus in their critique of Western consumption. Naomi Klein published her manifesto against global consumer culture, *No Logo*, in 2000, which resonated with a large audience, many of whom were nervous and angry at the sophisticated methods of contemporary advertising and branding and the seeming unstoppable presence of messages to consume, on billboards, in music videos, on the streets. Klein warned citizens to pay attention to "brands, not products," asking us to think deeper than the discrete consumer purchase and to look at how global capitalism structures our lives.[23] And, indeed, within the 21st century, branding and advertising strategies are increasingly complex, especially in a digital media environment where viral ads, guerrilla marketing, online consumer campaigns and competitions, and user feedback mechanisms are ways for corporations to script advertising messages that feel distinctly noncommercial, and therefore authentic.[24]

In this thoroughly branded landscape, two opposing schools of thought have emerged in the last few decades. I term these the "anticonsumerism" and the "consumer-as-agent" camps. The former is composed primarily of critical scholars, such as Klein, Kalle Lasn, Juliet Schor, Thomas Frank, and other anticonsumerism scholars and activists, who rightly point out the ubiquity of advertising, marketing, and branding in everyday life.

However, their critiques often maintain the same distinct boundary between a consumer capitalist space and an authentic one as Thoreau, Rousseau, and Marx did in earlier periods of capitalism.[25] For these contemporary thinkers, as with their predecessors, authenticity is still possible because they believe space exists outside of consumer capitalism.

This binary is particularly present in indictments over "selling cool," where marketers and advertisers have a long history of appropriating counterculture aesthetics, reformulating an aesthetics of resistance into something marketable, thus dissipating any fear or anxiety about what might be the consequences of such resistance.[26] Related to this, Michael Serazio, in his work on guerrilla marketing, makes a plea to citizens "for consumer restraint and reflection—advocating *true* discipline and *real* discovery external to commercial culture."[27] Klein calls advertisers and marketers who sell cool "cultural traitors," implying that the context for everyday living is one in which "selling out" is a viable, if undesirable, action to take. Lasn's anticonsumerist magazine *Adbusters* features strategies (in a kind of updated Situationist style) to help us expose advertising as an elaborate hoax, which manipulates and tricks consumers at every turn. These arguments all revolve around an accepted notion of corporate appropriation or a Marxist idea of alienated labor—either of which presumes a market determination and a dynamic of power that, albeit sophisticated and networked, nonetheless functions linearly.

Henry Jenkins, Clay Shirky, and Yochai Benkler (among others) are prominent representatives of the opposing camp. They argue that the anticonsumerism position gives too much power to advertisers and not enough to consumers.[28] For these theorists, "selling cool" is not always a manipulative corporate hoax or a co-optation of the authentic. Instead, they recognize the complicated ways in which cultural dynamics and media converge. In these accounts, the relationship between consumers and corporate power might be about profit motive, but it also can pave the way for a range of other kinds of relations to consumers. Consumers and advertisers coexist (though perhaps in contradiction) in this landscape. The problem in these accounts is that power clearly does not function on an equal playing field within advanced capitalism, so that a singular focus on *who* has more power—the corporate brand or the consumer—misses out on how power is created as a dynamic, often contradictory force, and similarly maintains a pristine definition of the authentic. Concentrating on individual and corporate uses of power within brand culture obscures the ways in which other entangled discourses in culture are deeply interrelated within it. In other words, power does not always work in a predictable, logical way, as something either corporations or individuals can possess and wield. Power is often exercised in contradictory ways, and brand cultures, like other cultures, are ambivalent, often holding possibility for individual resistance and corporate hegemony simultaneously. Individual resistance within consumer

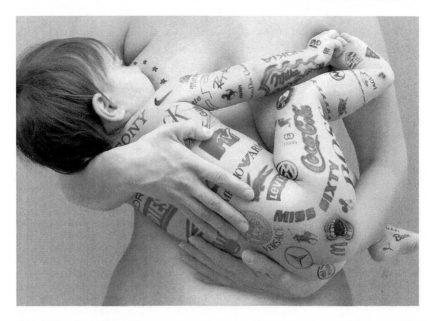

Brand Baby, featured in *Adbusters*, no. 91, Revolution Issue, 2009.

culture is defined and exercised within the parameters of that culture; to assume otherwise is to believe in a space outside consumerism that is somehow unfettered by profit motive and the political economy. This is nostalgia for authenticity.

I position the authentic differently from either an anticonsumerism or a consumer-as-agent position.[29] Brand culture is not defined by a smooth flow of content across media platforms or cooperation between multiple media industries, nor is it a context for consistent corporate appropriation. What other explanations can be found if we look beyond the authentic versus the fake, the empowered consumer versus corporate dominance? This kind of explanation needs to begin with an understanding of brand cultures as culture, complete with competing power relations and individual production and practice. And, this explanation is largely missing from scholarly discourse on consumption and branding, and allows us to analyze the cultural meanings of branding without resorting to a binary that is often unproductive. Within contemporary brand culture the separation between the authentic self and the commodity self not only is more blurred, but this blurring is more *expected and tolerated*. That is, within contemporary consumer culture we take it for granted that authenticity, like anything else, can be branded. In the current moment, rather than representing the loss of authentic humanity, the authentic and commodity self are intertwined within brand culture, where authenticity is itself a brand.

But authenticity is not only understood and experienced as the pure, inner self of the individual, it is also a relationship between individuals and commodity culture that is constructed as "authentic."[30] The organization of cultural meaning by economic exchange does not mean, by default, that the relationship individuals have with commodities is spurious or inauthentic; rather, that exchange is a construction of a relationship within the parameters of brand culture. Consider, for example, contemporary individuals' relationship with religion constituted through branded megachurches and burgeoning industries such as yoga; the revitalization of urban cities as branded, creative spaces for people to "authentically" express themselves; the amplifying mandate to develop a "self-brand" as a way to strategically market oneself personally and professionally. Appending "brand" to "culture," then, indicates not only the revaluation of culture but also a mapping out of the affective and authentic relationships that are formed *within* brand cultures—relationships that are unique to this historical moment, shaped by both the constraints and the possibilities of a brand-obsessed world.

While there is much to be said about how and why particular brand campaigns are successful and others are not, or about how marketers need to engage audiences through brand relationships, this book is not about how we react emotionally to particular brands like, say, Coke or Apple; nor is it about how to craft clever branding campaigns, or how to build a better or more fulfilling relationship between brands and consumers. Rather, I examine how areas of our lives that have historically been considered noncommercial and "authentic"—namely, religion, creativity, politics, the self—have recently become branded spaces. These cultural spaces of presumed authenticity not only are often created and sustained using the same kinds of marketing strategies that branding managers use to sell products but also are increasingly only legible in culture through and within the logic and vocabulary of the market. This book, then, is my attempt to think through what it means to live in advanced capitalism, to live a life through brands. The spaces I explore in the following pages are spaces that have been historically considered "authentic," that are now increasingly formed as branded spaces, undergirded by brand logic and articulated through the language of branding. Above all else, my argument here is that branding is different from commercialization or marketing: it is deeply, profoundly cultural. As culture, it is ambivalent. To understand what is at stake in living in brand cultures, we need to account for this ambivalence, explore its possibilities, and think about what the emergence of brand culture means for individual identities, the creation of culture, and the formation of power.

1

BRANDING CONSUMER CITIZENS

GENDER AND THE EMERGENCE OF BRAND CULTURE

Download our free self-esteem tools!
—Dove website

In October 2006, the promotion company Ogilvy & Mather created "Evolution," the first in a series of viral videos for Dove soap.[1] The ninety-five-second video advertisement depicts an ordinary woman going through elaborate technological processes to become a beautiful model: through time-lapse photography, we watch the woman having makeup applied and her hair curled and dried. The video then cuts to a computer screen, where the woman's face is airbrushed to make her cheeks and brow smooth, as well as Photoshopped and manipulated: her neck is elongated, her eyes widened, her nose narrowed.

The video is not subtle; it is a blatant critique of the artificiality and unreality of the women produced by the beauty industry. The concluding tagline reads, "No wonder our perception of beauty is distorted. Take part in the Dove Real Beauty Workshops for Girls."

According to its website, the Dove Campaign for Real Beauty is "a global effort that is intended to serve as a starting point for societal change and act as a catalyst for widening the definition and discussion of beauty."[2] It is

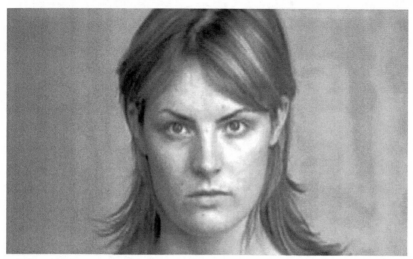

The "before" image of the Dove "Evolution" ad.

one of a growing number of brand efforts that harness the politicized rheto-ric of commodity activism. In short, the "Evolution" video makes a plea to consumers to act politically through consumer behavior—in this case, by establishing a very particular type of brand loyalty with Dove products. The company suggested that by purchasing Dove products, and by inserting themselves into this ad campaign, consumers could "own" their personalized message. Rather than the traditional advertising route of buying advertising slots to distribute the video, Dove posted it on YouTube. It quickly became a viral hit, with millions of viewers sharing the video through email and other media-sharing websites.[3] Well received outside of advertising, the video won the Viral and Film categories Grand Prix awards at Cannes Lions 2007.

With its self-esteem workshops and bold claim that the campaign can be a "starting point for societal change," the Dove Campaign for Real Beauty is a current example of commodity activism, one of the ways that advertisers and marketers use brands as lucrative avenues for social activism, and social movements in turn use brands as launch points for specific political issues.[4] Commodity activism reshapes and reimagines forms and practices of social (and political) activism into marketable commodities and takes specific form within brand culture.[5] It has a heightened presence in today's neoliberal era, which has seen an incorporation of politics and anticonsumption practices into the logics of merchandising, the ubiquity of celebrity activists and phi-lanthropists, and yet a new configuration of the consumer citizen. Like other forms of social or political activism, commodity activism hinges on a central

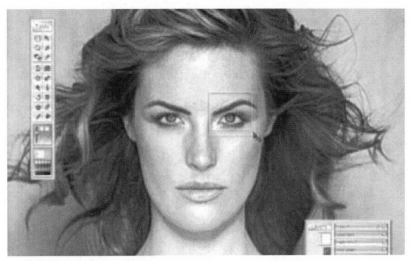

The "after" image of the Dove "Evolution" ad.

goal of empowerment. However, despite the social-change rhetoric framing much commodity activism, the empowerment aimed for is most often personal and individual, not one that emerges from collective struggle or civic participation. In this context of brand culture, the individual is a flexible commodity that can be packaged, made, and remade—a commodity that gains value through self-empowerment.

Commodity activism takes shape within the logic and language of branding and is a compelling example of the ambivalence that structures brand culture. This kind of activism not only illustrates the contradictions, contingencies, and paradoxes shaping consumer capital today but also exemplifies the connections—sometimes smooth, sometimes contradictory—between merchandising, political ideologies, and consumer citizenship. The Dove campaign represents a historical moment of transition, Joseé Johnston notes, characteristic of the kind of change unique to contemporary commodity activism: "While formal opportunities for citizenship seemed to retract under neoliberalism, opportunities for a lifestyle politics of consumption rose correspondingly."[6] Dove offers a productive lens not only into this rise but also into the concurrent retraction of social services and collective organizing that are characteristic of the current political economy—in other words, into the contemporary neoliberal world where anyone, apparently, can become a successful entrepreneur, can find and express their authentic self, or can be empowered by the seemingly endless possibilities in digital spaces, and yet where the divide between rich and poor continues to grow. In this context, personal empowerment is ostensibly realized through occupying the subject position of the consumer citizen. According to today's market logic, consumer citizens can satisfy their individual needs through consumer behavior, thus rendering unnecessary the collective responsibilities that have historically been expected from a citizen.[7]

Dove is merely one example of an increasingly visible kind of commodity activism in the 21st-century brand culture of the US. Certainly, commodity activism did not appear as a direct result of late 20th-century and early 21st-century neoliberal capitalism. Boycotts, such as those in US civil rights movements for equal African American and white consumer rights, Ralph Nader's consumer advocacy of the 1960s and 1970s, and the emergence of "ethical consumption" in the 1980s, could be accurately called commodity activism.[8] In this chapter, I am interested in tracing the relationships these histories have with contemporary definitions of branded activism.

Contemporary forms of commodity activism are often animated by and experienced through brand platforms. Individual consumers demonstrate their politics by purchasing particular brands over others in a competitive marketplace; specific brands are attached to political aims and goals, such as Starbucks coffee and fair trade, or a RED Gap T-shirt and fighting AIDS in Africa. Contemporary commodity activism positions political action as part of a competitive, capitalist brand culture, so that activism is reframed as realizable through supporting particular brands; activism is as easy as a swipe of your credit card. This competitive context for commodity activism, like the context for brands themselves, means that some forms of activism have a heightened visibility while others are rendered invisible. That is, if activism is retooled as a kind of product that either prospers or fails through capitalism's circuits of exchange, then some kinds of activism are more "brandable" than others. The vocabulary of brand culture is mapped onto social and political activism, so that the forces that propel and legitimate competition among and between brands also do the same kind of cultural work for activism.

Within these dynamics, the brand is the legitimating factor, no matter what the specific political ideology or practice in question. That is, the flexibility of branding enables a given brand to absorb politics, but that flexibility is subject to the market. In the case of Dove, the politics embraced by the company involves gender and self-esteem. To be blunt, girls' self-esteem is hot: there are best-selling books and Hollywood movies about "mean girls," eating disorders continue to be a problem for young girls (and one that is not confined to the white middle class), popular culture is constantly regaling the latest efforts by female celebrities to conform to an idealized feminine body. Girls' self-esteem in the early 21st century, in other words, is remarkably brandable.

While I argue in this book for a broad definition of brand cultures, experienced through expansive brand logics and strategies, in this chapter I examine broad ramifications through a focus on one specific brand. Dove, owned by the global personal care company Unilever, is currently the world's top-selling cleansing bar.[9] In the 1990s, Dove began to expand its product line beyond soap, and the line now includes shampoos, conditioners, deodorant, and other cleansing products for women. Dove began to attract global attention in 2004 for its marketing and branding; the company hired Ogilvy & Mather in that year to develop a series of ads portraying the "real beauty" of ordinary women. In 2006, Dove started the Dove Self-Esteem Fund, which purports to "be an agent of change" through educating girls and women on a "wider definition of beauty."[10] These brand campaigns have received much public attention for their efforts to intervene in advertising's standard representations of femininity, in which models are primarily white, thin, and blond, and thus exclude the majority of the world's citizens. As a challenge to this idealized image, Dove initially distributed ads that featured "real" women of different sizes and ethnicities, with slogans such as "tested on real curves." It is this reimagined brand identity of Dove, updated and experienced in 2010 as a multimedia, interactive campaign including videos, blogs, online resources for girls and women, and international workshops on self-esteem, that is the specific focus of this chapter, where I will trace the trajectory from selling products to selling identities to selling culture through an analysis of "real beauty" as well as Dove campaigns from two earlier eras.

Commodity Activism in Three Moments of Economic Transition

Commodity feminism, where feminist ideals such as self-empowerment and agency are attached to products as a selling point, is one specific element of commodity activism, which in turn is one part of the larger story of the historical emergence of brand culture. As an example of commodity feminism, or what some have called "power femininity,"[11] the Real Beauty campaign brings into relief a debate over the relationship between gender and consumer culture that has been taking place, in both national arguments and everyday interactions, since at least the 19th century. The question, in some ways, is simple: Have women "been empowered by access to the goods, sites, spectacles, and services associated with mass consumption"?[12] Writing about "power femininity" in ads, Michele Lazar characterizes this "knowledge as power" trope within contemporary marketing as an element of consumer-based empowerment, where brands like Dove offer educational services to consumers so that they can develop skills to become their own experts on self-esteem. The development of these skills is positioned, in turn, as a conduit to self-empowerment.[13] The Dove Real Beauty campaign, through its workshops and media resources, claims to enable girls to become confident and self-reliant through healthy self-esteem.

As Victoria de Grazia, Susan Bordo, Lynn Spigel, and many others have pointed out, there are a variety of points of entry into debates about consumer empowerment for women, ranging from historical analyses of consumer culture's empowering expansion of middle-class women's social and institutional boundaries to examinations of consumer culture representations of women and the "female" audience.[14] My examination of the Dove Real Beauty campaign approaches it as one of many contemporary examples of an advanced capitalist strategy that restages corporate and managerial practices (such as those of Unilever) into political, and in this case feminist, and social contexts. In the relentless search for profit, this retooled capitalism is built upon a restructuring of traditional identities (in this case, of gender) and social relations (in this case, between consumer and producer). Needless to say, some shifts in identity and relationships are easier to brand than others; wanting to improve girls' self-esteem is not a controversial political platform (unlike, say, immigration rights or same-sex marriage). In addition, the issue has a vast market—from self-help books to reality television shows to pedagogical initiatives—in the US that supports Dove's particular commodity activism. Nevertheless, it is worth reconsidering the logic of such brand campaigns. Why does a company driven by profit care about social issues? How did we get here? What is the historical context for this neoliberal recontextualization?

As much as marketers will tell you otherwise, the market itself is only part of the story. So when considering habits of consumption within advanced capitalism, and what that tells us about our identities and our relationships, we also must consider the equally important, but more abstract, notion of what constitutes a commodity in the first place. Is racial or gender identity a commodity? Can the pursuit of social justice be commodified? If the answer to these and similar questions is yes, what does that mean for individuals, institutions, and politics? What does it mean in terms of how cultural values are changing? Exploring the ramifications of commodification means considering what it means to be a social activist in an environment that above all else values self-empowerment and entrepreneurial individualism.

In order to address such questions, I examine commodity activism at three historical moments in US culture. These historical moments represent industry-defined transitions in relations of production, the creation of markets, and consumer culture. Crucial to each are technological shifts that are created, supported, and enabled by specific understandings of consumer capital as well as shifting notions of political and cultural subjectivity.

- First, I examine mass consumption within Fordist capitalism of the mid-20th century. In this era both broadcast media (such as film, broadcast television, and radio) and political subjectivity were often formulated collectively (from membership in one's social class or the imagined homogeneous, relatively undifferentiated audience).
- Second, I explore niche marketing and post-Fordist (or late) capitalism in the late 20th century. Here, new information technologies and narrowcast media (such as cable television and the Internet) fragment the formerly broad, mass audience into groups of more diverse communities. These audiences are differentiated by specific racialized or gendered groups (as well as other identity groups), and their "identities" are imagined (and marketed to) accordingly.
- Third, I examine individuated marketing and neoliberal labor practices of the late 20th century and early 21st century. These include immaterial labor, which is animated by the digital economy, and the blurring of consumer and producer identities (as with "viral" ads, user-generated online content, and brand culture), so that the individual cultural entrepreneur is celebrated as one who populates a radically "free" market.

To be clear, charting three economies is not an indication that one cultural and economic context ends as another begins; rather, there remains overlap between all three economies, and they both detract from and inherit legacies of their predecessors. These historical moments map transitions—some advancements, some retrenchments—in a longer history of culture, economy, and the construction of subjectivity within the capitalist episteme. It is often, as de Grazia reminds us, in the moments of transition—such as those I have outlined—that tensions around meanings of identities become especially visible.[15]

Getting "Creamed": Mid-20th-Century Mass Audiences and the Unified Subject

Interpreting advertisements targeted to women offers insight to the various ways in which gender and national identity intersect in different ways at different historical stages. Beauty and hygiene products have long been connected, by marketers and consumers alike, to broader relationships between personal identity, dominant racial and gender formations, and the nation. Soap, for instance, has historically been a rich vehicle for the notion of consumption as a kind of civic duty. Even in the 19th century, as Anne McClintock has shown, soap (and other commodities) stood in for values that traversed the cleanliness of the physical body into the "cleanliness" of the social body. Commodities were seen to represent cultural and social value, and through visual representations in advertising, they affirmed racial and gender hierarchies.[16] In particular, as McClintock demonstrates, in the colonial building of empire of the 19th century, "Soap flourished not only because it created and filled a spectacular gap in the domestic market but also because, as a cheap and portable domestic commodity, it could persuasively mediate the Victorian poetics of racial hygiene and imperial progress."[17]

Into the 20th century, feminine beauty products continued to be associated with national identity and rhetorics of American "progress."[18] Yet at the same time, the cultivation of a female consumer base authorized new social positions for women that disrupted traditional gender hierarchies in US society. Historian Kathy Peiss, for example, challenges a reductionist account of cosmetics as merely "masks" for apparent feminine shortcomings—whether these masks are imposed by patriarchal society (women needing artifice to compete) or by racist culture ("whiteners" and other means to affirm racist hierarchies among women). Rather, Peiss argues that women's consumption of cosmetics needs to be understood within a broader context of struggles between consumer conformity and female empowerment. While surely the marketing of cosmetics contributed to the commodification of gendered identity (where types of women are branded as products), it also, as Peiss argues, destabilized traditional gendered hierarchies based on notions of public and private and helped establish a kind of cultural legitimacy for women.[19] Cosmetics marketing in the early and mid-20th century was thus not only about capitalizing on individual insecurities for profit but also about creating and perpetuating a changing definition of womanhood; creating a market exclusively for women, and thus inviting women to participate in the market, shifted and challenged previously held notions of public and private spheres. Because of the changing position of the middle-class woman in postwar American culture (brought on by various social forces, including suburban migration, an emergent ideology of the ideal nuclear family, and marketing to the housewife), feminine beauty products reflect the dynamics of an era defined by the mass production and then mass consumption of consumer goods.[20]

The postwar context, federal housing policies that privileged white middle-class families, suburban development and the subsequent marginalization of racial and ethnic communities to urban spaces, the ideological solidification of the nuclear family, the role that white middle-class women played in the wartime workforce, the new and increasingly normative presence of the television in the privatized American home—all were factors in the shifting public and private terrain of consumer culture in this historical moment.[21] Advertising and marketing relied on cultural tropes that normalized and naturalized these dynamics, positioning them as conduits of access to national gendered identity. Marketers and artists alike increasingly turned to public space, such as buildings and billboards, to both create art and advertise wares. The public relations industry is born. Highway systems are built, automobiles are increasingly affordable, and with the two come a concomitant mobility and migration. Market-driven networks of communication, such as mass magazines, broadcast television, Hollywood film, and advertising, facilitated relationships between political and social identities and consumption behavior, a practice that only increased as new markets—for women, for African Americans, for families—were created and then capitalized upon.[22]

During this postwar period, then, the values of both citizenship and consumption began to merge in new ways. Consumption habits of white, middle-class Americans not only were framed as choices of what material goods to purchase but also were understood as larger symbols of individualism, freedom, and equality.[23] This is the context for what Lizabeth Cohen calls a "consumer's republic," where political and social values previously tied to more abstract political ideologies, such as freedom, democracy, and equality, were newly understood as accessible specifically through the promises of consumer capitalism.[24] As Marita Sturken and Lisa Cartwright write, "Thus individual consumerism, rather than social policy, was offered beginning in the 1950s in the United States as the means to achieve the promise of social change and prosperity."[25] It was not simply that purchasing goods signaled the storied upward economic mobility of the postwar years; consumption was now a means to construct a specific identity within the "consumer's republic" of the US.[26] This shift, this awareness that consumer choices could be political choices, is crucial to the later emergence of commodity activism.

For instance, consider a Dove soap television ad from 1957. We watch a white, blond, female actor in the bathtub, clearly enjoying herself beneath a hyperbolic, male voice-over: "From Lever House, in New York City, comes the greatest skin care discovery of our time! Its name is Dove! This amazing new bath and toilet bar is actually one-quarter cleansing cream. . . . Ordinary soap dries your skin. But Dove creams your skin while you wash."

From the opening shot of a towering New York City skyscraper to the dramatic appearance of a bar of Dove soap amid a flock of flying doves to the pseudoscientific demonstration of the amount of cleansing cream in the soap, the ad is typical for its late-fifties genre. The touted powers of Dove are then demonstrated by the female actor, who is depicted not only washing her face but also taking a luxurious bubble bath with Dove, promising its users that it will leave them with a "velvety, just-creamed feeling." The ad then turns to an "experiment" with the female actor, described by a female, vaguely British voice-over that contrasts Dove's powers against those of ordinary soap.

The ad is directed to a mass audience of consumers; though it is clear that Dove is a "beauty" bar, and therefore for feminine use, the ad has an otherwise general message to consumers. The ad is not explicitly directed toward any specific types of women—there is no ideal age, or race, or class for this potential consumer. Rather, in connection with current ideologies of mass consumption, it addresses the mass consumer as a unified subject. Yet, there are codes throughout the ad that signal race and class status: the visible

A 1957 Dove ad, highlighting the soap's cleansing power.

whiteness of the woman, the luxury of a bubble bath obviously taken in a private home, the cultural capital of the vague British accent. Thus, despite the appeal to the mass consumer (who happens, then as now, to be young, white, and middle-class), the ad nonetheless interpellates the individual consumer through its rhetoric (Dove "creams your skin while you wash"), constructing the relationship between the consumer and the product as one that is deep and highly personal, even as it is simultaneously overgeneralized. In other words, the ad is in fact directed toward a unified subject, one recognized as ideal in the mass-consumption/mass-production era.

As with all cultural meanings, commodities and the structure of marketing and advertising that supports them do not circulate in the same way in different spheres of life. So, while this historical moment is often defined by its homogeneity, the cultural meanings of gender, race, and socioeconomic class shape as well as limit the economization of social spheres. While the dominant image of femininity broadcast in American homes during the 1940s and 1950s resembled the young, white woman in the Dove ad, she was certainly not the only representation. As Lynn Spigel, George Lipsitz, and others have shown, television programs such as *I Love Lucy* and *The Honeymooners* often challenged dominant conceptions of gender and ethnicity through contradictory and alternative representations of female authority. While these representations posed a challenge to dominant forms, they were often subsumed by the new American advertising industry. Alternative media representations thus sat uneasily side by side with the newly built freeways that facilitated "white flight" to the suburbs. The nascent campaigns for sexual freedoms and racial equality occupied the same streets but were contradicted by the hegemony of what Lipsitz has called the "possessive investment in whiteness." As burgeoning feminist movements began to form in the late 1950s and early 1960s, during that same time the Nixon-Khrushchev Kitchen Debate celebrated abundance and convenience through consumer items (from lipstick to high-heeled shoes to dishwashers) as evidence of freedom and equality within American capitalism.[27]

Clearly, there were variances within the "consumer republic" of postwar US culture, and different communities used the context of consumerism in diverse ways to express empowerment.[28] Those excluded from the hegemonic consumer category, by race, class, or geography, for instance, were "invited" and encouraged through the mass media to aspire to be part of the consumer ideal. Communication technologies, such as the broadcast television on which the Dove commercial appeared, as well as mass-market magazines, in addition to new transportation systems and new patterns of suburban life, were critical to support mass consumption, providing venues for advertising not only to transmit information to mass audiences about products but also to sell ideologies about the ideal citizen consumer.[29] As advertisers used these new infrastructures to elaborate an image of this citizen consumer, the principles of choice, equality, and freedom were articulated as achievable via consumption. Within US society, these principles as political ideals have indicated exclusion as often as inclusion, so that choice, equality, and freedom are always contingent options, available primarily to those privileged enough to define what choice, equality, and freedom mean. Thus, the political ideals that were connected to consumerism during this era—democracy, freedom, choice, equality, empowerment—were based on a (relatively) homogeneous construction of the consumer. If not always literally white and middle-class, the ideological basis of the ideal consumer was supported by the mass-media technologies of the time and understood within a hegemonic construction of the American citizen, which was, by default, white and middle-class.

Mass production, and its attendant advertising industry, required a certain kind of management of difference so that the purported "free" choice and equality of the consumer citizen could remain intact. These ideologies manifested in the notion of abundance and conformity, so that the working class, people of color, and single parents (groups often confined to America's cities) were encouraged through ads, media, and marketing to strive to be "just like them"—white, middle-class suburbanites.[30] Advertisers' concerted efforts to capture a "mass consumer" base required a leveling of racial and gendered differences through the "objectivity" of purchasing power.[31] For example, the Dove ad exemplifies how though the "ideal" consumer was white and middle-class, the commercial and the image it conveyed were flexible enough to be embraced by a larger demographic (or at least aspire to it). While couched in a rhetoric of equality or equal access, needless to say these efforts were also profitable business decisions.[32]

The contradictions within this period of consumer capitalism—what Marx called the ruptures of capitalism—would eventually overwhelm mid-century advertising strategies (though not the insistence on mass production and consumption, which has proved far more durable). Such contradictions—between mass production and its concomitant homogeneity and standardization, dominant political ideologies of the "American dream," and material and racial inequalities—would just a few decades later form the context for a different era of consumption, the niche market era. Starting in the late 1960s and early 1970s, marketers and advertisers capitalized on these contradictions and "resolved" them through different marketing strategies. Indeed, the era of mass production and mass consumption was relatively short-lived. Its idealized image of a homogenized and standardized public also posed a great challenge to advertisers, as they strove to capture more and more differentiated demographic groups.

The transition from a unified subject targeted by advertising to a more niche-oriented market society can be seen in the era's growing critiques of mass culture. The reimagined links between consumerism and citizenship, and the increasing merging of commercial and political cultures, captured the attention of a generation of postwar intellectuals who, from various political vantage points, critiqued consumer society in general and the prominence of the American consumer in particular. Conservative and progressive intellectuals critiqued the mass audience imagined by the mid-20th-century US culture industries, likening American consumers to unthinking "sheep" and "pseudo-individuals."[33] They often situated their consumption arguments within Marxist frameworks positioning the consumer as passive and manipulable, functioning primarily (if not wholly) in the service of modern capitalism. Intellectuals mourned the loss of the "authentic" individual, an apparent casualty of mass consumerism. These critics largely saw consumer culture as a powerful distraction from rational public discourse, poisoning the spaces of "authentic" democracy, equality, and freedom.

Such intellectual arguments—even if they now seem moralistic, elitist, and nostalgic—by the mid-1960s resonated with emerging protest movements. The feminist and civil rights movements began to see the exclusionary practices of capitalism and consumer society as part of their specific struggles. But at the same time, such criticisms oversimplified the dynamics of production and consumption of mid-20th-century consumer culture. For instance, alongside the mass appeal of ads such as Dove's, beauty product marketing of this era also afforded opportunities for women excluded from representations of the mass consumer. Commercial beauty culture provided a context for reimagining social and political identities even as it simultaneously enforced a dominant femininity.[34]

Obviously, intention at the point of production is not always matched by intention at the point of consumption. Advertisers can, and do, have profit motive as their explicit goal—but consumers and their political ideals, then as now, can challenge and even exceed what advertisers want from them. As I argued in the introduction to this book, it is this excess of meaning that creates consumer (and, later, brand) culture as ambivalent. If the dynamic between producer and consumer is not inevitable, then we can move beyond the standard model—which sees the consumer either as a passive dupe of the brand's desires or as an active resister of these same desires—and instead see the nuances of this relationship between maker and buyer, a relationship often fraught with contradiction.

During the 1940s and 1950s, for instance, African Americans were targeted as niche consumers marked by racial identity and difference, long before the term "niche" came to characterize marketing discourse.[35] Some advertisers during the mid-20th century in the US recognized African Americans as potentially lucrative consumers and often used political ideals of equality and freedom in advertising as means through which to attract them and other nonwhite consumers. Walter Mack, the CEO of Pepsi-Cola from 1938 to 1950, was famous for enticing African American consumers and workers to white corporate America; as Stephanie Capparell points out, "When he looked at black, he also saw green."[36] Yet Pepsi-Cola was one of the first US corporations to hire African Americans in professional positions in the 1940s, forcing corporate America to acknowledge the complex issues that revolved around race and work. Consumer culture and political ideals, then, were connected in ways that extended beyond profit motive.

These connections also manifested in a form of consumer advocacy that differed from earlier historical moments, represented in Vance Packard's book *The Hidden Persuaders* (1957), which questioned the morality of the advertising industry and suggested that advertisers manipulate the American public into false desires.[37] Ralph Nader's *Unsafe at Any Speed*, published in 1965, also challenged advertising and consumer culture and argued that automobile manufacturers obfuscated issues of auto safety by focusing on style and comfort. Nader's crusading clearly struck a chord with an increasingly cynical American public (his book sold more than 400,000 copies in the first years after it was published), and he continued on the consumer advocacy path: in the next several decades he was behind the passage of two dozen consumer protection laws, including the National Traffic and Motor Vehicle Safety Act, the Consumer Products Safety Act, and the Freedom of Information Act.[38] One effect of this kind of advocacy was that consumers began to demand more from advertisers through their role as citizens, using the language of citizenship to insist on their "rights."[39] Both consumers and advertisers reinterpreted the way that 1950s consumer goods were marketed, then, so that the celebratory framing of abundance and convenience of that era became seen as an impediment to individuality and difference.[40] These kinds of critiques of consumer culture helped the US cultural economy transition into a liminal period, where there is a challenge to the unified subject of the mass audience and movement toward what would eventually become a fragmented, niche market landscape.

Midcentury consumer capitalism appealed to contradictory interests. The struggle on the part of both consumers and corporate producers to reconcile ideals of citizenship (freedom, equality, democracy) with the seemingly oppositional ideals of consumerism (individual satisfaction, profit) became particularly acute during this era of mass consumption and production. The unified subject that was the target of advertisers and marketers became increasingly disconnected from the US cultural and political environment in the latter half of the century. Rather than read this disconnect as a failure to adequately market to an audience, the advertising industry saw cultural and individual difference as an opportunity and reimagined its practices to capture an increasingly fragmented audience.

From Mass to Niche: Identity, Difference, and "The Truth" in Late Capitalism

The parceling of identities into markets in the late 1960s and early 1970s, complete with the rhetoric of "you deserve your own [insert artifact—channel, magazine, shop—here]" is a crucial next step in the trajectory that ultimately transitions to neoliberal brand culture and the commodification of social activism. The increasing emergence of niche marketing in the later part of the 20th century in the US had a complex focus: it was in part about recognizing communities (such as the African American or Latina/o communities), but at the same time, niche marketing reified identities into market categories. The double mobilization that characterized US counterculture, where difference was an important element of politicization and resistance cultures while simultaneously mobilized by consumer capitalism for individuated markets, also made possible niche marketing in the later part of the century.

Niche marketing, in connection with the emergence of identity politics of the 1970s and 1980s, helped to create a new understanding of "authenticity" as a desirable *market* category. The dominant category of the white, middle-class consumer of the 1950s—the mass audience—rendered a focus on "authentic" identity somewhat irrelevant, as the mass audience did not encourage comparison with others as a way to demonstrate one's "true" self. The "real" person, rather than a composite generalized consumer, became a dominant representation in advertising in the later part of the 20th century, tapping into a nostalgic longing for authenticity that apparently was missing in the era of mass consumption. Capitalizing on the fragmented market and the emergence of identity politics during this era, Dove in the 1980s created a new ad campaign that departed from the representational politics of the earlier ads, expertly incorporating "feminist criticisms against sexist advertising as well as elements of progressive social change."[41] The campaign used testimonials from "real" women, who did not tout the product's physical properties (e.g., the soap being one-quarter cleansing cream) but focused instead on how using Dove soap helped their "self-esteem." This move from product elements to ideological identity would prove crucial. The real, "authentic" women in the Dove ads gave their names and their testimony to Dove in a conversational, intimate rhetoric—quite different from the earlier male voice-over, blanketing the untouchable woman luxuriating in the bubble bath. Such a move toward "authenticity" was important for connecting female empowerment with consumption, especially beauty products. Dove's new strategy channeled second-wave feminist discourse about how male-dominated society suppressed or repressed women's "true" selves; being an empowered woman meant breaking free from constraint, being yourself. But, of course, Dove also wanted to convince its audience that authenticity is best brought forward through consuming products. Lazar describes how this operates "specifically in terms of a 'true beauty' and essentially 'bold personality' of women all over that make-up helps release (note that the action verbs 'reveal,' 'elevate,' and 'highlights' presupposed pre-existing feminine qualities that are drawn out through empowering cosmetics)." In short, "the pursuit of beauty becomes an extension of the feminist empowerment project."[42]

Dove maintained its commitment to the "feminist empowerment project" through advertising campaigns across the 1980s that relied on testimonials. In one ad, "Jean Shy" (1988), an African American woman named Jean Shy shares her use of Dove soap, and her reverend's noticing of her skin, with television viewers. Visually, the ad trades on intimacy and friendship; the hand-held camera, the close shots of the woman's face, the obvious home environment all work to give the sense the viewer is sharing a cup of coffee with a friend.

In fact, the ad begins with just that: Jean Shy having a cup of coffee, speaking intimately into the camera, as if in the middle of a conversation: "The other Sunday I went to church, and I wasn't wearing any makeup or anything. And Reverend Walker, he came up to me—cause we know each other really well—and he said, 'Jean, your skin looks really nice.' And I said, 'Well, I've been using Dove.' And he said, 'Well, it must be the Dove!'" Jean Shy laughs, and continues to talk intimately into the camera, sharing beauty "secrets" of Dove soap with viewers and ending with, "And when Reverend Walker gave me that compliment, I *loved* it." The ad is clearly meant to be a personal and intimate conversation with a real woman, not an actor, who used the product; the connection between Jean Shy as an African American woman and the notion of normative churchgoing (referenced by her familiarity with the reverend) help to position this ad as "authentic."

From Dove's "Truth" campaign, a 1988 ad featuring gospel singer Jean Shy.

Other Dove ads during this decade tap into the niche market mentality by focusing on explicitly defined feminine types. A series of ads titled "The Truth" featured "real" women defined by specific characteristics; one profiled women thirty-five years old or older, another focused on "brainy" women, another on women with freckles. Like Jean Shy, each woman speaks into the camera about the "truth" of attaining beauty: older women need certain products to stay beautiful, it's okay to be smart *and* pretty, freckles can be sexy. Identity categories that were the center of broader cultural struggles over visibility were easily collapsed into advertising typologies, so that the ads read as "authentic."

Within Dove's "Truth" is a larger truth about the shifting strategies of marketers. The ideal of the mass audience no longer held the same kind of profit potential; the focus of late capitalism was on narrow, discrete, and differentiated identities. These identities were presented and marketed as consumer categories—African American, women, gay or lesbian—in a shift that Fredric Jameson called "the death of the subject."[43] The general market that was both created and reflected by advertising became the topic of much intellectual and popular critique, as identity-based political movements gradually gained leverage in American culture.

Though consumer culture was often positioned as part of the white, male establishment against which so many groups protested, it was also consumer culture that provided the context—albeit in a reimagined way—for identity-based movements to articulate political and cultural aims.[44] A politicized notion of "difference"—especially in response to what some saw as the stifling conformity of mass production and consumption—was, in fact, doubly mobilized. The counterculture, civil rights movement, second-wave feminist movement, and others mobilized politicized difference in protest, but advertisers also recognized its flexibility and profitability in the marketplace. During the 1960s and 1970s, resistance to consumer capitalism had a heightened visibility, as different groups rethought consumerism and created alternative structures of exchange. As Fred Turner documents, the Whole Earth network experimented with gift and barter economies, one of many counterculture efforts to redirect and shape how consumer goods moved through the counterculture.[45] And, just as advertising continued to capitalize on feminine insecurities as a means through which to sell cosmetics, the 1960s and 1970s witnessed a cultural struggle over women's rights to sexual pleasure and the emergence of lesbian and other sexual identities.[46] Yet, the political ideologies seized upon by antiestablishment groups in the 1960s and 1970s—personal expression, equality, freedom—were precisely the kinds of ideologies that were also commodified and made into markets.

Thus, while being part of a "niche" meant in some ways that one was a member of a community rather than an individual consumer, the community in question was often reified as a market category. Identity-based movements have been properly credited with radically reshaping political culture, but they have been similarly essential fodder for consumer culture to capitalize upon. That is, identity politics and niche markets share an epistemological base, but they often move in very different directions from that point; for instance, the fact that a gay man is targeted as part of the gay male market does not mean that man is an engaged participant in marginalized gay communities.

Counterculture in general was a productive site for both identity politics and niche marketing. As Gary Cross points out, warnings against the dangers of co-optation by the establishment became material for clever promoters to create new markets: "Counter-culturalists became rebels through consumption: tie-dyed dresses, *as opposed to* cashmere sweaters and pleated skirts, defined them. The 'counter' in the culture was very much within the confines of consumerism."[47] From its beginnings, the counterculture was a movement deeply entrenched in materialist society and was "intensely entrepreneurial."[48] Advertisers during this time changed tactics, and rather than sell products with the overt message of "buy, because everyone else is, be the same," the message shifted to "buy our product, because it is different from everyone else's, be 'real,' be authentic." The message to "buy," of course, did not change; the value of buying shifted definition, as did the definition of the ideal consumer. In 1972, for instance, the Ms. Foundation for Women released *Free to Be . . . You and Me,* a record album and book that focused on issues of individuality, tolerance, and gender neutrality, which resonated with the decade's popular message to "be yourself."[49] Words such as "peace" and "revolution" were seamlessly incorporated into ads selling products ranging from crude oil to cosmetics; advertising capitalized on the politics of the real and the desire for authenticity as a new vehicle through which to sell products. A Tampax ad in the late 1970s, for example, promoted its product with the tagline "Free to be yourself"; another ad for Sylvania color television in the late 1970s capitalized on the market's growing attention to individual, "real" identities: "Presenting life the way it really is. White people aren't white, black people aren't black, yellow people aren't yellow, brown people aren't brown. Not in real life. Not on Sylvania Color TV."[50] Just as changing forms of citizenship and political subjectivity inform the consumer market and how it addresses its audience(s), so, too, do transformations in consumer capitalism shift modes of citizenship and political subjectivity. Harnessing the now familiar triptych of broad political ideologies—equality, freedom, and democracy—that characterized consumer culture at midcentury, consumer markets used these ideals as a way to both strategize and manage the increasingly public ideologies of "difference" emerging in the cultural economy. Thus, the mass market of the 1950s and early 1960s soon shifted to smaller, more differentiated markets that were mutually exclusive (and thus perpetuated an increasingly dominant understanding of "difference").[51]

In cultural politics, for example, "difference" manifested itself within the politics of visibility—in media, political spheres, and consumer practices alike. Women, African Americans, gays and lesbians, and many other marginalized groups struggled against the exclusionary strategies built into mass production and fought to gain recognition of their discrete identities.[52] Conversations within both academia and the media industries were ignited along the lines of "difference," with considerable attention focused on the visibility of specific identities. Access to and representation on broadcast television became key mobilizing factors in struggles over issues of equality, signaling the importance of media visibility as a conduit for empowerment.[53] Indeed, the emphasis on the power of visibility provided a crucial point of entry for advertisers and marketers, who capitalized on these political struggles, working them into the logics of marketing to create specific niches that directly appealed to narrower groups of consumers based on identity, culture, and lifestyle.

The unity of the subject that had been so important to mass consumption and mass production was no longer always assumed or desired by producers or consumers within late capitalism. Corresponding to changes in culture at large, subjectivities came to be understood through categories of differ-ence, including race, gender, and sexuality, and a shifted definition of the citizen consumer. This new definition was, like that of the mass consumer, dependent on connecting consumption practices with liberal political ideals. Conflating individual consumption with the citizen consumer was part of advertisers' broader conflation of liberal ideals of choice and empowerment with consumption habits in the mid-20th century. Such conflation was no less crucial in the later 20th century; the difference, however, came in what and who the citizen consumer was. Consequently, the terms of the producer-consumer relationship changed too, increasingly crafted in relational terms, as an exchange between marketers and consumers rather than a top-down imposition of a corporate message.

Of course, the central goal of advertisers and marketers remained the selling of products. Yet, as I have argued, the meaning that individuals cre-ate through consumption often extends beyond this general immediate economic goal, so that the relationship between consumers and producers is often not as predictable as advertisers would like. Both marketers and consumers understand this relationship differently, in other words, which resulted in changing strategies within marketing. For marketers and adver-tisers, communicating messages to consumers was no longer thought of in a linear, transmission model, with a unified sender and a unified receiver, but rather in an encoding/decoding model, with a more active consumer, who often resisted advertising and branding messages.[54] Rather than imposing a message and hoping for a resultant purchase, advertisers sought to establish a relationship with consumers, the terms of which were based on individual identities and particular "needs."[55] Consider the Dove ads of this era in this regard: the intimate conversations with the camera, the confessional qual-ity of the women's "revelations." Consumers were thought to have newfound marketing savvy, a skill not lost on advertisers, who created increasingly sophisticated and personalized campaigns.

Alongside shifts in identity formation, new technological and media forms emerged in the 1970s and early 1980s to sell products. For example, cable television tapped into underserved consumer groups, namely, African Americans, children and teens, and women, and promised to directly brand identities through discrete programming niches, with channels such as Black Entertainment Television (BET), Nickelodeon, and Lifetime. The emergence and increased installation of cable television technology in the American home during the 1970s were positioned and celebrated by the industry, as well as consumers, in terms of cable's difference from broadcast television (though the true explosion in discrete channel niches would not occur until the 1980s). Cable could be a venue for "individual creativity" in juxtaposition to broadcast TV's "mass conformity."[56] Cable, it seemed, could offer less "lowest-common-denominator" and crassly commercialized programming, less intrusive advertising, more viewer interactivity, and more viewer empowerment in terms of choice. In particular, cable's increased number of channels tapped into the growing public discourse about "difference," emerging identity politics, and the rejection of postwar homogeneity. In fact, the cable industry proved to be a particularly profitable site for new niche markets and the commodification of identities. As Joseph Turow describes, cable television offered a place for advertisers' cultivation of "primary media communities," groups of consumers sought in order to nurture brand loyalty against a progressively more cluttered media landscape.[57]

Despite efforts to separate them ideologically, the new "primary media communities" of the 1970s and more overtly political, identity-based communities were not mutually exclusive. Political struggles over visibility and voice, for instance, did not merely motivate change in cultural values in the 1970s and 1980s but also were exploited by the mainstream commercial media. One of the rallying issues of the social and cultural upheavals of later 20th-century US culture was a perceived lack of "mattering" in contemporary culture: the values and standards that seemed to signify the "American way" were woefully out of touch with (and often literally beyond the reach of) those groups fighting to have their voices heard. Struggles for visibility were one response to this: being seen was a step toward inclusion and cultural significance. Cable channels positioned themselves as a more inclusive, more individual answer to Newton Minow's famous "vast wasteland" of broadcast television, cultivating a sense of belonging and a notion of community. Cable channels were often designed to capture an undermarketed part of broadcast television's viewership and were heralded as an important factor in recognizing audiences broadcast television had historically obscured. Cable, that is, capitalized on struggles over visibility and "solved" these struggles by offering niche channels. Such recognition is crucial in a media society that often equates social power with visibility, but it is a limiting visibility that also works to commodify identities within boundaries established by communication industries. Additionally, niche marketing has the tendency to marginalize distinct groups, identifying them as so different from the mainstream as to, for example, deserve their own channel.[58] This worked to render these groups (such as kids or African Americans) as distinct and closed, implying that they have no relationship to each other. The result is not a harmonious multichannel, multicultural media universe but one in which a host of niche channels stand in their discrete corners, while the mainstream audience channels continue to dominate the stage and define norms of representation.[59]

Certainly the segmented market and its focus on individual identities can be celebrated as a beneficial response to the exclusive (white, middle-class) homogeneity of mid-20th-century mass markets. Yet, transforming identity into a product and a market has enormous consequences. Commodifying identity reifies it. Commodities like gender or race become hegemonically constructed things rather than relational, intersectional qualities that are constantly subject to reinvention. Writing about the success of the cable channel BET, Beretta Smith-Shumade points out how, "on a scale never seen prior, BET promotes and presents African-Americans as a product. It sells black folks like any other merchandise—pop, detergent, or shoes."[60] While surely there are other historical dynamics that construct African Americans as products, Smith-Shumade's point is that a television channel dedicated to this practice furthers the commodification of identity as the norm. She also points to a now quite obvious dynamic of television (and other media industries): television not only serves programming to audiences but also serves audiences to advertisers, thus literally commodifying viewers. Audiences, within capitalist media industries, are not only the targets for products; they *are* the product, and they are both of these things simultaneously.

A corollary dynamic is found in advertising's deployment of commodity feminism.[61] Like the commodification of race, transforming the politics of feminism into a product to be sold means to reify feminism (and, through feminism, women)—to make identity into a kind of thing. Concepts of empowerment and choice are threaded through the commercial address, making it more complicated to tease out differences between and within women (let alone make the determination that these differences do, in fact, make a difference). As Lazar points out, "The appropriation of feminism especially by the advertising media is hardly surprising given that advertisers are adept at reading and responding to the signs of the time....They are able to assimilate feminist criticisms against sexist advertising as well as elements of progressive social change."[62]

During the 1970s and 1980s, consumer capitalism in the US moved from a focus on product efficiency to a more affective relationship with consumers, evidence that advertisers are indeed "adept at reading and responding to the signs of the time." This affective relationship is defined by advertisers' acknowledgment of identity differences, which allowed them to position "authenticity" as a key component of the relationship. The consumer-producer relationship became one of exchange, modeled after the principles of encoding/decoding, rather than a simple transmission of information. It also marked an emphasis on marketing "real" identities as an attempt to disrupt the increasingly public discourse about the manipulation and inauthenticity of advertising. Mobilizing the authentic, "real" consumer enabled the subsequent forging of a relationship between consumer and producer that is now central to the neoliberal strategy of building culture within the structures of branding and marketing.

"Real" Relationships and Neoliberal Branding as Culture

Clearly, the era of niche marketing, and the subsequent fragmenting and commodifying of identities, has not come to an end. However, the contemporary era needs to be theorized as more than an expanded development of niche marketing. While there are residual elements within advanced capitalist consumer culture that overlap with other periods of consumer culture, there are also profound differences.

The cultural economy of advanced capitalism, ever more rapid innovations in technologies and user interactivity, and the explosion of brand culture have shaped a commodity activism quite different than consumer cultures of the 1950s and 1960s, or even the 1970s and 1980s. The late 20th and early 21st centuries ushered in advanced or neoliberal capitalism, an environment that among other things enables a kind of brand strategy in its production of goods, services, and resources. These advanced capitalist dynamics manage, contain, and actually design identities, difference, and diversity as brands. Brand cultures facilitate "relationships" between consumers and branders and encourage an affective connection based on authenticity and sincerity.

The contemporary era is one that focuses on the individual entrepreneur, "free" to be an activist, a consumer, or both. This newly imagined entrepreneur is not defined in the traditional sense of being a business owner or investor, but rather is an entrepreneur of the *self*, a category that has exclusive hints to it but also gains traction as something that ostensibly can apply to anyone. At the same time, digital technologies and other media have also facilitated the emergence of "networked publics," where networks between individuals help form collective communities, such as those revolving around feminist, gay, or environmental issues, to name but a few.[63] The relationship between the individual entrepreneur and networked publics is structured by an ambivalence that is critical to the operation of brand culture. Brand cultures are not merely an economic strategy but are cultural spaces and often difficult to predict and characterize precisely. The tension between a neoliberal focus on the individual entrepreneur and the continuing demands of collective cultures is one that runs through brand culture and shapes commodity activism. The individual entrepreneur is encouraged to participate in collective action through brands like Dove, just as citizens have been encouraged throughout US history to exercise civic behavior such as voting and organizing (some citizens far more than others, of course). The contemporary moment, however, is characterized by the fact that brand culture profit will always trump collective politics and social issues, so that these same collective politics are authorized by the brand itself. It is this tension, among other things, that characterizes marketing in the early 21st century.[64]

In other words, if marketing in the mid-20th century was primarily about mass, homogeneous audiences, and in the later 20th century about niches and authenticity, in the early 21st century it is about increasingly elaborate relationships between producers and consumers through the principle of "engagement." The trick for contemporary marketers is how to create engagement that feels authentic while still privileging market exchange. As I argued in the introduction to this book, these two practices can seem incompatible. Social economist Viviana Zelizer has pointed out, "Market exchange, although perfectly compatible with the modern values of efficiency and equality, conflicts with human values that defy its impersonal, rational, and economizing influence."[65] How to manage or contain this conflict in the contemporary era? As many marketers have relayed to me, an increasingly normative way to address the tension that comes with marketizing human values is through "engagement." Marketer Denise Shiffman argues that creating products and brands in the 21st century US market necessitates building a kind of affective, authentic engagement into the product itself: "The goal is to create your own space, attract your own audience, and develop a deep and long-lasting relationship with customers. When you do this, your product will rise above the din of marketing messages."[66]

Consider the way Dove tries to rise "above the din" with its current ad campaign. The Dove Campaign for Real Beauty website, launched in 2004 by Ogilvy & Mather, expanded on the "authenticity" of its ads in the 1970s and 1980s. Part advertising, part pedagogy, part social activism—and made legible through brand culture—this campaign capitalized and built upon the consumer-producer relationship as the privileged identity of the neoliberal cultural economy. As a part of the website and a concurrent billboard campaign, Dove featured images of "real, everyday" women. Taglines asked consumers whether the woman pictured was "Fat/fabulous?" or "Withered/wonderful?" Consumers were invited to text in their "vote" for the best choice, with results displayed in real time, encouraging consumer participation in the development of the campaign. (In the Toronto campaign, 51 percent of consumers voted for "fat" in the choice between "fat" or "fabulous," perhaps giving even more empirical evidence to Dove to continue its quest for healthy self-esteem.) Ostensibly empowered by "choice," consumers were asked to vote for the not-so-subtle correct answer—"wonderful," "fabulous"—even in a brand context that has historically not only supported but created an entire industry around "fat" and "withered" as problems women need to address. With the click of a mouse, or the tap of a screen, female consumers cast a vote and become citizens in the Dove nation; through their consumer-generated content, they help build the brand.

The "real" women Dove targeted were now not simply media representations but also consumers who helped produce the ads. Indeed, the current manifestation of the Dove campaign utilizes new technology and social media, from uploading videos on YouTube, to texting votes, to signing up for workshops online. Dove's campaign has also capitalized on a broader postfeminist cultural milieu in which, among other things, girls and women are encouraged to empower themselves through consumption practices, heightened visibility, and self-improvement.[67] Dove, through its messages of self-empowerment and the importance of building self-esteem, builds upon and reroutes the work that feminists have been doing for generations: helping women free themselves from restraint, having a voice, taking action in the world. This rerouting takes shape on the platform of the brand; Dove certainly did not invent discourses of female self-empowerment, but the company does retool these discourses in the service of brand culture and commodity activism. The combination of these practices authorizes the consumer activist as a participant in, and ambassador for, both female empowerment and the Dove brand.

To wit, and furthering this participatory aim, soon after the campaign began, the brand launched a subsidiary initiative, the Dove Self-Esteem Fund, to address eating disorders and other issues among young women and girls. The pedagogical function of the campaign—educating women and girls on how to have "healthy self-esteem"—is an important element in the Dove campaign. Tapping into the blurry boundaries between consumer and producer, the Dove workshops imply that consumers not only are helping produce ads but are also charged with producing a better, healthier gender culture.[68] Thus, Dove positions itself as both the tool and platform through which women and girls can become not just individually empowered but also social activists.

Consumers can, then, participate in Dove online workshops and download "free self-esteem tools." The workshops provided on the website, which offer videos of workshops actually done in person as templates, ask

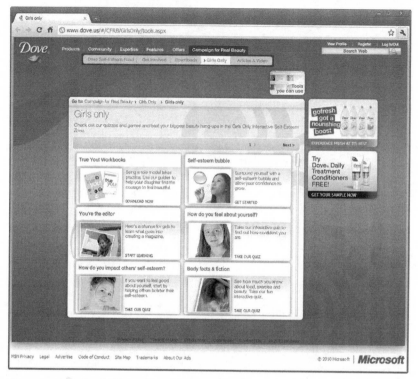

The 2011 website for the Dove Campaign for Real Beauty.

participants to think through questions and perform activities as a way to strengthen self-esteem. (Once a participant has completed three tools, she can "receive [her] very own self-esteem certificate," which thus acquires symbolic use-value for Dove consumer citizens.) The "self-esteem tools" include "True You!" workbooks that offer "simple self-esteem exercises for moms and girls to do together" that are guides to "help your daughter feel more beautiful."

The Dove campaign also includes "You're the Editor!," which offers tips for girls to create their own magazines, and a mother-daughter activity, "Boost Book," in which the participants are asked to "decorate a notebook or sketchpad together and keep a log of inspiring quotations, compliments and positive comments other people have made about the girl in your life.... Whenever she has a moment of uncertainty, bring out the book to get her self-esteem back on track." If users would rather participate in a workshop in person, one can sign up for the National Workshop Tour (through which apparently 3,308,796 "lives have been touched to date"). The company commissioned a report, *Real Girls, Real Pressure: A National Report on the State of Self-Esteem*, inviting consumers to "play a role in supporting and promoting a wider definition of beauty." The emphasis of the rhetoric on the individual consumer—"You're the Editor!," "play a role," "True You"—directs attention away from the role that capitalism in general and the beauty industry in particular have played in creating low female self-esteem, but also in the simultaneous creation of a market to help combat this issue. Indeed, on the same web page that offers "free self-esteem tools" are advertisements for Dove products, such as Dove Body Wash, which apparently gives its users a "nourishing boost," as well as an appeal to consumers to "try new Dove Daily Treatment Conditioners free!" Another, for Dove Beauty Bar, has the tagline "Just because the economy is drying up, it doesn't mean your skin should. With Dove Beauty Bar, beautiful skin is still affordable." These ads imply that larger social and economic problems—indeed, crises—need not be of concern as long as one attempts individual beauty. Or perhaps more precisely, that dismantling global issues that affect women is as easy as choosing the right face wash. It is difficult, in obvious ways, to reconcile the cultural work performed by Dove beauty products, which are created for women and girls to more closely approximate a feminine ideal, with the Dove Real Beauty workshops, with the campaign's invitations for consumer participation, and with its critique of the beauty industry.

But a seemingly impossible reconciliation is precisely the cultural work that postfeminism and commodity activism excel at. Moreover, reconciling consumption and social change is not a contradiction within brand culture but instead follows a political logic. This logic is neither objective nor neutral; rather, it is one strategy of advanced capitalism, where the logic of product differentiation allows Dove to relay feminist critiques of the beauty industry while at the same time deflecting those same critiques from Dove onto other brands. This deployment of feminist discourse structures the Dove brand culture as ambivalent, where the promise of feminist goals is held simultaneously with the logic of market exchange. Through brand culture, feminism is incorporated as part of the market; through brand culture, both the market and feminism itself are transformed.

Dove's repertoire of viral films has expanded since "Evolution"; another Dove viral video, "Onslaught," depicts a torrent of media images of distorted and unrealistic femininity seen through the eyes of an innocent white girl. The tagline reads, "Talk to your daughter before the beauty industry does." Another, "Amy," portrays a young girl who refuses to meet a boy because she has such low self-esteem. Its tagline: "Amy can name 12 things wrong with her appearance. He can't name one." As a way to further individualize this ad (after all, the boy—and by extension, masculine culture—apparently has nothing to do with Amy's low self-esteem), the video also invites viewers to insert their name in place of "Amy," thereby personalizing the representation. Dove's goal, it seems, is to make low self-esteem an individual problem, thereby emphasizing the distinction between all girls who suffer from low self-esteem and the personal suffering of the individual consumer citizen. The personalization privileges individual experience over systemic problems.

The Dove campaign is one example of a contemporary way of making culture that is dependent on the brand as a context for its production. In other words, brands, such as Dove, provide the context, or what Adam Arvidsson would call the "ambience," for the lived experience of culture.[69] Brand cultures are spaces in which politics are practiced, identities are made, art is created, and cultural value is deliberated. The Dove campaign is not simply about the acquisition of beauty knowledge (such as how to put on makeup or how to lose weight) that can be explained relatively easily as corporate appropriation of a kind of feminist pedagogy, or conversely, what might be expected from a beauty supply company. Rather, it is about creating and supporting a shifted manifestation of the citizen consumer, one who is critical of marketing and its unrealistic norms and is invited to develop this narrative in conjunction with corporate culture (and alongside the buying of beauty products).

The consumer coproduction at the heart of Dove's campaign reflects a labor practice characteristic of advanced capitalism in the early 21st century. Consumers contribute specific forms of production via voting, creating videos for the campaign, workshopping, and so forth, but the forms of their labor are generally not recognized as *labor* (e.g., participating in media production, DIY practices, consumer-generated content). This immaterial labor is defined by the Italian Marxist Maurizio Lazzarato as "the labor that produces the informational and cultural content of the commodity."[70] This kind of consumer labor does two rather contradictory things simultaneously: it both tightens the hold of the corporation over the consumer (in that the consumer is now performing labor with no compensation) and also reveals the contradictions within the structure of "informationalized capitalism," by loosening some of the control from the corporation as far as determining the final product.[71] In the context of the Dove campaign, the "cultural content" of immaterial labor produces affect, "healthy self-esteem," and gender identity. Obviously, the impulses of affect and gendered self-esteem existed before the Dove Campaign for Real Beauty, just as critiques of the beauty industry already existed within feminism. The practices of Web 2.0, however, seek to corral these impulses as part of broad consumer capitalism. Again, the transition to advanced capitalism and brand culture is not a teleological one, based in a linear history.

It is easy to accuse Dove of hypocrisy, and indeed, bloggers and cultural critics alike already have. After all, the company is utilizing the immaterial labor of participants for material gain—and to profit an industry, no less, that helped further the problem these participants are protesting. Immaterial labor, that is, emerges from the expansion of neoliberal cultural economies and is "part of a process of economic experimentation with the creation of monetary value out of knowledge/culture/affect."[72] However, this Dove campaign is not an insidious, manipulative attempt by advertisers to disrupt and co-opt an "authentic" formation of gender identity. It is a campaign that builds the Dove brand by "engaging" consumers and building "authentic" relationships with these consumers as social activists. Indeed, the Dove campaign is but one example from the contemporary marketing landscape that demonstrates the futility of a binary understanding of culture as authentic versus commercial.[73] To accuse the campaign of hypocrisy implies that non-hypocritical activities within capitalism (of which there are many, as capitalist practices are often quite bold about their motives and operations) are somehow nonexploitative. Brand culture is structured by ambivalence. Yet this does not deny the presence of power relations as a critical element in their formation. As Manuel Castells argues:

> It would be tempting to play with words and characterize the transformation of power in the network society as a shift from the ownership of the means of production to the ownership of the means of communication since, as some theorists propose, we have shifted from the production of goods to the production of culture. This is indeed an elegant proposition but it leaves us hanging in a discourse without precise reference to the actual dramas of power struggles in our world.[74]

The "actual dramas of power struggles in our world" have a role in the production and maintenance of brand cultures such as Dove, but not in the sense of the hypocrisy of the campaign, which implies that profit somehow trumps all other concerns. The perceived hypocrisy apparently embodied by Dove's parent company, Unilever, is actually not at all hypocritical given a context in which culture is a commodity and a resource made available for capitalization, and in which identities take on meaning at the precise moment they are recognized as market categories. Mark Andrejevic, in his work on participatory culture in Web 2.0 technologies, argues that the consumer empowerment promised by the openness and flexibility of new technologies needs to be understood as a coexistence between creative activity and exploitation.[75] The labor of Dove consumers *is* unacknowledged labor and, like all forms of labor, is exploitative. However, the practices of Web 2.0, as Andrejevic reminds us, exploit in a specific way. The labor of Dove consumers is also immaterial labor, work that produces affective relationships, and a form of creative knowledge. This creative knowledge is one that expands the flexibility (and consequently the ambivalence) of the brand itself. The labor of Dove consumers is ambivalent, about both creative activity and exploitation simultaneously: as a brand culture, the Dove consumer community expresses and validates both of these possibilities.

Within advanced capitalism, connections between consumerism and citizenship do not need to be justified or qualified. In the era of mass consumption, such connections had to be sold by advertisers (so that buying a product was crafted as a choice afforded by democratic freedoms); in the 1970s and 1980s such connections had to be justified by market segmentations (as identities became products like any other material good, marketers could naturalize the position of politics with commercialism, or citizenship with consumption, as a relationship). However, the consumer citizen *is* the central category of analysis for today's advanced capitalist culture. Individual freedoms are guaranteed not by the state or another institution but by the freedom of the market and of trade.[76]

An exploration of neoliberal brand culture reveals its overlaps and interrelationships with earlier historical consumer cultural formations and also its vast differences. Thus, the emphasis on "mass" in the earlier era of mass production and consumption and the focus on identity groups in the niche market era have been redefined as an emphasis on the "particular" (though of course enabled by the persistence of mass production). Within this economic and discursive context, systems of production and distribution that respond to smaller groups of consumers are framed within the cultural context of "individualism," "choice," and "freedoms." While niche marketing also capitalized on these concepts for marketing, in the neoliberal era they are reimagined to even more relentlessly focus on an individual person, one who has access to customized products and can become an entrepreneur of the self. The fact that these ideals continue to be shaped and defined by advertising and branding strategies is not contradictory; rather, politics and consumerism, advertising and art, individualism and entrepreneurship all become the contours of culture.

One significant contour of culture within this contemporary moment is a change from production of capital to the actual production of culture itself. George Yúdice, in *The Expediency of Culture*, argues that "the role of culture has expanded in an unprecedented way into the political and economic at the same time that conventional notions of culture largely have been emptied out."[77] Limiting his focus to political economy, Yúdice is not concerned with what he calls the "content" of culture. He is interested in "the question of culture in our period, characterized as one of accelerated globalization, as a resource. . . . Culture is increasingly wielded as a resource for both sociopolitical and economic amelioration, that is, for increasing participation in this era of waning political involvement, conflicts over citizenship, and the rise of what Jeremy Rifkin has called 'cultural capitalism.'"[78] In "cultural capitalism" more traditional forms of markets (such as those in operation in the mass-consumption or niche market eras) are replaced by a logic of networks, access, and affective economic relationships.[79] The "production of culture" within networked, capitalist society and the shift from production to communication is one in which, instead of "monetary" capital or the production of goods as driving forces, "concepts, ideas, and images—not things—are the real items of value in the new economy."[80] The production of culture also means that the expanding participation of consumers in this economy indicates a possibility for reshaping those concepts, ideas, and images—that is, culture has significance beyond materialism. Yet at the same time it becomes increasingly difficult to separate culture from materialism, or materialism from culture, as they are imbricated with each other.

Today's shifted role of culture as an item of value, produced through and within capitalist industries, has resulted in what Rifkin calls the "age of access."[81] Questions of access structure our relationships with not only capitalism but also other individuals. The Internet's most significant debates are no longer only about ownership of goods but about access to goods and their supporting production practices. Importantly, such debates evidence not a narrowing of the role of culture in society but an expansion. Within advanced capitalism, brand strategies and management are situated not as economic principles or good business but as the affective stuff of culture. Rather than insert brands into existing culture, brand managers use the emotive relationships we all have with material things, with products, with content, and seek to build culture around those brands.

Marketers talk incessantly of "engagement," new branches of advertising and marketing firms are devoted to using social media as a way to authentically interact with consumers, and marketers in general are strategizing how to "engage" consumers as a way of recouping a loosening of control over messaging. It is this "engagement," rather than any top-down work by brand managers themselves, that does the building of brand culture. As many brand marketers explained to me, branding strategies need to focus on affective, authentic relationships between consumers and producers, and to build culture out of these relationships.[82] Additionally, brand cultures need to be built "organically" with the authentic participation of consumers. Within brand culture, consumers produce identity, community, emotional attachments, affective practices, and relationships both with the brand and with each other; in turn, brand culture—not to mention the products of those brands—provides an infrastructure for this kind of social and political behavior.

As the consumer builds emotive relationships within brand culture, her work is enabled by media technologies and applauded by their surrounding rhetoric of empowerment. This infrastructure includes the various communication and technological apparatuses that have sustained, facilitated, and enhanced U.S. consumer culture historically not only by providing crucial platforms for marketing messages and images but also by offering cultural and political contexts that animate shifting versions of the consumer citizen. As I have described, in the era of mass consumption, broadcast television and mass magazines were two technologies crucial in constructing (and thus gendering and racializing) an imagined national consumer. When the standardized, mass consumer was challenged by political and cultural upheavals, emerging identity politics, and a focus on "difference," emerging media and new technology formats such as cable television and niche markets facilitated the transition. Now, in the contemporary era, the expansion of the digital economy, the rejuvenation of DIY forms of cultural production, the hegemony of brand culture, and other forms of new media have revised the consumer citizen as a specific kind of activist. Clearly there are important differences between these eras, and the flexibility between consumption and production that characterizes the contemporary moment may well pave the way for new forms of resistance to consumer culture. Nevertheless, like the other historical moments discussed in this chapter, the current nexus of political economies, technologies, and shifting formations of identity harness political ideals such as "freedom" and "empowerment" as motivating factors in establishing hegemonic dominance.

In particular, the current glamorization of the consumer-producer is important to consider when theorizing the empowerment of the contemporary consumer citizen. The blurring of boundaries between consumer-producer so celebrated in Web 2.0 discourse is often cited as a tipping point in the formation of individual subjectivity from a passive consumer to an active subject. The celebration of this boundary collapse, especially in the rhetoric of advertising and marketing, hinges upon the notion of the disruption of the traditional top-down delivery of information, from powerful producer to passive consumer. Consumers are afforded greater latitude and freedom than ever before to produce individually meaningful material. This also represents the "freedom" to engage in immaterial labor. Fixed distinctions between "production and consumption, labor and culture" are questioned and denaturalized, and the resulting space opened up becomes the space of individual empowerment.[83] Celebratory rhetoric about this new consumer-producer, coming from profit-seeking advertisers and marketers, enables a brand, such as Dove, to entreat its consumers to "download your free self-esteem tools."[84]

What, exactly, is the consumer producing? Arvidsson's work on brands is useful here; he points out that contemporary brands enable consumers in different ways and toward different ends than traditional forms of advertising that imposed messages on consumers. Brands engage with consumers in a context of "freedom," whereby consumers are expected to have a say in the coproduction of brands.[85] The consumer "empowerment" afforded by brands is one that is at least partly the product of the immateriality of brands; they enable the coproduction of an experience with consumers rather than dictate an already determined experience for consumers. More than that, the relationship brand companies cultivate with their consumers is one defined not by consumer purchase as much as it is by identity construction and validation. As such, brand cultures shift the very notion of cultural value.[86] Generating profit does not necessarily mean there is no community, that the "freedom" to participate in culture never does anything but produce individually, rather than collectively, meaningful material. Rather, a tension or ambivalence is produced between the individual entrepreneur and activist and the increasing presence of networked publics, both animated by advanced capitalism. In the 21st century, this tension and its underlying ambivalence underscore efforts both to create a sense of self in the branded world and to establish a sense of community.

The Compromise of Cultural Capitalism

Following Terranova's logic, I am not proposing that our current moment represents a logical progression in consumer culture, whereby one cultural economy has plausibly transformed to the next. Rather, I am proposing that the contemporary cultural economy both embodies and materializes a different logic of value, one that provides a fertile context for the emergence of brand culture and a specific definition of commodity activism. I try to resist overemphasizing either the incorporation of individual subjectivities by advanced capitalism or the autonomy of the consumer citizen within this economy. Terranova sees the contemporary context as one based "in a difficult, experimental compromise between the historically rooted cultural and affective desire for creative production [and] the current capitalist emphasis on knowledge as the main source of value-added."[87] It is important that contemporary culture be understood as a compromise rather than a dichotomy or a binary. It disrupts the theoretical paralysis of binary thinking—as in the critique of Dove's Real Beauty campaign as hypocritical—and allows for rethinking the consumer-as-empowered-citizen, emphasizing the ambivalence and contradictions of the current context rather than explaining these qualities away as insignificant outliers.

It should not then come as a surprise that, within advanced capitalist culture, social activism is understood and experienced as a material good, as an object that has exchange value with other products. Like other identities, such as race and gender, the social activist in its current manifestation is managed, organized, and exchanged not simply as a commodity but as a brand. And, like other manifestations of marketing and advertising in recent US history, political ideals such as social equality, freedom, and empowerment are realized through the practices of consumption and consumer citizenship. Furthermore, when current identities are configured as "posts" (as in postfeminist, postracial, or post-Fordist), older political paradigms that once mobilized social activism no longer have the same cultural or economic capital; their community-centered struggles are easier to dismiss, their community-won victories easier to ignore. The central subjectivity within advanced capitalism is now the individual entrepreneur, working on his or her own in a radically "free" market.

The activist in neoliberal culture can be *anyone* (another of its utopic promises), as long as she or he is willing to shift from social to commodity activism, and as long as brand culture supports and sustains that activism. Indeed, contemporary marketers deploy new strategies as a way to both recognize and exploit these changing identities, resulting in an increasingly more sophisticated and complicated exchange between the consumer and the brand. When Dove criticizes the beauty industry for damaging girls' self-esteem through a very visible, social activist campaign that is funded through the selling of beauty products, the relationship between political (read: individual) empowerment and consumer culture is intricately, and often ambivalently, configured within the contours of the brand.

It thus makes sense to think about this exchange as at least partly a result of the contradictions within advanced capitalism and to consider this relation as a strain of ambivalence. Rather than lingering on the various ways in which contemporary brand culture is flush economically, politically, and culturally but lacking in morality or ethics, we need to critically interrogate the concepts that have been historically used to distinguish between commercial culture and political citizenship, such as consumer and producer, or brand manager and activist. This interrogation needs to begin with an understanding of brand cultures as cultures writ large—not as purely a form of individualism, or personalization. Terranova's idea of compromise, between creativity and capitalism, between affect and profit, requires that we understand what exactly is being compromised, and what consumers gain as well as lose through such transactions.

What is at stake is not simply revisiting these terms to theorize what place they might hold in a cultural debate about the making of identity. A new conceptualization of these terms and the contradictions between them is needed as a way to account for changing practices of cultural production and identity formation within a shifting economy. The mechanisms of capitalism have indeed addressed inequalities between certain groups of consumers. Yet, the logic of market capitalism is that it often masks inequalities while simultaneously claiming to address and alleviate them. This masking is never complete; its contradictions are visible in the context of other social and cultural forces, such as social activist movements, consumer advocacy, and self-empowerment. The market is always a possibility and a refusal, but the nature of its possibilities and kinds of refusals depend on the larger cultural context of technology, politics, and the construction of individual identity. In brand culture, with its attendant Web 2.0 technologies for consumer-generated content and DIY production, the outgrowths of neoliberalism's radically "free" markets are knowledge and affect—the stuff of identity—as well as culture itself.

2

BRANDING THE POSTFEMINIST SELF

THE LABOR OF FEMININITY

The brand is a gift, and it will set you free.
—Self-branding seminar, Los Angeles, 2010

More than a decade ago, on April 14, 1996, a young college student named Jennifer Ringley began uploading a constant stream of pictures of herself on the Web. Filmed from her dorm room, a new photograph was taken every three minutes and automatically posted to a website. The result was a catalog of a young woman's life, detailing her daily activities: Jennifer with friends, Jennifer studying, Jennifer having sex. Named "JenniCam," this project attracted up to 4 million views a day at its peak. A few months after she started, Ringley realized the economic potential of this kind of involvement; she began charging for "full" entry into her site. Through automatic credit card payments by means of another nascent Web phenomenon—PayPal—paying customers gained "premium" access to (even) more frequent updates on her life. According to the mission statement of JenniCam.org, Ringley sought to create "a window into a virtual human zoo."[1] Ringley might be said to be the first web-based "lifecaster." Within the decade, her lone stream of images would become a deluge; as *Wired* magazine states, "Ringley's pioneering adventure in self-exposure anticipated the appetite for reality-based voyeurtainment."[2] Why this kind of relentless self-exposure is a "pioneering adventure" is not raised as a question; rather, JenniCam heralded a new era of media production.

Indeed, this "appetite" has certainly been whetted; a more contemporary manifestation of "voyeurtainment" occurred in the fall of 2008, when a twenty-two-year old American woman named Natalie Dylan attempted to sell her virginity on the online auction site eBay. According to a press release, Dylan hoped that selling her virginity on the immensely popular website would help pay for graduate school; she has a bachelor's degree in women's studies and expected to fund her master's degree program with the profit made from this unique auctioning. "We live in a capitalist society," she said in a later interview. "Why shouldn't I be able to capitalize on my virginity?"[3] According to Dylan, eBay refused to host her auction (and other sales like it, such as the sale of one's kidneys or one's parents) on the grounds stated in the site's regulations: eBay prohibits the sale of anything "immoral, illegal, or just plain distasteful."[4]

Dylan then took her virginity to the Moonlite Bunny Ranch, an infamous brothel in Reno, Nevada. According to her own account, she was taking "the ancient notion that a woman's virginity is priceless and [using] it as a vehicle for capitalism."[5] She has said that she has been congratulated by a CEO of a Fortune 500 company for her "entrepreneurial gumption" (although she apparently was not hired by this company) and has argued, using the language of business, that she might even be an "early adopter of a future trend."[6] While it is certainly easy to see Dylan's virginity auction as a publicity stunt (after all, she announced her sale on the Howard Stern radio show)—or even a kind of performance art, like JenniCam—Dylan's "project" nonetheless raises questions about what elements of the corporeal can (or should) be saleable.

Two years before Dylan's display of "entrepreneurial gumption," another woman, Tila Tequila (neé Tila Nguyen) became famous for a different kind of entrepreneurship. In 2006, she had more than 1.5 million "friends" on MySpace, her MySpace profile had been viewed more than 50 million times, and she was receiving between 3,000 and 5,000 new friend requests every day. In an article detailing Tequila's MySpace fame, *Time* reporter Lev Grossman wrote, "She is something entirely new, a celebrity created not by a studio or a network but fan by fan, click by click, from the ground up on MySpace."[7]

Tila Tequila has become the exemplar of the use and power of social network sites to create brand visibility. As she herself said, "Once they saw how I worked it, everyone did what I did and started promoting themselves."[8] Her popularity on MySpace soon led to a record deal with MySpace music and

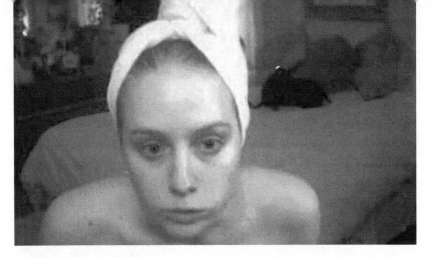

A shot from JenniCam.

then to a popular MTV reality show, *A Shot of Love with Tila Tequila,* where, in the spirit of reality dating shows, she sought a life partner from thirty-two well-screened contestants—sixteen straight men and sixteen lesbian-identified women. (Her first choice apparently did not work out, so the show ran for two seasons, in 2007 and 2008.) As Tequila says, over the course of her stay on MySpace, she turned her online persona into a full-fledged business. "This is my job," she said before the start of her MTV show. "That's how you maintain your popularity and keep it alive." Grossman continues by saying that Tequila "clearly grasps the logic of Web 2.0 in a way that would make many CEOs weep."[9]

The fact that Tequila claims the maintenance of her online brand as a "job" clearly situates her project as labor: she labors to create and maintain her self-brand. From this kind of work, questions inevitably arise: What kind of job is it? Who pays? And for whom does one self-brand?

I begin this chapter with these anecdotes not to make a reductionist collapse between the JenniCam project, Natalie Dylan's sale of her virginity, and Tia Tequila's self-promotion but to point out a shift manifest in contemporary brand culture. "Selling" yourself, or your virginity, is understood as illegitimate—"immoral, illegal, or just plain distasteful"—at least by eBay (and, again, even though the Fortune 500 CEO "admired her gumption," he did not actually offer Dylan a job). To accomplish her goal, to "capitalize on her virginity," and perhaps to increase the shelf life of her publicity stunt, Dylan turned to the Moonlite Bunny Ranch, and to what is still seen as an illegitimate career choice: prostitution. Ringley's JenniCam is positioned somewhere between Dylan and Tequila; her endeavor was acceptable because she did not prostitute herself, but she did not yet have the ability, knowledge, or

NATALIE DYLAN OFFICIAL MYSPACE PAGE

"THE BEAUTY OF CAPITALISM"

Female
22 years old
San Diego, California
United States

Last Login: 2/3/2009

mood: blessed
View My: Pics | Videos

Natalie Dylan's MySpace page.

cultural context to brand herself like Tequila and was rather content with making immediate money from her visitors. Tequila, on the other hand, is recognized as successfully parlaying her life online into a lucrative career.[10] While few people can maintain a personal profile on social network sites with the ferocious energy of Tequila, "branding" oneself is today understood not only as legitimate but as a goal to strive for. Indeed, self-branding is positioned by marketers and brand managers as the proper way—perhaps even the necessary way—to "take care of oneself" in contemporary advanced capitalist economy.

In this chapter, I turn my attention to the self as a brand. I focus on the technological capacities of the Internet and the creative possibilities of the interactive user as primary contexts that animate strategies of self-branding. Additionally, the processes, and the consequences, of self-branding are well

Tila Tequila's MySpace page.

illustrated by looking at the work of girls and young women. The vast cultural, political, and economic shifts within advanced capitalist consumer culture that I explore in this book are also accompanied by significant shifts in gender constructions. It is the intersection between shifts that become important for the legibility of self-branding as a normative strategy. Foucault spoke in 1978 of the "technology of the self": sets of practices, or methods, that "permit individuals to effect by their own means or with the help of others a certain number of operations on their own bodies and souls, thoughts, conduct, and way of being, so as to transform themselves in order to attain a certain state of happiness, purity, wisdom, perfection, or immortality."[11] These "operations," in the context of brand culture, involve economic principles such as brand management strategies, self-promotion, and advertising techniques that help to explain the self within a set of social and cultural conditions. Technologies of the self have vast and often contradictory implications for women in the 21st century, where "putting oneself out there," and the ensuing quest for visibility, is an ever more normative practice.[12]

The visible self on global display gains traction in the contemporary context of postfeminism. Here, as I discussed in the previous chapter, in the US, postfeminism is both an ideology and an increasingly normative strategy of engaging with the world. These practices—theoretical and practical alike—connect traditional liberal feminist ideas about everything from freedom to choice to independence, to an expansive and distinctly contemporary capitalist engagement with media, merchandise, and consumption.[13] Certainly postfeminism is not the only feminist practice available in the early 21st century, but it is one that has appeal and purchase on many levels, and has in relatively few years been absorbed into everything from political ideology to popular culture to consumption habits.

Because postfeminism has been almost seamlessly incorporated into consumer culture, it is a particularly rich context for girls and young women to build a self-brand. Postfeminism marks a historical shift in representation, as Anita Harris, Angela McRobbie, and others have pointed out, from women as a vague mass of passive consumers to girls and young women as active, increasingly individualized entrepreneurs. As we saw with Dove soap, the act of consumption is configured as an act of self-empowerment. With the normalization of postfeminism comes an increasing cultural recognition of girls and young women as both powerful citizens and consumers; such recognition can seem a radical disruption of the gender relations that have dominated American culture for the past century. The reality, of course, is far more complicated. Postfeminism in practice is often individualized and constructed as personal choice rather than collective action; its ideal manifestation, in turn, is not struggle for social change but rather capacity for entrepreneurship. Within the guise of empowerment, the "girl entrepreneur is the ultimate self-inventing young woman who represents a fantasy of achievement accomplished by good ideas, hard work, and self-confidence."[14] Importantly, the ideals and accomplishments of the postfeminist subject—independence, capacity, empowerment—are entangled with similar ideals about the contemporary media-savvy interactive subject who is at ease in navigating the ostensibly flexible, open architectures of online spaces.

This interactive subject, like the postfeminist subject, realizes self-empowerment through her capacity and productivity. I define the interactive subject as an individual who can move between and within media platforms with ease, and who can produce media online, whether in the form of videos, blogs, or even through comments and feedback. Interactivity here also implies the design of the technology that is engaged. That is, the interactive subject participates in and through interactive technology; she "finds" a self and broadcasts that self, through those spaces that authorize and encourage user activity.[15] These two cultural formations—postfeminism and interactivity—both enabled by advanced capitalism, make self-branding seem not only logical but perhaps necessary. Postfeminism and interactivity create what I would call a neoliberal *moral* framework, where each of us has a duty to ourselves to cultivate a self-brand.

"me & Nicole crazyyy" YouTube video, with 654,033 views.

In the following pages, I trace the entangled discourses and spaces of self-branding, postfeminism, and interactivity as a way to account for new configurations of gender identity in contemporary culture. As I discussed in the previous chapter, brand cultures are increasingly formed around discourses and practices traditionally seen as outside the market, in "authentic" spaces. The practice of branding the "self" is legible in such discourses and occurs in the context of certain specific cultural ideals of selfhood. These ideals include not only traditional liberal feminist ideals of freedom, self-determination, and self-improvement but also residual notions of sexual freedom and sexual confidence for women. Cultural ideals of selfhood are richly supported in online social network sites, which are increasingly spaces to ask and answer the question: Who am I? Even if girls and young women do not set out to strategically, or intentionally, build a self-brand, the logic of online sites and the presence of feedback mean that one's online presence will be viewed by others using the same rubric to judge brands: through evaluation, ranking, and judgment, and with the ideal of visibility in mind. Thus, I focus on social network sites as complex, technologically mediated venues for the branding of the postfeminist self, attending to three subgenres within the realm of such sites: amateur videos by girls and young women engaged in everyday, mundane activities (dancing, singing, playing) on YouTube; the emergence of the "lifecaster" on digital platforms as a lucrative career; and personal profiles on sites such as Facebook.[16]

At the self-branding seminar referenced earlier, an impassioned marketer told his audience, "The brand will set you free." But what, exactly, does it mean to be free in the current moment, amid the market-driven promises of postfeminism, within the seemingly limitless spaces of media interactivity? And why is building a self-brand understood as not only the most efficacious but also an increasingly moral way to achieve this kind of freedom? To address these questions, it is necessary to first account for the perspective of branders themselves. That is, a dedicated market for the self-brand, an industry for a seemingly never-ending consumer base, needs to be established by brand marketers.

The Brander's Perspective: The Industry of Self-Branding

Though certainly not everyone is invested in crafting a self-brand, more and more people in the US in the 21st century seem to agree with Tila Tequila: branding yourself is important. College graduates are counseled on the necessity of building a self-brand when entering the job market. Self-branding experts and professional Facebook photographers provide support services for the job of building a self-brand. Trade books with titles such as *Be Your Own Brand: A Breakthrough Formula for Standing Out from the Crowd; Managing Brand You: 7 Steps to Creating Your Most Successful Self; Make a Name for Yourself: 8 Steps Every Woman Needs to Create a Personal Brand Strategy for Success;* and *Me 2.0: Build a Powerful Brand to Achieve Career Success* now occupy a weighty bookshelf on a topic that barely existed fifty years ago. These physical books coexist with countless "how-to" forums online, where amateurs and experts alike debate the dos and don'ts of self-branding. Academics and intellectuals (and even those who study branding and consumer culture) are increasingly advised to further professionalize by developing personal brands as a way to strategically market both career and personal identities.

The marketing books on self-branding are useful archives for thinking through what, exactly, it means to embrace the practice of self-branding. Most of the books begin with the premise that because branding has been such an effective business strategy for corporations, it is perfectly logical to apply this business model to the crafting of oneself. David McNally and Karl D. Speak, the authors of *Be Your Own Brand,* have a chapter titled "Becoming More of Who You Are," in which they state:

Many of the proven, successful loyalty-building ideas and tactics used by businesses in managing their brands can be brought to bear on your own personal relationships, with outstanding results. As you learn to understand and apply sensible, practical brand-development and self-management principles, you will gain tools you can use to create and progressively strengthen your relationships with the people you interact with on a daily basis.[17]

Another marketer, Catherine Kaputa, in her book *U R a Brand!*, promises that readers will "learn how the branding principles and strategies developed for the commercial world may be used to achieve your business and personal potential....In short, you are a brand....savvy professionals, businesspeople, and entrepreneurs are also using self-, or personal, branding, so that they can be more successful."[18]

The self-brand, as the branding strategists continually remind us, is a complex relationship one has not only with the outside world but also within oneself. Marketers McNally and Speak define the personal brand in this way: "Your brand is a perception or emotion, maintained by somebody other than you, that describes the total experience of having a relationship with you."[19] By this definition, self-branding is an expression of a moral framework, a means to access "authenticity," and crucially important in order to become "more of who you are" as well as who "you were meant to be."[20] Brand strategists emphasize that businesses employ brand management principles and techniques by focusing on building relationships between products and consumers. If an individual were to utilize these same principles and techniques, she or he could have one's family, friends, and coworkers "truly understand and fully acknowledge who you are and what you do."[21] Brand strategists and marketers desire the brand relationship to be the most loyal kind of relationship for an individual—indeed, the entire brand industry, composed of brand marketers, strategists, and consultants, depends on this relationship being understood as both profound and loyal.

But because there is tremendous unpredictability in consumer culture in terms of what brands will actually inspire loyal relationships, marketers and branders are often anxious and insecure about which brands will succeed and which will fail. The relationship between brands and consumers needs to be constantly made and remade, and this continuous process creates yet another demonstration of the ambivalence in brand cultures. Especially in an era of seemingly constant new media options for not only branding, there is a precariousness to the brand relationship, one that marketers and branders struggle to secure in an ever-changing environment.[22] One strategy in securing this relationship involves collapsing brand strategy and personal identity. The collapse between business brand strategy and personal identity construction that these marketers assume has logic in an economic context where the individual is privileged as a commodity, and where cultural and social life is increasingly organized and experienced through the terms and conditions of business models. This means that cultural values, such as morals and personal standards, are harnessed and reshaped within these same business conditions, so that building a brand is often promoted by marketers as a moral obligation to oneself.

Clearly, the line between commodifying one's body and branding one's body is slippery. Traditionally, a Marxist critique of commodification has rested in part on the ways this process does not acknowledge the (human) labor that is necessary for the production process. But in the practice of branding the self, the construction of the self-brand *necessarily* acknowledges the individual's role as the producer of her individual life narrative. A crucial difference between commodification and branding is thus the self-conscious role of individual labor in the production of the self-brand. This labor of the individual is a necessary element in the "enterprising self," even more so on digital platforms that rely on self-disclosure as part of self-branding.

Self-Disclosure and Postfeminism as Brand Strategy

The practices of self-disclosure typical of building a self-brand, of "putting oneself out there," and transparency are both part of what Foucault would call "the proper care of the self."[23] Disclosure and transparency in this context are part of one's moral obligation to oneself. By disclosure I mean the detailing of one's everyday life for others' consumption; transparency is the effect of this kind of disclosure, ostensibly giving viewers a complete view of one's "authentic" self. Digitally aided disclosure, such as building a self-brand on MySpace or Facebook, relies on traditional discourses of the "authentic" self as one that is transparent, without artifice, open to others. As I discussed in the introduction, authenticity not only is viewed as residing inside the self but also is demonstrated by allowing the outside world access to one's inner self. For example, Jean-Jacques Rousseau implied that authenticity is built upon a collapse of one's outer appearance and inner sentiment, to be "true" to oneself. But, as Andrew Potter points out, "This project was never about merely telling facts about yourself. More than that, it was seen as a moral achievement, the result of a long, arduous, and artistic process of self-creation."[24] In the contemporary context, the creation of the "authentic self" continues to be understood as a kind of moral achievement, but moralism itself has metamorphosed into a fun-house mirror version of Rousseau's conviction, where to truly understand and experience the "authentic" self is to *brand* this self.

Principles of contemporary branding—such as engagement, building relationships, and consumer coproduction—authorize branding the self as authentic, because self-branding is seen not as an imposition of a concept or product by corporate culture but rather as the individual taking on the project herself as a way to access her "true" self. This branded self then becomes publicly legible in a surrounding brand culture. For the contemporary virtuous self, individual entrepreneurship is the conduit for self-realization, and online spaces are a perfect site for realizing this entrepreneurship.[25] Individual entrepreneurship, such as that demonstrated by Tila Tequila, within online spaces is legible within the broader cultural context of postfeminism, a context that is animated by neoliberal capitalism and by the participatory culture that structures much online activity.

Postfeminism can be seen as many things: as ideologies, a set of practices, and strategies. I find Angela McRobbie's formulation the most useful: starting in the late 1990s, she argues, postfeminism has formed a "cultural space," or "a field of transformation in which feminist values come to be engaged with, and to some extent incorporated across, civil society in institutional practices, in education, in the work environment, and in the media."[26] McRobbie calls this engagement of feminism by contemporary culture "feminism taken into account" because it is a process in which feminist values and ideologies are initially considered, only to then be found dated and passé and thus repudiated. McRobbie characterizes this dynamic—acknowledging feminism only to discount it—as a "double-movement," noting the paradox of how the dissemination of discourses about freedom and equality provides the context for the retrenchment of gender and gendered relations. In other words, young women are able to progress in society (in the realms of education, work, sexual freedom, etc.) on the condition that feminism "fades away."[27] Once again, as women are encouraged to "put themselves out there," we confront the notion of visibility. While feminism fades from vision, the individual entrepreneur takes its place.

Postfeminism is also what Rosalind Gill calls a "sensibility" that shapes everything from products to media representation to digital media.[28] This postfeminist sensibility authorizes the individualism of women more than anything else. The individual entrepreneur becomes the signature of a postfeminist woman, where individual success and personal consumption habits are the expected behaviors of the ideal feminine subject. According to Anita Harris, "The image of successful, individualized girlhood itself is one of the most profitable products being sold to them and others."[29] Importantly, this is a *commodity* image—that is, within a postfeminist sensibility, femininity is defined as a "bodily property." As Gill elaborates, "The body is presented simultaneously as women's source of power and as always already unruly and requiring constant monitoring, surveillance, discipline and remodeling (and consumer spending) in order to conform to ever narrower judgments of female attractiveness."[30] One way in which bodily property is manifest is in the encouragement of what Harris calls the "can-do" girl, who is identified by her ambition and career goals, her overt self-confidence, and her commitment to an explicit consumer lifestyle.[31]

The "can-do" girl finds a supportive environment online. Indeed, it is clear that, in the early 21st century, young people increasingly "live" in online spaces,[32] and "living online" has differently gendered stakes and consequences for young women and men.[33] Because of a previous historical context that situated girls and their practices as outside, both literally and intellectually, the realm of technology (usually because of girls' assumed "natural" deficiency when it comes to technology), the ever-increasing presence of girls online—and what they do when they are there—has been the focus of recent scholarly analysis.[34] Much of this work has challenged traditional communication research that links technological use (ranging from watching television to participating in chat rooms) to harmful social effects, where technology has been blamed for everything from violence to hypersexuality to "growing up too soon." Instead, feminist scholars are now exploring the potential benefits, especially for girls, of exploring the Internet as a space in which creative identity-making, among other things, might be possible. This work has detailed not only the various ways in which girls participate in online practices but also the increase in video production by girls in the last several decades.[35] The notion that girls can be producers as well as consumers has been embraced, albeit with many hesitations, as a kind of empowerment.

The fact that young people, and girls and young women in particular, are using social media in increasing numbers raises questions about empowerment, voice, and self-expression. The answers, needless to say, are not simple. Not all online spaces are the same; nor do they contain the same possibilities for self-presentation and self-expression. Personal home pages, blogs, and self-produced videos all capitalize in different ways on the flexible architecture of the Internet as well as on its potential for user interactivity. Young women's self-presentation online is a contradictory practice, one that does not demonstrate an unfettered freedom in crafting identity any more than it is completely controlled and determined by the media and cultural industries. As Mark Andrejevic has pointed out in his work on surveillance and corporate control in the online era, "The point of exploring the ways in which the interactivity of viewers doubles as a form of labor is to point out that, in the interactive era, the binary opposition between complicit passivity and subversive participation needs to be revisited and revised."[36] Focusing on the opposing forces of passive and active participation, as I have discussed, distracts us from the ways in which consumption and production are imbricated practices, or, as Mary Celeste Kearney argues, a kind of relationship, rather than isolated, discrete activities.[37]

Heeding the call of Kearney and others to avoid the simplified binaries of consumption/production is critical when parsing the deep interrelations between these categories. It is convincing, as many scholars have argued, that online spaces afford creative possibilities in terms of production.[38] However, the argument that creativity is defined, understood, and made legible within the commercial parameters of the online spaces in which it is enacted is equally convincing. Of course, neither extreme is true; nor does critical exploration necessitate a one-sided argument. If we question the celebratory discourse about gendered empowerment enabled by online technological formats, that does not in turn indicate that all forms and genres of online media production function in the service of consumer capital. Nor are all girls' media productions mere masquerades rather than socially and culturally significant practices.

YouTube is a rich online space for exploring these kinds of ambivalences. On July 25, 2008, the user kpal527 posted "i kissed a girl" to YouTube. In the two-and-a-half-minute video, two young white girls, likely twelve or thirteen years old, dance and sing to the popular song by teen idol Katy Perry, "I Kissed a Girl." The video seems to have been filmed with a webcam, a fairly low-quality image and no close-ups or any camera movement. The girls, wearing shorts and T-shirts branded with popular commercial logos, are clearly having fun in front of the camera—at times the dance turns silly, they giggle throughout, interrupting their own singing, making faces to the camera. In the grainy background we see what looks to be a typical middle-class teenage girl's bedroom: a nondescript bed and dresser, toys, books, and pink blankets strewn on the floor. At the time of writing, there were forty-two comments evaluating the dance performance in the feedback section beneath the video feed. One comment, from sophieluvzu, states: "LMAO! I can't say anything bad about them, because I remember when I was this young I made dances up like this but suppose its for fun, although I didn't know what youtube was back then."[39]

YouTube has established itself as a clearinghouse for the posting of videos that chronicle everyday life. The Katy Perry sing-along is one of thousands of amateur videos posted on YouTube featuring young women dancing and singing to popular music, referencing commercial popular culture, and presenting themselves for display.

YouTube was the most popular entertainment website in Britain in 2007, and it was consistently in the top ten most visited websites globally in early 2011.[40] Of course, YouTube is not only a video site for youth video exhibition; the site is a platform for audiovisual content of all kinds, from user-created videos to commercial advertisements to pirated broadcast media content to presidential addresses.

YouTube was launched in 2005 as a user-friendly means to upload, store, and share individual videos. It was acquired by Google in 2006 for $1.65 billion and has expanded to become a primary commercial venue for marketing music, movies, and television, while managing to retain its original identity as a site for amateur users. As Jean Burgess and Joshua Green state, YouTube is a "particularly unstable object of study," in part because of its "double function as both a 'top-down' platform for the distribution of popular culture and a 'bottom-up' platform for vernacular creativity."[41] The website's "double function" offers an opportunity to think critically about how YouTube helps with the creation of the self-brand.

The double function of YouTube also mimics the dialectic between the public and private with regard to subject formation, making it a particularly rich site for self-branding. In particular, some user-created YouTube videos specifically invoke what I am calling the "postfeminist" self-brand. These videos, like "i kissed a girl" mentioned earlier, both support and perpetuate a commercial postfeminist discourse in which girls and young women are ostensibly "empowered" through public bodily performances and the production of user-generated content. This may not always be a strategic positioning of the video for self-branding by the poster but rather a consequence of the way YouTube videos are situated in the context of postfeminism and online user interactivity. That is, the transition of YouTube from its earlier incarnation as a personal "digital video repository" to its now well-known function as a platform from which each of us can "broadcast yourself" cannot be seen as merely part of the expansion of Web 2.0 technologies.[42] Because of the site's dynamic capacity for displaying both individual public performances and viewers' comments and feedback, it has become an ideal space to craft a self-brand.[43]

For instance, a YouTube video by Uzsikapicics called "13 year old Barbie Girls," had, at the time of writing, 777,085 views and 1,226 feedback comments. The video, featuring six white girls, opens with a shot of a Barbie and a Ken doll (and a tube of toothpaste adorned with images of Disney princesses) arranged on a chair. A young girl sits on the dolls, nonchalantly fastens her shoes, stands up, turns on the stereo and begins to dance. She moves to the front door, opening it to two other girls, dramatically involved in putting on lipstick and other makeup. The girls, clearly mocking celebrity as well as beauty culture, air-kiss each other and also begin dancing to the song. The camera pans to two other girls: one girl is looking at a teen magazine with Paris Hilton on the cover, while the other is occupied by dramatically brushing the hair of a small toy dog. In the next shot, the five girls sit together on a couch, performing a choreographed routine of crossing and uncrossing their legs. Another girl enters the room, and with a dramatic gesture sprays the girls with a spray can. The five then collapse on the floor. As they get up together, they begin singing the popular song by Aqua, "I'm a Barbie Girl." One girl brandishes what looks like a steak knife. The video ends with a last shot of the Barbie and Ken dolls, with one exception: Ken's head has been cut off, and the aforementioned steak knife sticks out of his neck. The violent, vaguely political ending of the video is offset by the silliness of the girls, who are obviously having fun, and demonstrates a central contradiction of a kind of public femininity.

YouTube affords girls, such as the "13 year old Barbie Girls," an opportunity to experiment with performance as a way to craft gender identity. The possibilities here are indeed profound. And it is clear that the technological space of the Internet is also a cultural and social space that is potentially expansive in its ability to reimagine gender identity. New media seem to provide every adolescent's fantasy: a space—both culturally sanctioned and a little risky—in which to bring identities "into being" (and share them with friends). With playful parody, these girls explore the challenges involved in being a "Barbie Girl"; the girls both perform a stereotypical gendered identity and point out its contradictions. Popular cultural artifacts, Barbie not least among them, are often used in this way by individuals, their original use transformed into an object of resistance, a statement of challenge.[44]

Yet, despite the potential of YouTube and related sites, many of the YouTube videos created by young girls depend upon conventional, and nearly always gendered, brand contexts. For every radical statement, there are many more that are shaped by a confluence of commercial and sexual codes: Disney princesses feature prominently in girls' bedrooms and on clothing; the songs most often danced to, or sung along with, are commercially produced pop confections, made for profit by Beyoncé, Jennifer Lopez, Katy Perry, and others, released by a media industry that has made billions on a hegemonic female sexuality; posters on the walls in girls' rooms seem a steady repeat of heteronormative teen celebrities, mainstream movies and television programs, and retail outlets such as Abercrombie and Fitch. The girls producing these videos are certainly engaging in identity formation, but they also are engaged in immaterial labor, where branded performances do promotional work for the corporations or celebrities referenced (Disney, Beyoncé, Abercrombie and Fitch). A case in point: Beyoncé's video of her hit single "Single Ladies" became immeasurably more visible because of the number of people who copied its choreography (both sincerely and as parody) and posted their videos on YouTube.

The almost inevitable presence of commercial brands as structuring narratives for YouTube videos indicates that self-presentation does not imply simply *any* narrative of the self, created within an endlessly open cultural script, but one that makes sense within a cultural and economic context of recognizable and predetermined texts and values. Of course, an individual's use and combination of these texts and values may be unexpected, as there is no such thing as a truly "open cultural script" apart from cultural artifacts already in circulation. However, the script that is often relied on in these videos utilizes familiar branded elements.[45] Thus, the fact that girls produce media—and thus ostensibly produce themselves through their self-presentation—within the context of a commercially driven technological space is not only evidence of a kind of empowering self-work but also a way to self-brand in an increasingly ubiquitous brand culture (even if self-branding is not the overt intention of the producers). Videos are produced in ways that mimic MTV and other commercial music videos, and girls dance to Beyoncé, Jennifer Lopez, Katy Perry, and other pop artists, reaffirming the brands of the artists even as they create their own self-brands.

This is not to say that this commercialized script always dictates a heavily stylized image of traditional femininity—indeed, Beyoncé has been recognized as a strong icon of postfeminism, one who challenges hierarchies of gender. But this sort of "girl power" also relies on commercially popular music and gendered images. The result is a fixed cycle: postfeminism offers a cultural context that celebrates the production of the self but is shaped by an economic context that relies on that self to be a brand. In other words, young women can articulate, craft, and broadcast identities on YouTube, but they do so within the commercial context of branding and advertising, and this context can contain and limit young women. The empowerment that ostensibly results from identity construction is then logical within a commercial context. Therefore, adolescents' questions of "Who am I?" become more about "How do I sell myself?," especially for young women, precisely as a process of figuring out personal identity.[46]

The Internet is typically promoted as an open site, unfettered by the messiness of "real" life, by the entrenched power dynamics—gendered and otherwise—of the "real" world. Such an ideal situates technology, and technological mechanisms such as online feedback, as conduits to empowerment. However, there are two particularly relevant critiques of online empowerment in the context of the self-brand: one focusing on labor, the other on depoliticization. From an economic perspective, the empowered consumer who is also a producer (even if the "yield" of that production is just online feedback) has an additional, less celebrated, function: aside from helping to build brands by featuring them within video productions, the meaning-making and work of consumers can also be exploited by service providers eager to aggregate and sell large sets of data regarding user behavior.[47] The work of these active consumers is also seen in what Andrejevic calls an "off-loading of corporate labor," where consumers advertise for corporations through blogging, product placement, online competitions, and so on.[48]

The depoliticization critique is found in Jodi Dean's theory of "communicative capitalism." According to Dean, the "fantasies" of empowerment that characterize Web 2.0 technologies need to be understood within a broader context of late capitalism, "in which values heralded as central to democracy take material form in networked communications technologies."[49] These values include abundance, communication, and, of course, personal empowerment. Dean is primarily concerned with the ways in which abundance, or circulation of communication—demonstrated by the amount of information and the number of online messages in which a person can locate herself—"stands in" as political activity without ever actually achieving engaged political discourse. She argues that ultimately the "micropolitics of the everyday," the kinds of debate and activity that characterize online interaction, distracts individuals from engaging in broader political issues.[50]

While Dean overgeneralizes in her indictment of activity within online spaces as mere "stand-ins" for politics, her argument is helpful for thinking about the role of user feedback in self-branding. It is not that attention to everyday micropolitics in itself counteracts engaged political discourse; after all, in the historical context of feminism, it is precisely such attention to everyday life that encouraged millions of women to critique the dominant relations of power. The daily, just like the personal, is indeed political. But in the context of digital technologies and a postfeminist environment, attention to everyday politics becomes less a reason to collectively challenge power structures and more a reason to embrace self-branding.

The abundance of user feedback online exemplifies what Dean would call a "post-political" practice characteristic of Web 2.0 environments. The cultural and social value of online self-brands is partly measured through the number of views and comments these self-productions (be they personal profiles or YouTube videos) receive. While certainly the sheer quantity of "hits" one receives is not synonymous with social value, the number of comments, views, and "friends" a webpage garners means visibility, a necessary component to the self-brand. After all, it was Tila Tequila's 1.5 million MySpace friends who paved the way for her other entertainment possibilities. Feedback is critical to creating a self-brand; to sell oneself as a brand, there must be a conscious recognition of the fact that other users are "buying," even if feedback is negative (the Internet embodies the maxim that "all press is good press"). Feedback functions on YouTube as a way to create a continuous dynamic between consumer and producer. This dynamic is neither top-down nor bottom-up but ostensibly a meeting between the two, and thus implies a nonlinear power distribution between producer and consumer, with neither system controlling the other.

The interplay between media production and feedback is far murkier than this optimistic view, however. Feedback can easily replicate a culture's (offline) strategies of surveillance, judgment, and evaluation—practices signaling consumer agency, but simultaneously disciplining and constituting subjects. Just as not all online media productions are the same or have the same purpose, not all feedback is the same. To take YouTube as an example, feedback on girls' videos I examined on the site functions often as a disciplinary strategy, where through comments, videos are judged according to how well their creators fit normative standards of femininity.

This kind of comparative feedback is often positioned by marketers as evidence of user interactivity. Across the web, users engage in ranking products (such as customer rankings on Amazon.com), individuals (such as the website Hot or Not, the logic of which is self-explanatory), and media texts (such as those found on the TV review website Television without Pity).[51] Posting a video on YouTube is both an explicit and an implicit request for this kind of feedback and situates videos (and, implicitly, their makers) as products to be evaluated by customers. Importantly, feedback on YouTube forms a crucial element in the relationship between consumer and producer; in the logic of the web—just as in "real" lives—evaluation, judgment, and ranking are necessary components of the self-brand.

Recall the YouTube video "13 year old Barbie Girls." Below the video, feedback ran the gamut from the creepy ("I love all of u young girls") to the more embracing ("LOL 13 year old boys aren't like this! Women are just too sweethearted. Makes me sad to think of the way women are treated in this world"). Others commented on the high number of views: "763,292 views!!!! Anyway the girls are cute. . .but 763,292 views!!! For God sake the video is so stupid. . .sorry this is my opinion."[52]

Almost invariably, feedback on YouTube videos featuring young women eventually focuses on normative physical appearance, "hotness," and dancing skill. Comments on a variety of videos I examined ranged from "Damn girl, keep them coming" ("Stair Dance") to "excellent body" (Lissawentworth) to "god help me & have mercy on my soul, this is so goddamn hot" (irisverygood) to "I wanna do these little snots" (coolcokeify). Though again running the gamut of intention, each of these judgments exercises a kind of control over the girls' self-presentations, situating videos like this one squarely within a familiar script of objectifying the bodies of young women. Indeed, feedback for these videos does not invoke interactive dialogue. YouTube's comment system, in fact, makes it difficult to reply to other commenters. Instead, not unlike other ways of objectifying young women, these comments are nearly always a one-way discussion, in which the producer absorbs these judgments but has little venue to respond to them.

In some ways, in a manner similar to the notion of what McRobbie calls "feminism taken into account," the YouTube context (including both posting videos and supplying feedback) also provides a platform for the self-branding of girls and young women based on what Dean calls the "fantasy of empowerment."[53] Yet, alongside the position of the Internet as a key component in a gendered economy of visibility, there is another, more subtle issue here. In the use of the term "fantasy of empowerment," Dean presumes the existence of a nonfantasy version—that is, an empowerment that is more real, more authentic. Such a critique unintentionally reifies the simplistic binary that I have been arguing against—here between authentic empowerment and fantasy empowerment—rather than parsing their deep interrelations. I would like to suggest that the contrast between an offline empowerment that is "real" and an online empowerment that is "fake" is ultimately beside the point, since it misses the logic of digital technologies, simultaneously dynamic and disciplinary. Instead, the reality is far murkier. The ideals shaping the discursive and ideological space of the Internet—freedom, equality, innovation, entrepreneurship—are the same discourses that provide the logic for girls' self-branding, a practice that situates girls ever more securely into the norms and values of hegemonic gendered consumer culture, as they also reshape definitions of a new, interactive femininity.

Self-branding is thus not just a tired rehashing of the objectification of female bodies but rather a new social arrangement that relies on different strategies for identity construction and hinges on more progressive ideals such as capability, empowerment, and imagination.[54] The culture of self-branding, like other brand cultures, is structured by such ambivalence; self-branding is fraught with tensions between empowering oneself as a producer and occupying this empowered position within the terms and definitions set up by broader brand and commercial culture. Thus, like the "new category of womanhood" McRobbie describes, the self-branded girl is encouraged to be self-reliant, to embody the "can-do" spirit. Indeed, self-branding strategist Kaputa argues in *U R a Brand!* that while all people need to be self-brand "builders" in the contemporary marketplace, this is particularly true for women and girls: self-branding "is especially for women, women like myself, who were told as children, 'Don't upstage your brother' or 'It's not nice to call attention to yourself.' The truth is, if you don't brand yourself, someone else will, and it probably won't be the brand you had in mind."[55] This sentiment exemplifies the postfeminist vision of empowerment, acknowledging that there have been historical obstacles for women to be independent, but that in the contemporary context it is up to women to carve out space for themselves—and the best way to do so is to develop a brand.

For some girls, and some women, Web 2.0 culture does provide a perfect space to realize this particular kind of empowerment. Tila Tequila, by most accounts, is a success in the contemporary economy. Similarly, digital technology has enabled the self-branding of Rebecca Black, the much-maligned but very successful California teenager who in 2011 created the song "Friday, Friday" (dubbed by many critics as the worst song ever) through the record label ARK music factory and became an immediate online phenomenon. Because of the structure and definition of an empowerment animated by the Internet, the web becomes the perfect space for a heightened kind of self-monitoring and self-improvement undergirding self-branding. In other words, online empowerment is not always false proposition or hope; rather, it is defined and circumscribed precisely by the architecture of the Internet, as well as by the cultural and political conditions that make the Internet seem an appropriate vehicle for gender empowerment. Again, empowerment may be realized, but it is realized within the context of brand culture. Girls, then, are constructing themselves as gendered beings within this context, where their performances of visibility and spectacular femininity are subject not only to the evaluative feedback of others but also to their own self-evaluation.[56]

Brands, Not Products: The Self as Brand

In order to theorize the self-brand, it makes sense to first turn to the deceptively simple notion of the branded product within an advanced capitalist political economy. If self-branding is about branding the self as a product, what is the substance of the product itself? How does it register in time and space? Or perhaps even more basic: What counts as a product?

Typically, a product is a thing, a tangible object made through labor (human or mechanical). While certainly conventional products continue to be exchanged within advanced capitalism, as Naomi Klein has argued in her oft-cited antiglobalization manifesto *No Logo*, the central organizing feature of contemporary corporate culture was no longer products but rather brands.[57] Others have also noted the gradual shift in the marketplace from a tangible product to a more symbolic articulation of the brand; for instance, Jeremy Rifkin and others have argued that the contemporary economy is an economy of attention and access rather than one built on the more traditional notion of ownership of products. Henry Jenkins argues that the world can today be defined by "affective economics," in which brand culture has shifted how consumers relate to products, so that commercial culture is not merely about the profit a product makes but rather is more open-ended; the result is an expansive milieu in which new, affective relationships forge "networked publics."[58]

The replacement of things with affective practices, or, as Arjun Appadurai terms it, the "social relations of things," calls attention to the ways in which symbolic narratives of the brand, or the brand experience, have become more resonant with consumers than actual products.[59] If Ogilvy & Mather are successful, as I have discussed in chapter 1, buying a Dove product today is about far more than just choosing a soap. With these affective practices, the successful brand becomes more diffuse, more permeable, and therefore more wide-reaching in the influence it can have on each consumer, and the way each consumer, in turn, can influence it.

These shifting dynamics between tangible and intangible products and labor practices point to the dynamism of the concept of the product itself. The product has not disappeared from this affective, experiential landscape but has expanded to encompass a range of new phenomena that are characteristic of the contemporary US political economy—affect, emotion, the self. In other words, the product itself has a different value in this political economy, as do labor practices. The neoliberal digital economy privileges forms of labor that are not generally recognized as labor by a more conventional capitalist exchange system, such as affective relationships, emotion, and brand experiences.[60] This kind of "immaterial labor," as I argued in chapter 1, not only involves new characteristics of production, such as digital technologies and flexibility, but also "involves a series of activities that are not normally recognized as 'work'—in other words, the kinds of activities involved in defining and fixing cultural and artistic standards, fashions, tastes, consumer norms, and more strategically, public opinion."[61] As a result, the relationship between labor, products, and capitalism has a new dynamic, so that affect, attention, and culture itself are available as part of capitalist exchange.[62] Because labor is now understood as flexible, ephemeral, and continuous, the product in turn is flexible and "becomes more of a process than a finished product."[63] The commercial exchange of products is thus more difficult to capture and quantify with concrete numerical value.

The relationship of immaterial labor to self-branding involves, as Alison Hearn points out, an understanding of the self as a kind of product, as flexible, fragmented, and saleable.[64] Thus, branding the self is not simply a function and effect of economic structures but also a result of changing cultural outlooks. Economic structures and cultural norms form a deeply interrelated framework for branding the self; the labor of self-branding is thus economic in the sense that it relies on conditions of production of advanced capitalist societies, and it is cultural in that it involves a more diffuse, immaterial labor that creates new cultural norms and outlooks about the "authentic" self. These economic and cultural conditions can produce collaboration among communities, but they also privilege individual entrepreneurialism.

Within this context, the self-brand functions as a kind of social and cultural trace, or a palimpsest of a more conventional notion of a tangible, saleable object. The product is still present, but the practices of labor that produce it also make the product ephemeral, emotional, and affective. Thus, the "producer" ostensibly enabled by a context of user interactivity could as easily be considered a "marketer" for the product of the self. As Kaputa, a marketer and brand strategist, argues, "In many ways, brands are like people: They have qualities, attributes, and personalities. And people are like brands. They are products that can be nurtured and cultivated to become winning brands."[65]

This slippage between people and brands, where "brands are like people" and "people are like brands," is validated within the variegated practices of advanced capitalism and its ever-expanding markets. The marketization of the self, and indeed of social life in general, indicates that economic practices have been retooled to reach not just a generic audience but ever-more-individualized communities, utilizing key strategies of emotional engagement, authenticity, and affect. In turn, cultural practices have also been retooled, so that the conditions of labor in the contemporary moment imply not so much the "prescription and definition of tasks" but rather involve the production of subjectivities: immaterial labor is about "becoming subjects."[66] Discourses of empowerment and self-improvement that provide an ontological framework for current understandings of subjectivity are embedded within these labor practices, which insist that the subject maintains an authoritative discourse about herself. Importantly, the self-as-commodity involves a "social relationship" with oneself, one of innovation, production, and consumption, charged with ideally producing a unique, "authentic" self. Consider again the example of Tila Tequila. As Tequila said, it is her "job" to cultivate popularity through her self-brand, part of what Laurie Ouellette and James Hay call a larger ongoing "self-work," where individuals "create biographical 'narratives' that will explain themselves to themselves, and hence sustain a coherent and consistent identity."[67] But this self-work relies also on explaining oneself *to the users*—audiences, viewers, peers—who view and evaluate the self-brand, so that self-presentation is a dynamic between production and consumption, between the individual and the culture at large.

Self-Work: I Want to Be a Lifecaster When I Grow Up

What does this self-work look like in practice? While the process of selling is often incidental (and, indeed, can be unknown) to many of the YouTube video producers discussed earlier, for those individual entrepreneurs who recognize the potential of online sites such as YouTube as a platform for a more consistent and constant narrativizing of the self, a new career option, the "lifecaster" has emerged. A case in point: a comment on a video of a young girl dancing on YouTube, "13 year old MiSS Delazee," states: "You are a very cute girl and you can dance very well. Ue seem a little camera shy but ii hope that you will get over that. Ii love the cargos & ii could like to see more videos from you. Hoping you get discovered with both hands & feet crossed!!—Pretty&Not paid." This comment, like hundreds of others on similar YouTube videos, explicitly makes reference to the function of YouTube in "getting discovered," ostensibly by the commercial media industries, and gives value to the YouTube brand. Indeed, youth talent agencies for kids now often specialize in making online stars (often through social networking sites), thus institutionally legitimating YouTube as well as social networking sites as lucrative venues for self-branding.

As but one example of this kind of legitimation, the popular "how-to" website eHow.com contains an article titled "How to Be a Star on YouTube." One "step" in the path to YouTube stardom is: "Come up with a concept that others will become addicted to when watching. It must be presentable as a series. It should be controversial, sensational or shocking. If it isn't any of these then inject it with your sex appeal, your incredible sense of humor or be bizarre. Each episode must terminate in suspense."[68] Alongside "how-to" tips like these, the business media have become involved as well. For example, the Business Insider website, in August 2010, published an article, "Meet the YouTube Stars Making $100,000 Plus a Year." that features ten YouTube stars, the majority of whom video blog about their everyday lives and have their own channel on YouTube (and sometimes more than one).[69]

Other stories about online stardom circulate in culture, functioning much like the generations of celebrity dream narratives where unknowns "get discovered" by producers and are made into Hollywood stars. Perhaps the most recent is the teen pop idol Justin Bieber, whose YouTube videos were discovered by a music agent, who then connected him with music star Usher and an eventual contract with RBMG studio. Both of Bieber's albums have since gone platinum—and, as perhaps a subconscious nod to the power of self-branding, were titled *My World* and *My World 2.0*, respectively. In 2010, Bieber had 17 million Facebook fans, had the most-viewed YouTube video of all time, made $100 million, and published a memoir (and he was sixteen years old).[70]

On the tails of Bieber's success, perhaps the most recent iteration of the discovery narrative is acceptance into YouTube Partner Program, through which amateur video bloggers and video makers are invited to become "partners" with YouTube once their videos receive a certain number of hits. Here again, visibility is a key to success. Once an individual has been accepted into the Partner Program, advertisements begin to appear overlaid on or next to the uploaded videos, and YouTube then splits the revenue generated by those ads with the partner. The more the videos are viewed, the more revenue they generate.[71] According to the press release about its new program, YouTube positioned the Partner Program as "an exclusive development program for up-and-coming YouTube Partners who are well on their way to star success."[72] Part of the program offers YouTube partners "training and mentoring to build their brands and improve their content, global promotion across the platform, and an invitation to what will become a global community of leading content creators." In this same press release, a YouTube spokesperson lauded the online site as a mode of self-expression *and* a business; my argument is that for YouTube, and for an increasing number of social network sites, self-expression *is* a business.

This has been an especially appealing program for young people. YouTube estimates that 10 percent of its most-subscribed users are nineteen or younger, and that "as a whole, more than one-third of the most successful participants in its revenue-sharing Partner Program are under 25."[73] Girls and young women have found a space amenable to global visibility in YouTube, where videos on how to shop (often called "haulers"), how to put on makeup, how to dance, and other tutorials in hegemonic femininity seem to generate hits in the millions.[74] A central logic of discovery narratives is that *anyone* can be discovered; the YouTube Partner Program clearly ascribes to this egalitarian rhetoric. And certainly, it is not the case that only, say, white middle-class girls are invited to become partners in YouTube's program. However, brand culture, social media as a site of empowerment, and the privilege of the "can-do" girl together form a context for a selective typology of girl video makers to be invited as partners and to be legible as branded citizens.

Indeed, the Partners Program is one small hint of the hierarchies that are characteristic of YouTube, just as they are everywhere on the Internet. It is often declared—and sites like YouTube, not to mention derivative "how-to" manuals, insist—that the web is open to everyone. But the notion that there are clear—and accessible—steps one can simply follow in order "to be a star" renders invisible how bounded those steps are in terms of age, race, and class. Individuals who are culturally marginalized (through law, policy, media representation, etc.) because of race or class, for instance, do not have the same access to the practice of self-branding as white, middle-class girls and young women. Like the discourse of postfeminism, the normalization of self-branding necessarily relies on practices of exclusion and is available primarily to "can-do" girls.

The YouTube Partner Program is part of the emergence of the career of "lifecasting" as an increasingly visible niche. Lifecasting, defined as a live video programming on the Web, "shows life in unabridged form, programming without a thematic concept, without a casting director, without an editor, without anything in the subject's life that is much different than the audience's, other than the willingness to be on view."[75] Lifecasting takes various forms, of course, but the basic skill set needed for a successful "career" in this field is merely a "willingness" to broadcast every moment of one's everyday life in real time. Lifecasting is cheap in comparison to other media-related endeavors; video streaming is all but free for those who have access to a computer and the Internet, and the only equipment needed is basically a webcam on a laptop.

I began this chapter with one of the most famous lifecasters, Jennifer Ringley, whose "JenniCam" livecast detailed her life from a webcam from 1996 to 2003. Launched from Ringley's dorm room, JenniCam was on twenty-four hours a day, focusing viewers' attention on the apparently unfiltered minute details of her life, including using the bathroom, having sex, and masturbating. As I mentioned, at the height of JenniCam's popularity, the video received 3 to 4 million viewers daily and was soon expanded into a pay-for-service site, where viewers who wanted "full" access to Ringley's life had to pay. Ringley thus positions herself, and is positioned by context, as occupying a space between Natalie Dylan and Tia Tequila; she engaged in both "selling" and branding herself. Seven years after JenniCam was launched, the online banking system PayPal shut down Ringley's account, citing its new antinudity policies, leading to the demise of the entire site.

As Mark Andrejevic points out, JenniCam "seemed to demonstrate the revolutionary potential of the Internet."[76] JenniCam was a popular show produced with almost no resources, and as such, it seemed to be an exemplar of the boundary-breaking power of the Internet, where media producers are no longer needed in the same way, where "uncut" reality can be aired without the messy clutter and crass commercialization of advertising, and where a young female college student can make a profit from her entrepreneurialism and her "empowered" postfeminist sexual identity.

However, as Andrejevic further points out, while webcams of the late 1990s and, for my purposes, the emergence of the lifecaster as a potentially lucrative career choice in the early 21st century, do mark a transformation in the way we use media, the transformation is not necessarily one that endows users and producers with newfound power. Rather, "the use of webcam pages for perpetual self-disclosure (personal 'reality TV,' as it were) anticipates the emerging surveillance-based rationalization of the online economy."[77] Webcam culture, argues Andrejevic, allows for the "exploitation of the work of being watched," where marketers and data miners keep a watch on lifecasters in order to ever more closely determine their profit potential. Among other things, this means that within the "digital enclosure," the spatial division critical to modern capitalism between work and leisure is rendered obsolete. Work, or labor, as I have discussed throughout this chapter, becomes immaterial, and this process "does not make work more like 'free time,' but, rather, tends to commodify free time by transforming it into time that can be monitored, recorded, repackaged, and sold."[78] This is especially true in an era of data mining, where individuals' personal information is mined for its commercial value to corporations.

The core logic of the lifecaster involves the transformation of quotidian and personal existence into a commodity that is packaged and sold. This is also why lifecasting is perhaps the quintessential example of the self-brand. The idea that one's everyday life should be not only recorded but *broadcast*, with every detail laden with significant meaning, is one that makes sense in a culture of branding, where the self is a product, promoted and sold by individual entrepreneurs. Branding strategist Kaputa points out that although brands are "wordless, a brand's packaging and design speak to us in color, shape, and material. Brands speak through imagery and symbols in logos, packaging, and advertising. It's the same with people."[79] A self-brand depends on an individual's willingness to be viewed for "purchase," a willingness aided by the normative use of marketing strategies and lexicons, demonstrated bluntly by Kaputa, as a way to construct the self. Lifecasting is a perfect mechanism for the self-brand, as the practice uses video to describe one's life on the Web and has a dedicated market category and an increasing consumer base to support it.

Justine Ezarik, for instance, is a lifecaster with a very popular YouTube channel, "iJustine," and has made more than 300 videos and posted them on YouTube, including skits, satires of television shows, and spontaneous dancing in the middle of an Apple store. Her video about wanting to order a cheeseburger was viewed more than 600,000 times on YouTube in one week and, at the time of writing, had more than 2 million views.[80]

Ezarik began her career in 2006 on Justin.tv, a website that facilitates continual live webcam streaming supplied by anyone wanting to broadcast their lives through video. Justin Kan, the founder of Justin.tv, pioneered the technique of wearing a camera on his head while he livecast, thus inviting the viewers to see his life as he does, in a constant stream. Justin.tv was attractive to lifecasters because, unlike YouTube at the time, it did not have a time limit. It was also attractive because the new practice of lifecasting was seen as a conduit to stardom; as the *San Francisco Chronicle* headline about Justin.tv put it clearly: "It's Justin, Live! All Day, All Night! S.F. Startup Puts Camera on Founder's Head for Real-Time Feed, and a Star Is Born."[81]

Unlike Kan, Ezarik turned the camera on herself, thus changing the narrative of the lifecast from one that is about capturing the personal experience of a lifecaster from his or her point of view to one that is about turning the attention—and the media visibility—on the lifecaster. Ezarik is the visible center of attention in her lifecast. And, by turning the camera on herself, Ezarik positions the feminine body as the crux of her self-brand.[82] Ezarik is the postfemininist self-brand, "putting herself out there," capitalizing on the visibility of global online sites for display, the camera's optic focusing on her body. Indeed, a desire to be noticed or recognized is perhaps the quintessential element to the branded postfeminist self; this desire mobilizes young women to "come forward" as feminism "fades away." Displaying self-work, whether through consumption practices, popular culture, or digital technologies, is key to branding the self in the contemporary moment. In this sense, lifecasting can be connected to a broader normalization of "confessional culture," spaces that provide venues for individuals to tell the truth about themselves as a way to construct subjectivities.[83] Confessional culture depends on the exposure of the self, and the normalization of this culture in digital media can renovate everyday, mundane practices into items for consumption.[84] As iJustine demonstrates, ordering a cheeseburger, paying the bills, and dancing in the Apple store are practices that are "worthy" of posting on a global site for display; they are practices made saleable through the logic of lifecasting. This kind of transparency and disclosure blurs traditional divisions between the public and the private, so that one's private life is a central feature of popular entertainment, and immaterial labor—the work on the self, affect, and emotion—is the primary form of labor within the practice of self-branding. And the public, accessed through the 24/7 camera, gets compulsively incorporated into the private.[85]

The emerging practice of lifecasting calls to mind other sorts of performances of femininity. For instance, in 1991, Sandra Lee Bartky detailed the various ways in which women discipline their bodies, from training themselves to move in certain "feminine" ways to ornamenting their bodies with makeup and jewelry.[86] As a theoretical framework, she used Foucault's notion of the panopticon, the means by which individuals in contemporary society are disciplined through constant surveillance and observation. Bartky noted that women are especially susceptible to such disciplinary practices. On the one hand, women's bodies are more "docile" than men's, due to historical and cultural constructions of gender. On the other, mastering the practices of self-construction can be understood as a kind of empowerment in the face of external pressures:

> Whatever its ultimate effect, discipline can provide the individual upon whom it is imposed with a sense of mastery as well as a secure sense of identity. There is a certain contradiction here: While its imposition may promote a larger disempowerment, discipline may bring with it a certain development of a person's powers. Women, then, like other skilled individuals, have a stake in the perpetuation of their skills, whatever it may have cost to acquire them and quite apart from the question whether, as a gender, they would have been better off had they never had to acquire them in the first place.[87]

I would like to extend Bartky's analysis of the docile feminine body and consider what female lifecasting means in this context. Today, twenty years after Bartky's essay was published, this external gaze has expanded to encompass an even more relentless internal gaze. A self-policing and self-absorbed gaze is animated both by new digital technologies and by an increasing belief that visibility leads to a reimagined self-empowerment. The docile body, as a result, has been transformed. In the postfeminist milieu, the ideal feminine

The iJustine YouTube channel.

subject is often understood as precisely *not* the docile body but rather the "can-do girl," who is "flexible, individualized, resilient, self-driven, and self-made and who easily follows nonlinear trajectories to fulfillment and success."[88] Feminine bodies, however, are still docile bodies. Indeed, the idea of the docile body is crucial for the articulation of the "can-do girl." This mastery also disciplines the feminine body in a different way: as a self-brand. Justine Ezarik (as well as many others) is a "can-do girl," a necessary condition to developing a successful self-brand. Her body—thin, white, conventionally attractive—is "brandable" in the current media economy of visibility.

The practice of self-branding by women and girls in the contemporary moment requires an updated sort of contradiction from the one identified by Bartky: while the practice of self-branding subjects one to processes of judgment and evaluation (through "feedback" mechanisms, among other things), mastering the practice of self-branding is expressive of a definition of empowerment in the current technological and postfeminist environment. As I explored earlier, the blurring of boundaries between producer and consumer, enabled by interactive technologies, has been undeniably empowering for girls and women. Again, girls and women have historically been excluded from the realms of production (especially technological production), so creating media is an important challenge to their long-standing position as primarily consumers of media.[89] Online "production," though, is often inseparable from "self-production," thus offering a new complication in the spectrum between production and consumption; self-production online can position girls and women as specific kinds of products for consumption. This is evident in the YouTube videos I examined (even if that was not the video maker's intention), as well as in the burgeoning career category of lifecasting.

Will You Add Me? Facebook and the Self-Brand

To craft a successful self-brand, one not only has to brand oneself *as* authentic but literally has to *be* authentic. This is a shift from historical liberal values where being true to the self is solely an internal process (think of parental lectures to children influenced by peer pressure: "It's not about what others think about you, but what you think about yourself"). The contemporary context of self-branding encompasses both these strategies, but their order is reversed, so in order to access one's authentic self, one must be true to others. To be authentic to yourself, one must first be authentic to others; it is about external gratification. As marketers McNally and Speak state, "It matters a whole lot what other people think. Your brand, just like the brand of a product, exists on the basis of a set of perceptions and emotions stored in someone else's head."[90] Alison Hearn points out that this kind of "outer-directed self-presentation . . . trades on the very stuff of lived experience in the service of promotion and profit."[91] This reimagines a traditional notion of authenticity, one based on intrinsic motivation, which values uniqueness, original expression, and independence from the market.

Online spaces provide a potentially expansive opportunity for young people to explore and express this "outer-directed self-presentation," this version of the "authentic" self. In a postfeminist context, this "authenticity" is tied to a particular version of femininity, so that it is increasingly normative for gender and sexual identities to be expressed through girl-oriented websites, personal profiles, and YouTube videos.[92] As Susannah Stern points out about personal profiles online, girls often use these spaces as "a forum of self-disclosure, especially as a place to engage in self-expression."[93] Sandra Weber and Claudia Mitchell have similarly argued that online youth productions are examples of "identities-in-action," where young users combine old and new images to establish creative, multifaceted identities. Like other scholars investigating identity-making online, Weber and Mitchell see online youth productions as self-reflexive, where media made by youth are also viewed primarily by those youth, so that users constantly revisit their own web productions and update them, as well as see how many "hits" or comments they might have generated. The fact that young people producing media online are their own audience demonstrates, for Weber and Mitchell, a "conscious looking, not only at their production (themselves), but how others are looking at their production."[94] danah boyd takes this self-conscious looking a step further and sees online spaces as formative of "networked publics," places where "teens are modeling identity through social network profiles so that they can write themselves and their community into being."[95]

As boyd's notion of "networked publics" implies, and as we have already seen, digital technologies sit at the intersection of the public and private; so too does self-branding, which is about both a private and a public performance. Constructing oneself as what Hearn calls a "detachable, saleable image or narrative" necessarily entails a private disclosure—*this is who "I" am*.[96] Yet the "I" that is created is marketed to a public of both known and anonymous subjects. Digital technologies are intended to communicate the self to others—the Internet and its innumerable appendages rely on a dynamic between self and others that results in self-construction. This dynamic, often expressed through feedback, works to legitimate personal profiles as sites for self-branding and regulates girls and their gendered self-presentations. While personal profile sites are not the same as YouTube videos, in that ostensibly one chooses one's audience by "friending" people or inviting them to the site, personal profile sites are nonetheless both a public and a private performance—public because they are displayed to an audience, and private because they purport to answer the intensely personal question of "Who am I?" Answering this personal question occurs in public, in a space that positions itself as a kind of constantly surveilled, yet seemingly intimate, public sphere.

The questions of "Who am I?" and "Who do you think I am?" are the central mobilizers of online personal profiles. For instance, besides encouraging users to brand themselves as "they really are," personal profiles encourage communication and feedback between user and producer that then validates the self-brand. To take just a few examples of how this "authenticity" in self-branding is maintained: the social networking site Friendster kicked out "fakester" fake profiles; Facebook requires users to post under their "real" names (or at least individual status updates must carry the same name as that profile does at the time of posting); and Twitter maintains "verified" celebrity accounts (though it does not eliminate fake accounts).[97] This maintenance of "authentic" communication enhances the notion that such communication is empowering for the user, as it ostensibly presents users as "they really are." However, as I have discussed, the empowerment supposedly gained by such participation can only be understood within specific online contexts. This potentially distracts individuals from what empowerment might mean in a broader sense. That is, in online spaces, media debates center on empowerment but often rely on a limited, binaristic understanding of participation—say, whether or not one posts a video. This is especially evident within the public performances of girls' personal lives—the communicative act involved in self-disclosure works as a technique of self-branding, thus objectifying young women precisely through the act of authorizing them as subjects.

To take one example, Facebook personal profiles rely on a commercially recognized script that invokes and validates brands and brand strategies. Facebook is a global social networking site that is privately owned and operated by Facebook, Inc. Created by Mark Zuckerberg as a tool to connect and reconnect college friends, the site initially included only college students, then opened access to high school students, and now is available to anyone over the age of thirteen. It currently has more than 300 million active users worldwide and is seen (at least for the moment) as an important tool of communication—clearly no longer limited to helping college students get to know each other, Facebook is now widely used by employers, businesses, and brands as a way to distribute information about people, groups, and products. (The ubiquity of the site is evidenced by the critically and popularly acclaimed film *The Social Network* (2010), which narrates Facebook's success—along with just enough controversy to make it fit with Web 2.0's paradigm for media success.) According to the web trafficking monitor Compete. com, Facebook was, in 2009, the most used social network worldwide, followed by MySpace.[98]

Facebook's origin story is not insignificant to its current position as a preeminent site for self-branding. The college newspaper the *Harvard Crimson* reported that Zuckerberg, a Harvard undergraduate student, created a website called Facemash as a version of the popular online rating site "Hot or Not" (one in the aforementioned genre of Internet personal rating sites, including others such as RateMyFace and AmIHot.com), where users rate the "attractiveness" of photos voluntarily submitted by other users. These sites, aside from the insidious and highly gendered practice of rating "attractiveness" and "hotness," depend on an online definition of "popularity" that is determined by the rating numbers and user votes (the site BecauseImHot. com launched in 2007 and simply deleted anyone with a rating lower than 7 out of 10). As I have argued, self-branding is often legible within a context of a culture of commercial hypersexuality, so we then witness things like the normalization of "hotness" as both a category of analysis and an inspirational and aspirational subject position. This kind of sexualized objectification, seen historically as a misogynist practice that contained and managed women, is legible in new ways within brand culture.[99] For instance, many online sites evaluate women based on physical attractiveness, using the concept of "hot" as defining ideal femininity. Sites such as Hot or Not, Because I'm Hot, AmIHot, and RateMyFace, as well as the assignation of icons such as chili peppers next to professors' names on the student evaluation site RateMyProfessor, legitimate the concept of hot as a desired feature of a "can-do girl." These rating sites and the normalization of "hotness" as an aspirational subject position also situate "hotness" as an important factor in self-branding of white, middle-class girls, where the "hotter" one is, the more one will be noticed.[100]

The prehistory and cultural context of these social network sites are significant because of the way in which the sites privilege a specific sort of logic: evaluating and comparing people (primarily women) is the purpose of the site. And, although Facebook is not explicitly designed for side-by-side comparison like these other examples, it purportedly did originate as a site that evaluated and compared women (a history that plays a central role in *The Social Network*: in the film's opening scene, Zuckerberg creates Facemash as a vicious, public revenge against his ex-girlfriend). There is a base aspect to the logic of rating sites: the evaluation of hotness is translated into the "right" to visibility—the lower-ranked faces on some of these sites are simply deleted, rendered invisible. This practice of evaluation and user feedback is enabled by the web's most basic norms—indeed, many users simply expect to be able to leave a comment on a given site, or to rate its contents. Of course, Facebook has evolved since these origins and has other clear uses aside from evaluating women or developing self-brands. Indeed, the flexibility of new media opens up spaces such as Facebook that facilitate empowerment; it is, however, important to understand empowerment as a concept that exists within a context of social network sites. The ethos of individual entrepreneurship and postfeminism, both emerging from advanced capitalist cultures, works to situate the hypersexualized female body as the conduit for this kind of empowerment on social network sites.

As implied both by its user statistics and by its origins as a site to rate physical attractiveness, Facebook epitomizes how visibility is at the heart of digital technology. A brief tour of Facebook is helpful in situating the site as a rich context for self-branding: an individual's Facebook page consists of a personal profile, organized around a series of one's choice of "boxes." Standard boxes on profile pages include a headline box, where users can put a quote or video that defines them or a short self-description; a "mutual friends" box, where users can view friends in common; a "friends" box, which lists how many Facebook "friends" one has (a person needs to request or be invited to be a person's "friend"); a status box, where the Facebook user can describe what she is doing or thinking at that moment (thus connecting with Twitter, which can be linked to people's Facebook accounts, so that they update simultaneously, communicating one's status of, say, "doing homework" or "having a beer" or sharing important news clips with different audiences); and, finally, the "Wall," upon which other posts about the user are located along with past status updates, photos, videos, links, and notes (this varies depending on which applications the user and her friends have added to the site). Anything that is posted to the Wall also has a comments field, wherein friends can leave comments and feedback.

Finally, there is an "Information" box that displays whatever subsections the user has filled in: basic information, personal information, contact information, education and work, groups one has joined, links to fan pages, and so forth. The topics in the "Information" box are wide-ranging, but the response options are quite narrow, from sex (one can select only male or female), to home neighborhood, to relationship status (the choices are single, in a relationship, engaged, married, it's complicated, in an open relationship, and widowed). The user can list her "favorites," including books, movies, TV shows, and music. However, the "favorites" mechanism was revised in 2010, so that one's personal favorites are linked to existing Facebook pages as a way to help Facebook sell advertising, and the site deletes any favorites that are not brand names, which motivated many users to stop using the site. Throughout any of the information sections, users can post photographs or videos of themselves, friends, bands they enjoy, and so on.

Despite the fact that personal profile pages on Facebook are customizable, there remain standard elements that most people include in their profiles.[101] Interestingly, Facebook makes a distinction between a user's personal profile and other, more commercial uses for the site. The site directly stipulates that a user cannot use a personal profile page to engage in commercial activity: "You will not send or otherwise post unauthorized commercial communications to users."[102] But within a context in which the self-brand has become normalized, it is murky indeed to determine what is "unauthorized commercial communication." The distinctions between this kind of communication and branding oneself are vague at best. In addition, Facebook recognizes the porous boundaries between commercial communication and self-branding: according to a website specializing in navigating social media, "Facebook wants all commercial activity to take place from Business Pages and they want you to pay them for the rights to advertise to their users. This doesn't mean you can't engage in indirect marketing from your profile or group, it just means you need to be much more careful and adopt conversational marketing tactics rather than direct sales pitches."[103] While I am supportive of individual users not adding to the Facebook coffers, there is no way, if one has a Facebook account, *not* to add value for Facebook if one uses the site. In the terms of use, Facebook claims ownership to *everything* that users post to the site. These divisions between conversation and commerce are fused, so that there is not a clear difference between the two but rather just a cautionary note to "be careful" about not being too direct in one's sales pitch. Importantly, this caution is offered not because it is a troubling trend to craft identities using business or commercial language but so that a user does not violate Facebook's official rules.

Self-Branding: Identity as Industry

Marketer Catherine Kaputa advises her readers that successful entrepreneurs achieve their success as personal brands because "of a conscious process, a strategic branding process, often undertaken with the assistance of advisers, coaches, and other mentors who propelled their achievements and celebrity."[104] The process that results in the crafting of an "authentic" self within the contemporary context, then, may remain a "long, arduous, and artistic process of self-creation," but it is increasingly achieved through a business plan, through a reliance on "experts," and legitimated within an industry of self-branding. Brand culture validates and supports shifting boundaries of what can and cannot be configured as a product to be sold; we now take for granted that the self is (and should be) branded, managed, and distributed.

Yet there are limits to what kind of self is brandable. The hypersexualized female body is particularly brandable in the current economy of visibility, but "hotness" is not "empowering" for all young women, who might not have the same kind of access to their own bodily property. Some women, notably women of color and working-class women, are identified by precisely the opposite position—they are girls "at risk" of failing economically and socially, signaled in part by "bad choices" regarding drugs, alcohol, early maternity, and inappropriate sexual behavior. While postfeminism claims to be inclusive, women and girls of color and the working class are often excluded from the "can-do" category; racialized and classed identities are always already "at risk" of falling into the "can't-do" category.[105] While other feminisms, such as critical race feminism and third-wave feminism, have shown how mainstream US culture marginalizes certain bodies while making others normative, it is postfeminism that has recently achieved the greatest visibility in contemporary consumer culture, global culture, and the workplace.

As McRobbie points out, a postfeminist subjectivity (what she calls the "post-feminist masquerade"), created and experienced in large part through consumption choices that are clearly articulated as free choices, is also by definition a reinstatement of white femininity as the ideal: "The 'un-doing' of feminism in the present moment intersects with the 'undoing of racism,' a process that, like the un-doing of feminism, is animated and enabled by fantasies of empowerment."[106] Thus, we can find a moralist framework that undergirds the postfeminist context in which girls and women construct their subjectivities: some postfeminist practices are pathologized and considered immoral, while others are seen as the proper care of the self. Not surprisingly, those women who have mastered the skills of properly caring for the self, or building successful self-brands, are those who are the most socially and culturally valuable: white, middle-class women and girls. This is a shift from previous moments in feminism, where part of "taking care of the self" was political action that challenged patriarchal and misogynist culture. From the second-wave feminist insistence that the "personal is the political" to *Our Bodies, Ourselves* (1973), a pathbreaking book on women's health and sexuality, to the early 1990s feminist punk underground movement Riot Grrrls, taking care of one's self, and "owning" one's body was a specifically feminist issue, one that revolved around freeing women from patriarchal restraint.[107]

Importantly, the successful postfeminist self-brand relies not on obscuring any failures or immoral behavior that comes as part of the process—Tila Tequila, after all, knows that her success relies in large part on playing a scandalous role. Brand culture loves controversy; key, however, is to juxtapose normative self-branding practices (including personal or moral failures) against those behaviors that are seen as pathological. The fine line between behavior that is merely immoral and that which is pathological, in the context of the "enterprising self," exposes the high stakes involved in mastering the skills of self-branding, or being capable of branding oneself at all. Clearly, for example, the teenage girls who are featured on MTV's *Teen Moms*, or the many women who do not have access to Facebook or other social network sites, or those who have neither the technology nor the skills to upload a video of themselves on YouTube are not simply not skilled at self-branding—they cannot possibly brand themselves. These young women are a necessary contrast to the "can-do girl." Self-branding, in the postfeminist context, becomes the selective hallmark of how to insert oneself into the future, as savvy, technologically astute, and invested in visibility.

This kind of comparing and evaluating oneself in relation to others, represented in the distinct spaces of personal profiles and online personal ranking sites, relies on feedback as a normative mechanism in the creation (intentional or not) of a self-brand. That is, if self-branding is part of a "project of the self," then the conceptual crux of this project is feedback. Evaluating or commenting on others' self-disclosures empowers one as a consumer-cum-producer of content, yet it also reproduces normative identities and relations. Self-branding, much like the branding of other products, only works if you enable other people to rank your product, which in this case is yourself. As each user is given the ability to reconstitute *someone* as some*thing*—whether "hot" or "not," whether perfect or pathological—is as much a telling of one's own story as a judgment of another's. Self-branding does not merely involve self-presentation but is a layered process of judging, assessment, and valuation taking place in a media economy of visibility.

This media economy of visibility, with its accompanying texts of how-to guides for "how to be a star" online, as well as the normalization of self-branding as both an industry and a practice, taps into what Jean Twenge has discussed as the extreme narcissism of contemporary young people.[108] At its core, narcissism is about total self-importance, an importance that authorizes entitlement, self-absorption, lack of personal accountability, and a whole host of other undesirable qualities. If narcissism is one of the defining personality characteristics of this generation, digital media are its official method; after all, where—or when—else was it this easy for an individual, with relatively few resources to have his or her own media channel?[109] Indeed, the most substantial manifestation of this kind of narcissism is the expectation and assumption of an audience, implying not simply the right to speak but the right to be heard. Twenge, in her book *The Narcissism Epidemic*, situates social networking sites as just another example (albeit an extreme one) of teens' and tweens' quests for attention, adding cumulatively to a culture of celebrity, materialism, and entitlement to produce a completely narcissistic demographic. Online spaces such as MySpace function as effective sites for self-promotion, Twenge argues, adding to a general culture that values visibility and self-worship. Twenge sees this pull toward narcissism as enabled and exacerbated by the Internet; as she argues, the availability of online sites to both users and producers "encourages narcissism, and, while we like an idiotic YouTube video as much as anyone, an Internet without rampant narcissism would be a much better place."[110] Regardless of whether one agrees with this last statement, it is important to point out that Twenge sees narcissism as an unfortunate side effect of the Internet, one that can be ostensibly corrected by shifting social values from "me" to "us." Of course, social network sites are also used to communicate and share thoughts with others, and they can facilitate the formation of networked publics to rally support for politics and events that are important to individuals far beyond self-image; we need only look at events such as Arab Spring 2011 to realize the import of social media in forming networks both on- and offline. This collective online world exists in constant tension with its individualizing tendencies, a tension that is struggled over constantly through efforts to regulate online spaces, the creation of alternative community spaces online, and the imposition of commercial platforms to structure these spaces. But while certainly the Internet affords possibility for collectivities, communities, and networked publics, it also enables and facilitates a focus on the individual; that is, it is no easy move to switch from "me" to "us" in the current moment of self-marketing and self-branding.

Indeed, considering the possibility of merely switching focus from "me" to "us" is already to be theorizing social network sites and the people who participate on these sites in an acontexual manner. Narcissism is part of the very *structure* of online technologies. Today's messy (and profitable) mixture—advanced capitalism and its attending labor practices, the flexible architecture of the Internet, and the ideal of the individual entrepreneur—validates a specific kind of narcissism and, related, the logic for the practice of self-branding. Narcissism, while identified by people like Twenge as a kind of pathology, something that can be "fixed" through refocusing social values, is reimagined within the context of self-branding and social media not only as a moral duty to oneself but also as a new kind of business model.

For example, in their book on YouTube, Jean Burgess and Joshua Green argue that in order to understand the cultural impact of social media such as YouTube, we need to think about all users, "whether they are businesses, organizations, or private individuals, as *participants*."[111] They advocate moving away from thinking in terms of binaries—amateur versus professional, commercial versus community—in order to truly understand the kind of cultural work that YouTube does for individuals, corporations, and communities. To wit:

> To understand YouTube's popular culture, it is not helpful to draw sharp distinctions between professional and amateur production, or between commercial and community practices. These distinctions are based in industrial logics more at home in the context of the broadcast media rather than an understanding of how people use media in their everyday lives, or a knowledge of how YouTube actually works as a cultural system. It is more helpful to shift from thinking about media production, distribution,

and consumption to thinking about YouTube in terms of a continuum of cultural participation.[112]

While I fully agree with Burgess and Green about the inefficacy of conventional cultural distinctions as a starting point for analysis, we need to push further. Drawing sharp distinctions in culture is limiting *not only* because individuals and companies interact on a "continuum of cultural participation" but also because "cultural participation" is increasingly only legible in the language of business—and, more specifically, through the lexicon of the brand. While Burgess and Green recognize the blurriness within cultural formations, this indistinctness needs to be articulated in the context of broader shifts in culture and the economy. This is precisely an example of how YouTube works within a context of advanced capitalism; because it is understood as "a cultural system," then "older" models of commercial media—including the logics of branding—are seen as antiquated and somehow, in the current era, not useful as analytics. The industry of self-branding and the consumer base for this new market, of which YouTube is a part, constitute a "cultural system." Self-branding firmly situates the key actor in this "cultural system"—the individual entrepreneur—as an essential element in the maintenance of the broader landscape of brand culture. Recall Natalie Dylan, whose "project" of selling her virginity online was marked by (at least some) as entrepreneurial gumption. This individual entrepreneur, validated within postfeminism and interactive digital media, unfolds within preexisting gendered and racial scripts and their attendant grammars of exclusion. Certainly, as I have argued, producing a self-brand *is* cultural participation, but this kind of participation—what it does, and for whom—needs to be critiqued as a commercial practice.

3

BRANDING CREATIVITY

CREATIVE CITIES, STREET ART,
AND "MAKING YOUR NAME SING"

Brandalism: the people who run our cities don't understand graffiti
because they think nothing has the right to exist unless it makes
a profit....the people who truly deface our neighborhoods are the
companies that scrawl giant slogans across buildings and buses
trying to make us feel inadequate unless we buy their stuff....Any
advertisement in public space that gives you no choice whether you
see it or not is yours. It belongs to you. It's yours to take, rearrange
and re-use. Asking for permission is like asking to keep a rock
someone just threw at your head.
—Banksy

In the spring of 2010, a film about street art debuted at the Sundance Film
Festival.[1] The film was eagerly anticipated, as it starred and was directed by
perhaps the most infamous street artist of the decade, Banksy. *Exit through
the Gift Shop,* purportedly a documentary, tells the story of Thierry Guetta,
a Frenchman living in Los Angeles in 1999, who is obsessed with filming
everyday life. He happens on the street art scene while visiting his cousin, the
renowned Parisian street artist Space Invader, and begins documenting street
artists as they create their art, putting up stencils, posters, stickers in urban
spaces all around the globe. Guetta films Space Invader, Shepard Fairey, and
other street artists, but the real coup here is a chance to document the infamous Banksy, whose true identity is unknown.

When Guetta is finally allowed access to Banksy, he films him obsessively,
and the remainder of the film revolves around Guetta's eventual collaboration with the street artist. However, it turns out that Guetta is not a particularly skilled filmmaker (although he has great quantities of filmed material,
ultimately it is useless because he does not know how to edit it), so Banksy

steps in and begins directing the action. The film's narrative then engages in a kind of reversal, as Guetta decides to become a street artist himself—not because of a registered talent, passion, or history but simply by virtue of his relationship with other street artists. Guetta gives himself the tag name Mr. Brainwash and in a matter of weeks creates not only a successful self-brand but enough street art to open a show in Los Angeles entitled *Life Is Beautiful,* where his work is sold for tens of thousands of dollars.

The trajectory of the film, through the figure of Guetta, and narrated at times through a hooded, voice-distorted Banksy, loosely maps the recent, contradictory history of street art more generally. The voice-over of the film calls street art "a hybrid form of graffiti…driven by a new generation, using stickers, stencils, posters and sculptures to make their mark by any means necessary. Street art was poised to become the biggest countercultural movement since punk."[2] Yet, through Guetta's narrative, Banksy also critiques the branding of street art. His comments force viewers' attention to the uneasy, yet in some ways inevitable, entanglement of art and commerce, of branding and the imagined authenticity of "the street." The film both validates and mocks the market for street art; Guetta's capricious choice to be a street artist and his subsequent ability to open a successful show are enabled not by inherent talent but by promotional culture and the insatiable demands of neoliberal capitalism. Banksy comments on Guetta's revealing role at the end of the film, saying, "Maybe the joke's on him. Maybe the joke's on us. Maybe there is no fucking joke."[3] A review in the *New York Times* points out that the film

> certainly asks real questions: about the value of authenticity, financially and aesthetically; about what it means to be a superstar in a subculture built on shunning the mainstream; about how sensibly that culture judges, and monetizes, talent.…Asked whether a film that takes shots at the commercialization of street art would devalue his own work, Banksy wrote: "It seemed fitting that a film questioning the art world was paid for with proceeds directly from the art world. Maybe it should have been called 'Don't Bite the Hand That Feeds You.'"[4]

Even as Banksy "questions" the art world, and even as he critiques the political economy of street art, the film itself is part of the branding of street art. The brand of street art is developed in the film not despite its critique but *because* of it. That is, as I discussed in the introduction to this book, critique and commentary on branding in advanced capitalism do not lessen the value of the brand but rather expand it as something that is ambivalent, a recognizable part of culture, indeed, a recognizable part of ourselves. *Exit through the Gift Shop* is a compelling film because it is located in the echo chamber between the art market, individual entrepreneurship, and the street as a canvas. This chapter, in turn, explores that echo chamber further and examines the branding of creativity as one characteristic of contemporary US culture.

Banksy's satirical and subversive street art has been displayed all over the world, recognizable for its stenciled style and political commentary. His work critiques a wide range of contemporary global issues, from homophobia, represented in images of, for example, two London policemen kissing each other and an image of Queen Victoria having oral sex with another woman; to war and violence, imagined in a variety of ways, from stencils of young girls hugging bombs on concrete walls to soldiers painted with bright yellow happy faces to images of police and soldiers furtively painting peace signs and anarchy symbols. As Banksy sardonically says in his book *Wall and Piece,* "I like to think I have the guts to stand up anonymously in a western democracy and call for things no one else believes in—like peace and justice and freedom."[5] Statements like this (as well as embracing critiques by other artists of his work) are also part of managing his brand, so that he simultaneously accounts for and neutralizes critiques of his anonymity. The politicized rhetoric both by and about street artists like Banksy and others does not undermine their value as brands but rather illuminates the ways that brands work in contemporary culture, where critique and ambivalence are elements of self-brand management.

Banksy's most famous productions include nine images painted on the Palestinian side of the wall enclosing the West Bank, several of which were crafted in the tromp l'oeil style. For instance, one image features an idyllic portrait of a white child playing at the beach, shovel and pail in hand, standing in the middle of a cracked window of blue skies, white clouds and bright sunshine above his head, a clear contradiction of the stark concrete walls and rubble surrounding the Palestinian side of the wall. Another image is much simpler, featuring a silhouette of a young girl lifted in the air by a bunch of balloons; it seems that she is about to fly over the wall.

As Banksy comments about what he labels "The Segregation Wall," "Palestine is now the world's largest open-air prison and the ultimate activity holiday destination for graffiti artists."[6] This deliberately loaded statement calls attention not only to the conflict between Palestine and Israel but also to the street art tradition of pilfering from disenfranchised spaces and marginalized populations—and the statement is made while Banksy is actually doing that very thing. While most of Banksy's work is created on walls and

Banksy art on the Israeli West Bank barrier.

urban spaces, he also is known for hanging his own versions of oil paintings in museums, replicating landscapes but adding surveillance lights or military helicopters, placing a human bomb on the baby Jesus or an iPod on the Virgin Mary.

Banksy's work is political and is arguably subversive. His work challenges hegemonic institutions such as the military and state practices, exposes hypocrisy in advertising and marketing, and questions the fundamental premises of advanced capitalism. Yet while he critiques the world of advertising and branding—calling such practices "brandalism"—he is clearly a brand in and of himself. Auction houses like Sotheby's feature Banksy art, which sells for anywhere between $10,000 and $200,000 (he is clear to point out that he does not sell his work himself but is just as clearly capitalizing on

Another example of Banksy art on the Israeli West Bank barrier

the fact that it does sell for high prices); there recently was an "identity auction" on eBay, where Banksy's identity (apparently based on tax records from art sales obtained by the seller) received bids up to $1 million before eBay removed the auction;[7] and in 2006 a CNN reporter coined the phrase "the Banksy effect" as a way to demonstrate how Banksy was partly responsible for the rapid commodification of and popular interest in street art. The recognizable anonymity of Banksy is an important, if not the crucial, element in his self-brand. His work is supported by brand culture and the creative economy, even as he critiques these cultures. In his critique of advertising, he is establishing his own brand, using similar strategies of recognizable images and slogans, catchy phrases, his name featured as a brand itself. Indeed, his work is perhaps the quintessential neoliberal creative practice, as it relentlessly puts forward the idea of the "free" enterprising individual—who does not ask for permission but rather takes and rearranges and reuses. This neoliberal freedom is advocated both in the content of the art and in the position of Banksy as an artist.

Like Banksy, the street artist Shepard Fairey is similarly at home with entrepreneurship and progressive cultural politics. His marketing strategies for his clothing line, Obey Giant, critique the persuasive power of advertising while simultaneously doing the work of selling clothes. In a 2009 ad campaign for Saks Fifth Avenue, for example, Fairey deliberately uses the codes of anticonsumerist socialist art. This play with art and commerce, and recoding of the language of capitalist critique into campaigns that are playfully yet directly about marketing consumerism, are key characteristics of contemporary street artists. Fairey's creation of a recognizable "nonbrand" brand, one that resonates most prominently with a hip, presumably urban youth culture, exemplifies many aspects of contemporary brand culture, in which individuals create, experience, resist, and challenge identities through and within the visual aesthetics and the political culture of branding. Fairey is successful at negotiating these multiple, seemingly contradictory roles— from the artist who is credentialed by his arrest record as retaining the authenticity of the street to the manager of a clothing brand who runs a large factory in Los Angeles; from the artist of weekly produced and quickly run political posters to an artist whose work is sold in limited editions and featured in museum retrospectives.[8]

Reminiscent of Banksy, Shepard Fairey himself is a flexible, neoliberal brand. His Obama "Hope" political poster was acquired by the Smithsonian; his style mixes political poses with brands in an unapologetic way, accompanied by a discourse that roams from the abstractions of Heidegger to marketing code words like "flexibility." For instance, in his widely circulated "Manifesto," Fairey describes his early artwork, the Obey sticker campaign, as "an experiment in Phenomenology," referencing Heidegger's notion that phenomenology is "the process of letting things manifest themselves." He states, "The first aim of phenomenology is to reawaken a sense of wonder about one's environment. The Obey sticker attempts to stimulate curiosity and bring people to question both the sticker and their relationship with their surroundings."[9] He aims, often quite successfully, to straddle both this artistic aim of reawakening a sense of wonder and the market goal of selling commodities through the dissemination of ideas and slogans.

Street art is a brand culture that is mobilized by the ethos and morality of antibranding. As branding becomes part of an everyday lexicon in all cultural realms, expressed in creative production as dynamic play within and between residual and emergent codes of capital and aesthetics, street art becomes its own definition of a brand: it associates with graffiti and tagging not just aesthetically but also in terms of the ethos of vandalism, secrecy, illegality, risk. But it also takes shape within the environment of the brand, so that it borrows from advertising and promotional culture. Street artists become brands in and of themselves, and their art is produced and distributed as a recognized commodified form and practice: when Los Angeles–based street artist Man One was asked if he considered himself a brand, he replied, "Yeah, I consider myself a brand! I want to see my name on everything."[10]

Branding and street art have a conflicted and tumultuous history; their relationship to each other does not indicate merely the melding of two or more previously distinct cultural and economic artifacts, media, or everyday

Shepard Fairey's Obey sticker, Harvard Square.

practices. Rather, the branding of street art is mobilized by political, economic, cultural, and historical transitions that centrally involve what Angela McRobbie calls the "entrepreneurialisation of arts and culture."[11] How and in what ways does "creativity" matter differently—indeed, have a different value—in the contemporary moment of brand culture and neoliberal capitalism?

In this chapter, I interrogate the stakes involved in thinking about the ways in which contemporary street art is branded, as well as how the dynamic and shifting definitions of "creativity" in the context of the US cultivate the branding process. I focus on the relationships within and between three central factors in contemporary creative brand culture: the branding of creativity, the newly imagined creative city, and the individual entrepreneur-artist. Brand culture and the creative city have authorized and animated a new form of individual entrepreneurship whose profile reveals the current relationship of brand culture, creativity, and advanced capitalism. This relationship involves the means by which contemporary capitalist logic underwrites the discourse of creative economies, and the resulting legitimation of the role of the individual entrepreneur within brand culture. The "creative city," signaled materially by public-private partnerships and a redirection of city funding away from low-income housing, immigrant communities, and social services, and toward art galleries, museums, and renovated city

walks, is the venue for the branded individual entrepreneur.[12] In this context, individual entrepreneurship takes on new dimensions, as an increasing
number of artists and musicians move seamlessly between making art, creating brands, running small businesses, and selling their cultural capital, all
while working to retain status as radical, and sometimes street, artists. The
conventions and logic of brand culture, such as local and global campaigns
and the use of repetitive logos, but also more diffused sets of logic, such as
the "freedom" to be creative and a validation of individual entrepreneurship,
have shaped contemporary street artists and their cultural productions.

A Brief History: The Brand of Street Art

The contradictions highlighted in the film *Exit through the Gift Shop* and
Fairey's work not only are characteristic of street art but also signal a more
general branding of creativity. The creative practice of street art exemplifies
the dynamics taking shape in a neoliberal context where social domains are
recoded as economic ones. The convergences between art and commerce,
between creativity and the market, that typify street art in the 21st century
are not new; as *Exit through the Gift Shop* demonstrates, street art has important historical legacies. The historical antecedents to street art are as political
as they are aesthetic: from Federal Art Project (FAP) murals in the 1930s and
1940s to pop art in the 1950s and 1960s to the emerging graffiti scene in the
1970s and 1980s. The street and public office murals created during the Great
Depression abound with critique of state and local politics;[13] pop artists of
the 1960s such as Robert Rauschenberg and Roy Lichtenstein insisted on
the mundane and the everyday as works of art, offering a coded critique of
elitist hierarchies in the art world as well as the increasing normalization of
advertising in public spaces; and graffiti artists in the 1970s and 1980s, often
under cover of night, challenged the invisibility of working-class communities and communities of color by writing on walls, subways, and other urban
surfaces.[14] In each of these historical manifestations, artists used the street as
an opening to critique local, state, and federal policies and to advocate for a
public space liberated from profit-driven commerce.

Street art, too, calls attention to the corporate-driven legitimation of
advertising at the expense of other artistic uses for public space.[15] Yet
despite this clear history, contemporary street art is also, as *Exit through the
Gift Shop* claims, an "explosive new movement." In the first decade of the
21st century, street art has found a unique new manifestation. Street art is
increasingly sponsored by corporations; street artists have been commissioned to design products ranging from T-shirts to album covers to political

campaign posters; and museums have gradually featured street art as central exhibitions.[16] As a Los Angeles–based street artist, Retna, said in 2011 about the recent cultural phenomenon of street art, "We always knew it [was a phenomenon]…it just took the public a while."[17] The "explosion" and visibility of the cultural phenomenon of street art in the early 21st century are not just the result of more street artists or creatively talented people tapping into the genre of street art, or the result of more public space suddenly becoming available. Rather, contemporary street art is authorized and made legible through and within the increasingly normative logic of the brand. Street art is itself part of a brand culture that takes shape not only as a multiformat aesthetic production but also as a validation of the celebrity culture that surrounds individual entrepreneurs such as Banksy and Shepard Fairey.[18]

Street art, broadly defined, exists in the historical tradition of graffiti and murals: in other words, anything that is painted, stenciled, stickered, or pasted on public spaces—from walls to trains, from fences to lampposts—that is clearly intended by its producers as art and not advertising. Defining "art" has historically depended on the ideological and aesthetic separation of artistic creativity and commerce. In a Western episteme, art was defined as an avenue toward enlightenment, transcendence, and the sublime, with commerce set up as its opposite, defined by instrumental goals of rational governance and profit. In Walter Benjamin's famous indictment of the commercialization of art, he argued that within a context of mechanical reproduction and commerce, the aura of original art "withers away," leaving art to be created for politics rather than ritual.[19] In the context of contemporary advanced capitalism, when someone refers to street art as "authentic," that means the piece is original, made by an artist who has not "sold out." Surely this idea of the authentic has never accurately defined the relationship of art and commerce, in that artists have always been involved in collaboration with those industries and organizations that finance, distribute, and sell their work. From simpler relationships such as the artist as apprentice and that of artists and art dealers to the much more complex market for books, music, television, and film, artistic creativity has been imbricated throughout its history in commercial interests.[20] Yet, the idea that commercialization corrupts the authenticity of art appears to continue to structure tastes, policy decisions about funding federal artwork, and cultural boundaries.

Given this imbrication with other forms of public creative practice, why street art specifically? Surely there are a number of kinds of cultural productions that might characterize creative brand culture. For instance, in a 2010 article in the *New York Times,* reporter Ben Sisario documents a new relationship between indie music and brands, focusing on a newly developed underground recording studio in Brooklyn that is entirely funded and maintained by the iconic sneaker company Converse. As Sisario points out, Converse is only one company among many that are becoming modern-day patrons of underground music; as he states: "Lifestyle brands are becoming the new record labels. Looking to infiltrate the lives of their customers on an ever deeper cultural level, they are starting imprints, scouting for talent and writing checks for nearly every line item on a band's budget. And as the traditional record industry crumbles, plenty of musicians are welcoming these new rock 'n' roll Medici."[21] Indeed, brand marketers characterize the 21st century creative economy not only by the increasing normalization and flexibility of relations of digital production but also by, as Sisario points out, the accompanying "crumbling" of traditional creative industries such as the record industry (a nostalgic—but nonetheless common—view, to be sure, given the control mechanisms historically employed by studios over their artists).

Converse's new venture is orchestrated by the media and marketing company Cornerstone, which also is the producer of the *Fader* (a magazine dedicated to independent musicians) and its record label, and has found success in the gaps left by the struggling music industry. As Jon Cohen, one of the founders of Cornerstone, states, "A brand now has the ability to really break an artist."[22] Another founder of Cornerstone, Rob Stone, argues that the key to contemporary branding is transparency; branding creative productions is not about hoodwinking the consumer but rather about "activating real people as a market," instead of relying upon traditional concepts like imagined audiences or demographics.[23] Branders no longer buy media to promote brands but rather "let the brand grow organically" and think of themselves as not only "the curators but creators of content" through multimedia platforms, such as concerts, radio releases, YouTube postings, chat room discussions, and so on.

To return to the question, why focus on street art?, the idea of "activating real people as a market" is key to the branding of street art, an aesthetic practice that often plays upon a dichotomy between the authentic and the commercial, the real and the manipulative. Contemporary street art must thus be contextualized within the history of the political economy of creative industries. In 1997, in the UK, the focus of the arts policy documents of the British Labour Party changed from the "cultural industries" as a description of the activities involved in arts and cultural policies to the newly named "creative industries."[24] During this same period (and continuing to the contemporary moment), the US witnessed a more privatized, corporate-led movement in the arts and culture. Government officials and city planners, preoccupied with the promise of "creative cities," hope to increase city revenue by enticing talented, creative professionals to relocate to depressed urban areas, revive the media, arts, and culture industries, and thereby stimulate the tourist trade.[25] These shifts are indicative of the late 20th-century and early 21st-century Western worlds of marketing, urban planning, city policy, and nation building, where there has been a renewed emphasis on the creative industries as an economic and cultural force that can do the work of "revitalizing"—or, from another perspective, gentrifying—and transforming place and space through arts and culture.

During this same general period, while the creative industries were being economically restructured in Western contexts, creative production itself was undergoing major transformations. The rapid rise of social media and digital technologies raised the visibility and lowered the barriers of entry to participatory cultures, in which individuals are expected to "be creative."[26] As I discussed in chapter 1, "old" media such as broadcast television has been similarly restructured by widespread deregulation, global distribution, and the emergence of the cable industry, such that the audience is now fragmented into individuated niche markets. In the world of contemporary art, street art became a widely recognizable and commodified art form as part of this broader restructuring process. The artist-as-brand is thus legible not only within a history of traditional art but also as part of a broader neoliberal restructuring of urban spaces, media, and creative practices.

There are a number of other reasons that street art is a particularly useful optic to understand the various contradictions of brand culture within changing values of creativity and the creative industries in contemporary US culture. For instance, street art nurtures a nostalgic dichotomy between the authentic and the commercial, one that relies on street art's association with graffiti and tagging, which are not only deeply racialized in the US imagination but also often fetishized for their links to racial otherness, and therefore rendered "authentic." The "authentic" and "commercial" in this context thus command specific racial domains.

Miriam Greenberg, discussing graffiti in New York in the 1970s and 1980s, argues that the difference between graffiti and commercial culture is in part about differing needs for attention: in advertising, the mobilizing factor is about ever-greater product recognition, whereas for graffiti writers "whose activities were illegal and for whom survival depended on official anonymity, name recognition was an end in itself, or as Norman Mailer put it famously: 'the name was the faith of graffiti.'"[27] But such name recognition, like today's street art, is distinct from another strain of graffiti used by gangs. Street artist Man One claims that the central difference between street art and graffiti is one of intent: "We [street artists] maybe put on our names, but it's to make the city beautiful. When gangs do it, it's about marking their territory." However, making a city beautiful through art is also about marking one's territory; Man One also claimed he wanted to see his name on everything: "walls, Man One sneakers, the works."[28] In brand culture, products and names, beauty and cultural territory, are all part of the same cityscape.

Like graffiti, street art cannot be read as simply a sign of urban decay and rebellious youth, nor is it a pure form of cultural innovation. Street art is a hybrid form of graffiti, which itself emerged as a cultural art form in the US in the 1970s. The inspirations that caused youth to write their names on public spaces were numerous: the increasing ubiquity of advertising; the global economic crisis of the early 1970s; racial dynamics including widespread "white flight" in the decades following World War II;[29] the devastating aspects of urban "renewal," including the razing of housing and the building of highways through marginalized neighborhoods in cities from New York to Los Angeles; the vast federal and state defunding of urban centers like East LA, the South Bronx, and Philadelphia; and an explosive rise in gang activity in these same urban centers. This context authorized a kind of brokering for cultural territory that expressed itself not just in violence but also in creative practices. Writing your name anywhere became a form of currency, a way of gaining cultural value.[30]

Graffiti can thus be understood within the increasing proliferation, across the 20th century, of advertisements, signs, and brand names in the public and semipublic spaces of urban America.[31] (It is also part of a larger cultural milieu that birthed other creative practices, including the emergence of hip-hop music in the 1970s on the East Coast.)[32] Graffiti and street art, then, are both enabled and animated by struggles over the meaning of public space and the role of creative production within the tangle of commerce, economics, and racial identity.

Graffiti emerged in force, at least according to some, when a teenager from Washington Heights started writing his nickname, Taki, along with his street number, 183, on the outsides of buildings and the insides of subway stations across Manhattan.[33] As Craig Castleman argues, the subsequent trend in writing one's name eventually became more of an aesthetic style, so that "as hundreds of new writers emerged...new emphasis began to be placed on style, on 'making your name sing' among all those other names."[34] "Making one's name sing" became a complex activity, involving competition for space, regional differences (say, between Brooklyn writers and Bronx writers), changing artistic conventions in terms of letter shapes and perspective, and new developments in technology (from the evolving tops of spray cans to different kinds of paint). Significantly, graffiti was recognized, at least by its practitioners, as art.[35] While graffiti writers came from different racial communities and socioeconomic classes, as a politicized statement about the takeover of public space the practice was taken up most boisterously in urban, marginalized neighborhoods, and most often in communities of color.

This desire to take over public space was manifested by writing on subway trains that traveled far beyond the neighborhoods of the writers themselves, a way to infiltrate neighborhoods, and boroughs, that were otherwise inaccessible.[36] As Jeff Chang writes about New York in the 1970s, "All across the city youths were customizing their names or giving themselves new ones and scrawling them across the naked city surfaces. The young graffiti writers were the advance guard of a new culture; they literally blazed trails out of the gang generation. Crossing demarcated turfs to leave their aliases in marker and spray paint, they said 'I'm here' and 'Fuck all y'all' at the same time."[37] Graffiti writing was part of the cultural context that also nurtured the hip-hop scene, and like that creative practice, writing on urban walls was a political act: "Writing your name was like locating the edge of civil society and planting a flag there."[38]

But graffiti was also shaped by the conventions of commercial culture, and indeed, as Norman Mailer has famously pointed out, graffiti artists were, at some level, advertising themselves. It may have been a belligerent challenge to the encroachments of the state, but it was also a chance to self-represent.[39] As graffiti became more widespread in the late 1970s and early 1980s, it was subsequently institutionalized in organizations such as United Graffiti Artists and Nation of Graffiti Artists, which enabled graffiti artists to display their work in galleries. It was also demonized by city officials, especially New York mayor John V. Lindsay, who in 1972 established an antigraffiti force and declared "an all-out war" against graffiti artists, criminalizing both the practice and the artists themselves.[40]

This criminalization often took shape in racist and classist forms of policing nonwhite and working-class subjects. Indeed, as part of 1970s and 1980s "revitalization" efforts, the criminal charge for graffiti in the city of New York moved from a misdemeanor to a felony.[41] The "graffiti problem" that plagued urban US cities during these decades was largely attributed (by government officials, the mainstream media, and citizens) to an out-of-control youth population (most of whom were youth of color) whose members had "no respect" for their immediate environs.[42] Rudy Giuliani, the mayor of New York from 1994 to 2001, furthered this policy, employing the "broken windows" theory as a validating framework for criminalizing graffiti artists. The broken windows theory holds that ignoring relatively minor problems in a city, such as graffiti, will lead to a decline in civil behavior, leading to more and more crime. Criminalizing graffiti, then, became part of a "zero toler-ance" policy toward petty crime in New York.[43] And as important for the purposes of this chapter, eradicating "nuisances" like graffiti, so the theory went, would improve the city as a whole.

In the 21st century, the commercial potential of the "creative city" has dis-placed the broken windows theory and reversed the potential role of such "nuisance." Through the emergence of public-private partnerships within cities, as well as the general corporatization of cities, the "graffiti problem" became, at least for some marketers, a way to harness "street" creativity and, by association, a technique for regulating racialized creative practices. The aesthetic of street art—untainted by corporate influence, a willful expression of self—is now used in the image marketing of cities. Street art, mobilized by the earlier legitimation of hip-hop as popular music, attractive to middle-class, white, suburban audiences as well as the working class and people of color, emerges in the 21st century as a "white hot commodity." (The emphasis here is on the white: a recent article dubbed Banksy "white people's favorite graffiti artist.")[44]

This earlier demonization of graffiti, however, proved essential for its legit-imation as an urban creative practice. What better proof of the "authenticity" of graffiti, after all, than its illegality? Contemporary street art relies on a sim-ilar flirtation with illegality. To accumulate cultural and underground capital, the brand of creativity simultaneously relies on both institutional legitimacy and discursive marginalization. The seemingly contradictory quality of street art—its simultaneous reliance on a kind of "dangerous" street cred and its insistence on sustaining a "legitimate" place in contemporary culture—has proved to be lucrative, and subsequently accepted into legitimating institu-tions. Banksy would not be as subversive if his art was not explicitly illegal; but at the same time, Banksy would not be as successful if he did not have a recognizable signature look. Contemporary commercial culture poaches the signifiers of cool from street culture and hopes to attach this cachet to products; just as significant, however, is how the creative productions and personal identities of street and graffiti artists are shaped by the conventions of commercial culture, especially in the use of brand logics and strategies.[45]

In the cultural economy of the 21st-century US, street art is practiced within an increasingly normative brand culture, which both expands upon and capitalizes on residual and emergent meanings and practices, themselves the residual and emergent meanings of racial codes and values. Hegemonic power and ideologies privilege some creative practices over others (such as street art over graffiti), as well as cultivate technological and artistic forms that are accompanied by new configurations of labor and labor practices. Additionally, these same dynamics of corporate power reimagine codes for race and the urban so that they are palatable for a "mainstream" audience; some racialized expressions are more "brandable" than others. These entwined dynamics are manifest in new economic branding practices and strategies. Street art, graffiti, and advertising all compete for space in a context of advanced capitalism. Positioned within a history of such competition, some creative expressions are rendered visible while others are obscured.

During a public presentation titled "How Does Street Art Help Cities?," Aaron Rose, the cocurator of a 2010 street art exhibition at the Los Angeles Contemporary Museum of Art, articulates this play of meanings as "learning a common language." Street art, he claims, is caught between two worlds: "mainstream America" and "street America." "Street America" is a racial code; like "urban," the use of the term "street" conjures danger, transgression, and racialized constituencies. The language of "street America" needs to be, according to Rose, incorporated into mainstream America to form a lingua franca; "the artists who are the most successful . . . are the ones who can speak both 'street talk' and fluent corporate America."[46] Street art negotiates the exoticizing aspects of racial tourism with a white fear of the "urban," a classic tension found in media representation, popular culture, and entertainment. Those racialized expressions of "street America" that are non-threatening to white consumers are thus branded in the form of street art.

Focusing on contemporary street art, then, allows for a rereading of the relationship between the parallel and deeply interrelated industries of advertising and art. Through such a reading, it is possible to see how exclusionary practices structure this relationship; to succeed as an artist, it seems, you need to be fluent in the language of corporate branding. This relationship is not always about the mutual benefit of each but is rather about what forms of cultural capital are profitable for branding. Branding practices depend on the erasure of noncommercial public space—even if this space is precisely what gives street art both its logic and legitimation among artists. Contemporary street artists often rely on commercial privatization as part of the way in which they can create and display their work. LA-based street artist Man One recalls when corporations began approaching him for design work: "Whether it was for T-shirts or shoes . . . [I] never lost sight of what it was: It's a gig . . . I know how the game works and it's a game."[47] Many street artists see corporate interest as a crucial resource, an opportunity to gain more visibility. As Rose put it, the corporate attention to street art is indicative of "Andy Warhol's vision come true. We've actually gotten to the point where it has permeated the culture. Now we just have to convince certain city authorities that that's the case."[48]

The language of corporate determination and appropriation does, in fact, explain and define much contemporary creative production. Yet, street art is an artistic practice that shifts and expands within changing political-economic conditions and is an example of a kind of underground capital that corporate culture longs to appropriate as a selling strategy. The interaction between creativity and brand culture, just like that between girls and technology, is not simply another example of corporate co-optation. Resisting this binary formulation allows us to think in more complex ways about how creativity is understood and experienced within urban cities in the contemporary US. What is at stake in acknowledging that creativity itself is branded? What must we give up, or what might be gained, if we acknowledge brand culture as a complicated historical dynamic, involving both consumerism and creativity?

Creativity and authenticity are not situated here as players in a zero-sum game—reimagining the value of creativity in the contemporary moment necessarily means a retreat from either a focus on crass corporate appropriation or a search for a "real" art that can be found only in noncommercial spaces. Street art gives us purchase in thinking about changing definitions of value and the ambivalence of brand culture because its creative practices refuse an easy position as either predominantly about the consumer industries *or* about noncommercial cultural production. Because the context for street art is the city or the urban space, and given that many urban cities are aggressively rebranding themselves as "creative," through public-private partnerships, hiring marketers to "sell cities," and creating quantitative matrices for measuring levels of creativity (based on statistics such as the number of art galleries or coffee shops, and even the density of the gay population), the presence of visual representations of creativity in city spaces contributes to the process of "revitalization" that so often signals the "urban."[49] In creative cities that develop alongside processes of gentrification, "urban" street art signals a desirable racial presence to wealthy investors and tourists rather than actual raced, undesirable bodies. Street art, in other words, is a richly "brandable" creative practice for middle-class, white consumers.

The City and the Self-Branded Cultural Entrepreneur

Shifts in the wide-ranging practices of the cultural economy of the early 21st century signal a powerful turn in the modes, meanings, and available spaces of creativity.[50] In thinking about the complexities of flows of transnational capital and consumer products, Inderpal Grewal states: "Why certain products sell and others don't raises important issues of culture, identity and subjectivity. The cultural work required to create consumer desire for a product is not as simple as producing a marketing plan; rather, *the plan contributes to and participates in wider cultural changes within which the product can become meaningful (or not) in ways that often cannot be predicted.*"[51] What are some of the "wider cultural changes" that provide the backdrop for street art? The contours of the contemporary cultural economy—a "wide cultural change" over the past several decades—allow not only for very specific creative expressions to be branded "authentic" but also for public-private convergences to become legible and normalized.

In today's cultural economy, cities are increasingly branded.[52] Small cities have adopted branded taglines or mottoes to distinguish themselves, ranging from the descriptive "An Oasis of Recreation" (referring to Santee, South Carolina), to the aspirational "Ain't No Big Thing, But It's Growing" (for Gretna, Virginia) to the cryptic "The Salad Bowl of the World" (for Greenfield, California). Financial crises only compel cities to brand themselves even more aggressively as global centers—whether of bird watching or convenient public transportation or hipster coolness—in an effort to accumulate tourist and business dollars. As Greenberg details in her book *Branding New York*, the ideological transition from New Deal–style liberalism in the 1960s and 1970s to a free market ideology in the 1980s and 1990s "led most cities to turn to a new, entrepreneurial mode of economic development that combined political and economic restructuring with cultural strategies like image marketing."[53] This mode of development is two-pronged, according to Greenberg; it includes, on the one hand, marketing and image-making efforts and, on the other hand, public-private partnerships for the restructuring of government and the urban economy. Importantly, this kind of economic shift, through its reimagining of cities, also directs resources and priorities away from public and social services, such as housing, public sector employment, and the maintenance of working-class, nonwhite neighborhoods.

As Greenberg states, the priorities of branded cities like New York "shift from the provision of tangible use-values to the projection of intangible exchange-values, and the city itself is increasingly transformed from a real place of value and meaning to residents and workers to an abstract space for capital investment and profit-making, and a commodity for broader consumption."[54] Yet these two functions of a city—a "real place of value and meaning to residents and workers" and an "abstract space for capital investment" and commodity consumption—are not necessarily oppositional in

21st-century branded cities; street artists, for example, rely on the blurriness between these two categories.

In a meeting in 2009, I listened to marketers describe how they brainstorm ways to create a brand for their clients. In this case, their clients were cities. The question at hand: How do you find an appropriate "theme" for a city? Should we focus on nightlife?, the marketers asked. Or the city as oasis? Or the dating possibilities for single adults? I also wondered what happens to all the people, communities, and institutions—immigrants, the working class, racialized constituencies, prisons—that are inconsistent with a city's newly developed brand. The marketers were very honest about how few answers they had to these questions. But it was nonetheless clear that such answers would be sought using market strategies.[55]

As Greenberg details, during periods of crisis the branding of cities is especially important because this process can create a kind of "imagined consensus" of its citizens, a process that theoretically benefits everyone and that transcends issues of racial or class discrimination. This imagined consensus, however, can distract citizens from the ways in which urban "rebuilding" and "revitalization" are often elaborate forms of gentrification and displacement.[56] One of the clearest models for this kind of aestheticized and branded urban recovery is geographer Richard Florida's best-selling book *The Rise of the Creative Class* (2002). Florida's strategies for rebuilding urban centers as creative cities became a platform from which cities around the US and Canada launched new practices of urban planning that emphasized a "creative workforce."[57] For Florida, creativity means a whole range of activities and identities that intersect to create a highly energized, productive economy, one populated by "culturally creative" people.

Florida and others have been hired to consult with city planners to rebrand cities such as Des Moines and Toronto as newly energized and creative.[58] Cities that have utilized Florida's Creative Class Group also include Tacoma, Washington, which implemented as part of its rejuvenation project Love Tacoma, a social networking program that "coordinates and promotes events that bring young people to local venues to participate in cultural offerings—glass blowing, boutique tours, new neighborhood crawls, farmers' market." Another city on the consulting group's website, Tallahassee, Florida, is reimagined through strategies such as the three-day Tallahassee Film Festival, the Neighborhood Revitalization Advocacy program to revitalize the central business corridor of the city, and Greenovation, an environmental advocacy program.[59]

Critics of Florida abound.[60] While Florida recognizes material or cultural inequalities, shifting labor relations, and an increasingly immigrant service labor force, his privilege of a specific definition of the creative economy renders these "uncreative" elements of society all but invisible. As many critics have noted, one result of the renewed focus on the creative class and industries has been the off-loading of state responsibilities onto the individual. As the creative class "rises," the state abdicates its role supporting ordinary wage-earning workers to focus instead on those "innately creative" individuals who effectively become "entrepreneurs" (or temporary laborers) in an economy that increasingly privileges self-employed freelance labor.[61]

While these dynamics hardly seem new, what has shifted is the way in which this creative economy has enabled the branding of creativity and authenticity. Florida's promoting of "creative cities" and a creative workforce is a clear example of a kind of urban branding, a practice characterized by Greenberg as something that is "at once visual and material, and combines intensive marketing—in this case place marketing—with neoliberal political and economic restructuring."[62] As is clear, this economic restructuring hinges on gentrification. Transforming urban neighborhoods into creative hubs indicates the erasure of all those who fall outside of the creative class: the working poor, immigrants, service workers, or those marginalized by material or cultural inequalities and changing labor relations—anyone, in other words, who does not productively channel the "innate creativity of humans."[63]

How do street artists fit into this transformation of urban neighborhoods? How is their artwork positioned? City development is now nearly always the result of public-private mergers, so the corporation has far greater influence in the shaping of a city and its resources than it has ever before. Within this context, where the corporate world exerts so much power, street artists are increasingly looking toward corporate sponsorship. For instance, in 2009, street artist Shepard Fairey collaborated with Levi's to design a street art–inspired line centered around his clothing brand, Obey. To launch this collaboration, Fairey put up posters of his art in New York City's Times Square and tagged the Obey logo on the street outside the Levi's store.[64] Levi's sponsored the clothing collaboration and also the actual practice of creating street art as a way to highlight both the Levi's brand and Fairey's own creative brand. A poignant site for such collaboration, Times Square is now routinely celebrated as a family-friendly spot in part because of the assiduous removal of graffiti by the city government alongside the (racialized) removal of other "unwholesome" city sights such as pornography and prostitution.

In the creative economy, charting and measuring creativity becomes paramount and is a significant element in reimagining a creative city. Success requires the explicit marketing of the *idea* that there is a creative class.

Creativity itself is organized as a kind of brand, complete with not only corporate sponsors such as Levi's but also consultants such as Richard Florida's consulting group, the Creative Class Group. "Creative consultants" and brand managers are hired by city planners to produce a more creative city, which ostensibly then increases the value of a city in terms of actual revenue, tourist dollars, and reputation. As I witnessed, city branding is about "theming." Creativity is quantified and measured on various scales, such as Florida's "gay index," which sees the demographic of gays and lesbians as evidence of an open city, tolerant of "diverse" lifestyles and open to creativity as an economic force. (Of course, a numerical categorization of the gay population obscures class dynamics within gay communities as well as histories about why gays and lesbians migrate to urban centers in the first place, among other things.)

Through the presentations of indexes and scales, and the slick promotional materials of branders, creativity itself is reified, transformed into an object that is marketed, distributed, and exchanged within the contemporary neoliberal economy. Creativity takes on value as a lifestyle, as government policy, or political behavior. Even within the branded city, then, street and graffiti artists often use creative practice to create a "counterbrand," one that rejects and critiques the increasing privatization of city resources and shrinking public spaces. The challenge to the corporate takeover of public space, though explicitly anticorporate, is not necessarily outside the contours of brand culture but rather works as a kind of ambivalence within the branded city. So, for instance, brands are represented in the form of street artists Banksy or Shepard Fairey, brands that deliberately question the role of public space in capitalist societies and that signify street culture, which use savvy wordplay, and a pastiche of graphic image styles that signal dissent and a kind of outlaw, unapologetic individualism, which packages creativity into market items for art world consumers, hip youth, and ordinary citizens (or at least those "ordinary" folks wealthy enough to afford a creative city). Yet, in those cities where artists (like generations of artists in other cities before them) have begun to move into neighborhoods with cheap foreclosed homes—cheap real estate being a key incentive to low-paid artistic production—it is not the creative product, or even creativity itself, but the *promise* of creativity that is marketed.[65] This is one of the consequences of the Florida model: cities that are successful in fostering creative bourgeois economies tend to become too expensive for all but the most successful artists (or the independently wealthy) to live and thus quickly become environments where creativity is signaled by branding and marketing, but other forms of artistic production are in short supply.

The city is where the aspiration toward creativity can manifest itself. The city is key in the cultural circuit from brand to actual profit; there is a need for a specific place, a tangible location, if creative practices are going to yield revenue. In marketers' designs for creative cities, neighborhoods are planned around indexes of creativity. Art galleries, coffeehouses, theaters, well-kept walkways, and perhaps commissioned street art indicate not only a safe neighborhood but one where creativity attracts specific classes of people, namely, those who have the cultural and economic capital to visit art galleries and museums and spend time at coffeehouses. The creative city thus nurtures the individual entrepreneur, who is a central actor within brand culture.

Creating the Individual Entrepreneur

When creativity itself is organized as a brand, it is effectively reconfigured through commodity fetishism so that the relationship of labor to creativity is effaced and it is allied with broader social concepts and individual desires. Creativity itself (rather than the tangible products of creativity) thus becomes a means to accumulate profit. Indeed, as I have argued throughout this book, the political economy of advanced capitalism involves not only the decentralization of production but also the reorganization of labor and markets, including changing labor patterns (such as the normalization of the itinerant laborer, flexible production, and a multiskilled labor force).[66] Within this economic context, postindustrial capitalist practices develop systems of production and distribution that respond to smaller niche groups of consumers in order to maximize profit and are framed, as I argued in chapter 1, within a discourse of "equality," "freedom," and "democracy." The artistic endeavors of contemporary street artists such as Shepard Fairey or Banksy are a kind of logical outgrowth from this context; their skill at placing cultural critique, branding, and art dynamically side by side is not necessarily conceived of as a kind of anticapitalist activism. Rather, this brand of rebellious creativity—built on an inherent, and very profitable, ambivalence—is precisely the kind of branding nurtured by advanced capitalism.

Part of the marketing of an urban space now involves navigating the inherent tensions between corporate sponsorship of the arts and culture and maintaining a sense of "authenticity" to those same arts—especially to those creative practices such as street art and graffiti. Brand marketers relentlessly address these kinds of tensions about losing "authenticity," crafting business models that transform authenticity into a brand strategy. To brand authenticity and structure it as part of a business plan is to understand experiences and, importantly, the emotions that accompany experiences, as distinct economic offerings. As marketers James H. Gilmore and B. Joseph Pine explain in their book *Authenticity: What Consumers Really Want* (2007), in the contemporary economy, businesses have to develop new strategies and management expertise: "Organizations today must learn to understand, manage, and excel at *rendering authenticity*. Indeed, 'rendering authenticity' should one day roll trippingly off the tongue as easily as 'controlling costs' and 'improving quality.'"[67]

Rendering authenticity, as a specific business imperative enabled by contemporary capitalist practices, is in urban cities made possible by a convergence of creativity and commerce. Street artists, and their own histories as well as the histories of this creative practice, are coded as authentic precisely because of the way these histories are imbricated in discourses about reclaiming and taking over the street. The streets that are the canvasses of street artists, and the street artist him- or herself, are coded as both potentially "creative" and "authentic."

But, and importantly, the definitions of creativity and authenticity are increasingly understood within the logic of business. The idea that one can "excel" at "rendering authenticity"—to cite one of many examples of business logic—runs counter to any kind of conventional definition of authenticity. The reason so many seek out authenticity is precisely because it cannot be managed and rendered but is rather a state of being, a quality that most people hope to have. But, like other subjects within contemporary brand culture, the street artist must be managed and governed. When successful, those artists and their streets-cum-canvasses are potentially profitable, since they maintain "authenticity" while at the same time not threatening the business model of the branded city.[68]

Ritzy P, a contemporary street artist from Los Angeles, defines street art in the following way:

> To me street art is a term to cover art that is from and/or in the streets beyond graffiti since that has its own specific definition but does also include it. In the past years since "street art" has been the term *du jour*, it seems artists that might only do stencils or wheat pasting for instance, all seem to respect and know the basic history of graffiti and have figured out a medium to communicate their personal ideas in the streets. All of it to me seems to have a certain aesthetic and vibe, a non verbal understanding of the essence of the hustle and grind of the streets.[69]

The use of the terms "hustle" and "grind" by Ritzy P is a reminder of how the "street" is always a trope with race- and class-based assumptions. That is, Ritzy P also eloquently describes the "non verbal understanding of the essence" of the streets, an understanding that is marketed and branded for ordinary citizens using tropes of race and class that lend it authenticity and hipness. As I have discussed, the definition of street art is broad and encompassing, though it seems clear that street artists define it in ways that are in distinct opposition to advertising—it is an aesthetic, a vibe, an identity, something that is created often without permission, or, as street artist DJ | LA says, "any expression that transcends that need for attention only factor. gotta have some love behind it."[70] The "love" that is behind street art often comes in the form of pointed political critiques, especially those that question, mock, and critique its commercialization. Artists from Jean-Michel Basquiat and Keith Haring to Jennifer Holzer and Barbara Kruger have asked people, in various ways, to be critical and question the world around them. These artists as well as others used creative practice as an articulation of struggle and ambivalence over forms of cultural expression and uses of public space—and it is precisely this struggle, *not its resolution*, that characterizes contemporary brand culture.

As one example of this kind of struggle, Banksy's website features not only images of his own work but also images of other street and graffiti artists covering up his work (which is generally understood as a sign of disrespect within street art and graffiti communities). So, a Banksy work featured on his website presents a piece he created in London that depicts a young boy of color, wearing baggy clothes, a gaudy gold chain with a gun pendant, and a backward baseball cap while holding a boom box stereo—and implausibly carrying what looks to be a tattered and well-loved stuffed bunny. The next image in the website gallery features the same work, but this time the image is partly covered with graffiti that reads "love not money." A third image features the work again, this time completely covered by the words "Say No to Art Fags" and "Fuck Banksy," along with a few writers' names. These gestures of reflexivity are part of Banksy's cultivated commercial image. The 2010 film discussed at the beginning of this chapter, *Exit through the Gift Shop*, is subtitled *A Bansky Film* and chronicles, among other things, the brand of Banksy himself. It is a brand that trades on a recognizable unrecognizability, profiting from (even while admonishing) the codes of celebrity visibility. But this play is particularly profitable within the current creative economy because through its self-critique and reflexivity it is read as authentic. This reflexivity is indicative of the precariousness of the brand. That is, street artists operate with an awareness of the system; indeed, the most financially successful street artists (such as Banksy or Shepard Fairey) operate by acknowledging the limits of branding, which is what marks their work as critical in the contemporary context.

Consider another example. The Wooster Collective, founded in New York in 2001, is "dedicated to showcasing and celebrating ephemeral art placed on streets in cities around the world."[71] The collective's website features events (ranging from museum exhibitions to photos of new street art), asks viewers for feedback on what to include in the site, and solicits input about design. The collective nature of the group suggests that it is not a top-down organization but rather celebrates unknown and emerging artists and encourages critique of advertising. Yet, the Wooster Collective is clearly a brand in and of itself. The brand of a self-run, independent collective might have a different end goal (such as sustaining the collective) than that of corporate street art, but the logic of branding remains the same. The website offers collections of street art for sale, asks viewers to "become a fan" of the Wooster Collective on the social network site Facebook, provides a Twitter feed, and features links with other affiliations and artists. These are all ways the collective manages its online presence and are crucial elements of the way the Wooster Collective develops its brand.

In yet another example, on Fairey's website, ObeyGiant.com, one finds a similar brand environment: art for sale, links to other commercial websites, invitations to become a fan. Importantly, Fairey's work with corporate brands is in part enabled and authorized by his other street art, including work that directly criticizes capitalism, economic imperialism, and the fallacy of the "free market." Indeed, part of the reason Fairey makes an attractive partner for corporations such as Levi's is that Fairey has been arrested more than a dozen times for defacing public property (a fact the artist cites often as evidence of his street authenticity), and his street art frequently critiques issues ranging from capitalism to anti-immigration policies to the environment. In 2009 in Boston, Fairey was arrested for vandalism during a major retrospective of his work at the Institute for Contemporary Art. When he appeared in court a month later with his lawyer to fight what the *New York Times* called a "cascade" of vandalism charges, it prompted yet again a debate (one deliberately instigated by Fairey over the years) about the difference between street art, graffiti, and branding. "He's raising important issues about consent and who decides what we see in public spaces," Jill Medvedow, director of the Institute of Contemporary Art, told the *Times*.[72] Yet Fairey himself is a beneficiary of the "free market," where his status is made possible by the normalizing of the individual entrepreneur.

As these examples of street art and artists bear out, despite the conceptual and ideological differences between street art and advertising, the relationship between these two aesthetic forms is not one of binary opposites but one of ambivalence. This ambivalence supports the cultural narrative that street artists are "reclaiming the streets," where street art is an act of rebellion against the bullying power of commercial interests—such as Florida-inspired strategies to make a city more creative. Yet reclaiming the streets has a market value on its own. *Los Angeles Times* reporter Richard Winton claims the LA-based tagger crew MTA has firmly established its brand within the cultural marketplace of urban street art. Describing the leader of MTA, a street artist called Smear, selling street art to collectors, Winton reports, "[There] is so much demand for street art right now."[73] This demand not only recognizes the aesthetics of street art but also is a market demand, one for those artists and groups, such as MTA, who "have made a name for themselves" in the branded world of street art. As Cedar Lewisohn states about the political motivations of London street artists, "They are in competition with the fly posters and advertisers. They also know that as soon as they put their work up on the street, the advertisers and marketers are going to attempt to appropriate their ideas So the street artist in London must build a defence-shield against corporate theft. It's a constant cat-and-mouse game of artists innovating and advertisers assimilating."[74]

A scene from the Banksy opening of *The Simpsons*

In contemporary brand culture, however, the idea that corporate play-ers are focused on blatantly appropriating the ideas of street artists, who are clearly the mice in this "cat-and-mouse" game, does not have the same pur-chase. The myth of the "innovative" artist and the "assimilative" advertiser breaks down when the artists become the advertisers. The new game is one of competing for representation. Street artists are not just competing with representation through advertising, though, but also are competing with the police and with gangs and their own social invisibility. In other words, there is no street art without graffiti and tagging, there is no street art with-out murals, and there is no street art without advertising. Because of these dependencies, street art must cultivate and nurture an authentic/commer-cial divide: it resists the corporate consumerism to which street artists (along with all other people) are asked to commit; it challenges corporate and gov-ernmental efforts to contain and control creativity; and it both buys into and challenges a culture of anxiety about authenticity by engaging in illegal prac-tices that are specifically not sanctioned by commercial institutions. Seen from this angle, street art is one way of claiming space in a "creative city" where every space can be taken up, expanded, reimagined, and branded as authentic.

The tension between autonomy and subjugation that emerges when polit-ical work is embedded within (and often defined by) capitalist practices can even be seen on *The Simpsons*. As usual, the episode begins with the camera panning through the streets of Springfield accompanied by the theme song. As the camera passes through the town, however, there are a few different images: people defacing statues, the word "BANKSY" written over advertis-ing billboards, and Bart Simpson (in his typical pose, writing the sentence "I must not write all over the walls" multiple times on the chalkboard as pun-ishment for his perpetual crimes).

The theme song seems to end as it always does, with the Simpson fam-ily sitting on the couch, gathered to watch television together. But then the camera continues to pans out, away from the family, and the viewer finds herself instead in a dark sweatshop somewhere in Asia, where rows of som-ber, nearly identical women are shown, under the watchful gaze of a menac-ing guard, painstakingly painting the image of the Simpson family on tele-vision cels. Deep underneath the sweatshop, we are then shown a dimly lit basement, where other beleaguered workers manufacture other Simpsons merchandise: brightly colored T-shirts, and Bart Simpson dolls made out of shredded kittens. A head of a dead dolphin is used to seal boxes of Simpsons merchandise with its extended tongue, and a man uses the horn of an old, gray, sickly unicorn to form the hole in the middle of Simpsons DVDs. The scene ends with the Twentieth Century Fox logo behind barbed wire. An obvious critique of the network's outsourcing of labor to underpaid, overworked women and children in various Asian countries, the episode continues the satiric tradition of the program and its long-standing critique of capitalism, US hegemony in the global economy, and alienated labor.

However, the opening credits of this October 2010 episode were storyboarded and directed by Banksy. According to press reports, Banksy created the credits as a reaction to reports that the show outsources much of its labor to a South Korean company.[75] In typical Banksy fashion, he both critiques the neoliberal practice of outsourcing labor and also makes sure that his name is known throughout the opening scenes by plastering it on billboards around Springfield. Banksy thus participates in the discourse surrounding the practice of outsourcing labor; his critique of Fox serves to ameliorate outrage over the company's labor practices and therefore helps Fox continue to outsource labor. While creating and directing the opening credits for a wildly popular US commercial television show is not typical street art, the use of a space such as television to critique the infrastructure that enables its existence—capitalism—embodies the compelling and troubling ways Banksy has used the street as a politicized canvas. Here, Banksy demonstrates both his flexibility as an individual entrepreneur by creating in a mainstream media space and the ambivalence that structures the branding of creativity in the first place.

Labor in the Brand of Creativity

Is Banksy part of Richard Florida's "creative class," or at war with it? In many ways, the idea of the creative class rejuvenates—and rebrands—the historical notion of a meritocracy, where those who are the most "creative," like Banksy, will find a place in this economy. *Creative* laborers in the creative economy rely only or primarily on their individual talents; absent any state or federal support for "creativity," with creative labor romanticized as "cool" and "artistic," creative laborers are designated as "agents of the neoliberal order."[76] As with other manifestations of meritocracy, those laborers not considered creative are nonetheless crucial to the creative economy but are not privileged as entrepreneurs. For instance, the animators referred to by Banksy in the Simpsons episode are surely laborers in a creative economy, but (and this is part of Banksy's point) no employer imagines them to have creative talent, just exploitable labor.

Street artists such as Banksy or Fairey, not only through their creative artistic productions but also in their positions as people who take on the risks of bucking the system, occupy the subject position of the creative laborer. As Angela McRobbie points out, laborers even with creative talent (say, a street artist or a fashion designer) seem to be missing from articulations of the creative class, except as glorified individual entrepreneurs.[77] Indeed, the laborer, historically defined as someone who works for wages, or as an unskilled person who assists skilled workers in a particular trade, is dependent on an organized system of labor, revolving around state-defined wages, trade unions, and so on. The entrepreneur, in contrast, is understood as an ambitious individual, dependent on no one but him- or herself, a person who "owns" his or her own labor and is thus accountable for not only the profit but also the risks accumulated by this labor and is not officially "owed" anything by the state. Within an advanced capitalist environment, the individual entrepreneur is the archetypal laborer; the labor that is performed is proof that the individual can "free" him- or herself from the state. And as we have seen with the emergence of the self-brand, such "freedom" is synonymous with "finding oneself" and the other infinite possibilities inherent in branding oneself.

What looks like critique of state and corporate power by street artists functions rather as a *validation* of the neoliberal state because the critique aims at a state structure that no longer exists. The necessarily clandestine practice of street artists, the play with politics and art, and the characteristically audacious "street" attitude read as a well-crafted script for the individual entrepreneur within the current environment. The entrepreneur is at the center of today's creative economy, indicating, as Jamie Peck argues, that only a privileged class of consumer-producers has a place within the creative economy.[78] This is partly because the currency of this creative economy is authenticity, so that the "correct" affective articulations come from "authentic" people. The creative entrepreneur is celebrated and romanticized because of the kind of work produced: not the gritty, industrial products that workers care nothing about (but which are, of course, still necessary for all capitalist industries), but rather artistic and innovative expressions of "inner creativity," products that workers care intensely about, with passion driving the production process rather than a mind-numbing need for minimum wage.

Andrew Ross terms this creative class the "precariat," composed of workers whose precarious and itinerant labor is romanticized as existing outside the market (and thus denied the rights within it).[79] As I have argued, creativity (and its boundless possibilities) is presented as an incentive that reduces government's role as provider of social and cultural services. That is, self-employment is romanticized as a viable career option for many people rather than a lifestyle available to a very few: "Set up your own business. Be free to do your own thing. Live and work like an artist....This is the logic of 'everyone is creative.'"[80] Clearly, not everyone is creative—at least not in a form that will generate a profit—but the mobilizing ideology behind this idea becomes a normative mechanism, thus validating the practice of self-branding and glorifying the position of the entrepreneur. At the same time, this ideology obscures the class assumptions and requirements of being an entrepreneur.

Ross's point, along with McRobbie's, is not so much that "creativity" is lauded and rewarded in new ways but that the exploitative economic practices characterizing more traditional forms of labor, such as the denial of labor rights and oppressive managerial policies, now extend to creative labor. The discourse of creativity obscures the continued exploitation of many labor relationships and distances these creative types from the long history of labor unions and other efforts to protect workers from exploitation.[81]

Yet, the popular mythologies of creativity—as a passionate pursuit of innovation, an innate individual characteristic, or a skill set that is somehow outside the field of commerce—continue to define creative labor, resulting in a relentlessly individualist kind of work, absent of any kind of state involvement, such as workplace protection, job security, or health care. The mystique surrounding the creative laborer feels familiar, even as neoliberal infrastructures are the context for the creation and nurturing of this mystique. Most creative laborers, however, do not uncritically embrace the intersections and collapses between creativity and commerce. Rather, as David Hesmondhalgh argues, many creative workers have ambivalent feelings toward their creative work; the historical opposition between creativity and commerce is maintained, but creative labor is how creative workers make a living, so there must be compromises. As Hesmondhalgh shows, there is a great deal of anxiety and insecurity about pay in the creative economy—the romantic ideal of "living on the edge" becomes less appealing when trying to pay the bills, particularly in the midst of financial crisis.[82] The ostensible autonomy of creative labor—that one can, in Florida's concept, channel innate human creativity to make a living doing what one loves—is seen here as a kind of control mechanism, in which the overly romanticized notion of "creative autonomy" and the individual entrepreneur obfuscates the actual material realities of advanced capitalism. The discourse of creative autonomy additionally obscures the kind of privilege that is necessary to access this autonomy.

The Authentic and the Street Artist

Within the context of the branded city, street artists maintain an "authentic" aura to their creative productions precisely because authenticity is part of the brand. This authentic aura is present in Banksy's work that critiques the state and through Fairey's murals that challenge capitalism's norms. This authenticity is expansive; it also undergirds the "Hope" poster that the Obama campaign officially commissioned from Fairey. The anxiety potentially caused by the convergence of creativity with commerce ("selling out") is assuaged when street artists' cultural labor is performed in ostensible public spaces. This is despite the fact that these spaces are nonetheless branded, because the idea of selling out implies two discrete, bounded spaces, the creative and the commercial. Brand culture is enabled and supported by blurrings between the authentic and the commercial precisely by decentering consuming products as the crucial act of consumption and highlighting instead cultural practices as consumptive spaces in which individuals are "free" to practice politics, articulate lifestyles, and engage in creative acts. Crucial to the convergence of creativity and commercial culture is, ironically, the maintenance of a *distinction* between authenticity and the commercial, especially in terms of crafting a personal identity that is expressed as "freedom" from state power. Maintaining the distinction between authentic creativity and commercialized industry in turn maintains the idea that there is a space outside of the market in which authenticity can take root and flourish, a cultural space that has somehow escaped capitalism's unapologetic bullying.

Outside the realm of state responsibility and obligation, individuals are charged with taking care of their own needs and entrepreneurial ambitions. The street artist is one such individual, where the entrepreneurialism and innovation of the artist, previously understood and practiced as a cultural or political practice (one that is economic only out of sheer necessity), are situated within an enterprising cultural context, one in which artistic endeavors can be seen as "freedoms" in the marketing or branding of the self. Street artists brand themselves through their art, personal logos, social media, and websites, among other elements, as a way to enter the circuits of commodity exchange, but also to be visible in those circuits. To think of street artists as individual entrepreneurs forces us to think more deeply about how, and in what ways, the relationship between the market and the individual works: the contemporary cultural economy authorizes specific individuals, such as street artists, to be entrepreneurs, and clearly delineates creative productions, such as street art, as brands. This form of convergence is a relationship of struggle and ambivalence, of necessity and (not always) mutual benefit.

Street artists, in their attempts to reclaim city space, operate using similar strategies as those of branding companies: making one's personal mark on the environment, using logos that are instantly recognizable by other street artists and (hopefully) the general public, and taking great pains (sometimes

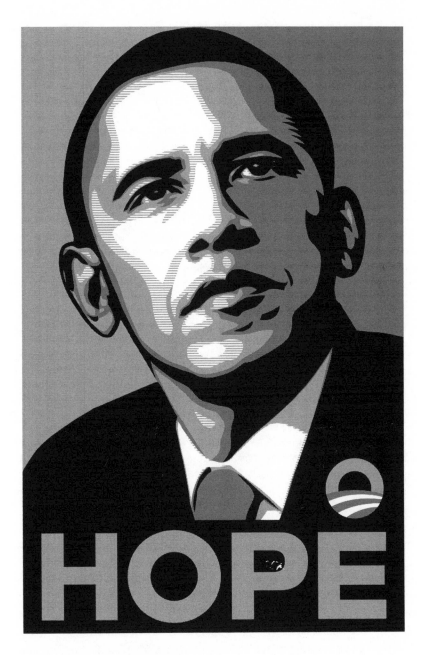

The Shepard Fairey Obama "Hope" poster.

illegal ones) to increase their cultural visibility. Of course, visibility is also a privilege: when street artists are racialized subjects, their visibility as artists becomes a complex negotiation with invisibility as well. That is, as with all self-brands, some bodies are more "brandable" than others.

As I've argued, Shepard Fairey is one example of the intersection of the creative class and the creative laborer. He is a street artist who has successfully branded himself, sells commodities of his brand, and regularly does commercial ad campaigns while also using his brand for various political causes such as environmentalism and human rights.

These different components of Fairey's creative labor—some political, others commercial—do not stand in contrast or opposition to each other but rather form complementary elements of the overall brand of Shepard Fairey. As he has stated, "I think to have these very impractical delineations between art, design, what's keeping it real, and what's commercial, is not very psychologically healthy for most artists and designers....it's just a reality that rather than being apologetic about it, we've put together a group of people who actually thrive on that overlap."[83]

Fairey's success is evidence of how cultural capital today trickles upward. The cultural capital of the street is now invaluable in the world of mainstream branding. Fairey negotiates this cultural capital through a constant publicizing of his arrests he often notes his arrest record when he speaks publicly, and it is invariably brought up in news stories about his art. He makes his illegal acts into a badge of his marginal status, one that has market value. Again, this market value is also connected to race, as the multiple arrests of a white man have a different cultural resonance than those of a man of color. Yet, Fairey's negotiation of these potential contradictions demonstrates a discourse that is decidedly different from historical tortured defenses of artists adamant that they are not selling out. He subtitles his massive coffee-table book *Supply and Demand*, he remakes dollar bills, and he talks constantly of flexibility, a key buzzword of the current creative economy and its redefinition of work. Indeed, his continued work in support of Barack Obama demonstrates how he negotiates these potential contradictions: the August 20, 2009, cover of *Rolling Stone* featured a new Shepard Fairey portrait of Obama, a more sober and ambivalent depiction than on his "Hope" poster. In the same red, white, and blue color palette as the earlier poster, Obama is shown on the *Rolling Stone* cover looking stern and determined, surrounded by what appears to be a halo of stars and the question: "Will he take bold action or compromise too easily?" Fairey claims his inspiration for the illustration was in part Gilbert Stuart's portrait of George Washington, which became the basis for the engraving on the dollar bill, thus both situating Obama among other significant US presidents (as well as reinforcing the connection between the president and currency) and also saying that "the jury still's out on whether this President will live up to his promise."[84]

This play between validating mainstream politics and simultaneously using art to ask questions about those politics is a hallmark of Fairey's work, as well as an embodiment of the ambivalence within creative brand cultures. When Fairey argues for the right to poster the streets with his Obey Giant images, he does so not through, say, a radical discourse about the street as a public space that should be decommercialized but rather through the discourse of a taxpayer's rights: "I became a street artist because I felt public space was the only option for free speech and expression without bureaucracy....I also found the whole idea that you could be arrested for stickering or postering as something I wanted to rebel against. In my opinion, the taxpayers are the bosses of the government. I'm a taxpayer—why can't I use public space for my imagery when corporations can use it for theirs?"[85] Though Fairey likes to refer to his relationship to corporate capitalism as an "inside/outside strategy" with a "Robin Hood effect," and, as I noted, his reputation as an artist of the street is crucial to his value as an artist, he also stakes out the position that "capitalism is a way for hard work to yield rewards."[86] It is precisely the context of creative economies and advanced capitalism that allows such comments to seem complementary rather than contradictory. It is also the case that Fairey's style has been enormously effective in creating these boundary crossings between the street and the mainstream.

In one sense, the brands of Banksy and Shepard Fairey and the rise of the individual entrepreneur can be understood as part of a larger commercial endeavor, where the branding of creativity demonstrates some of the latest business maneuvers in an increasingly competitive market. However, work by Banksy and Fairey, and its enthusiastic reception, also prompts questions about how, and in what ways, we need to account for branding strategies *as* creativity. The work of street artists demonstrates the importance of taking into account the complexities of consumer identity, affect, and desire that, as I have discussed, form the center of brand culture when discussing alternative systems of consumption. The work of these artists and others like them represents the complex contradictions of cultural entrepreneurship at large: both the potential for social activism to thrive under the guise of consumerism and the potential for artists and workers to be incorporated, in new yet similarly disabling ways, into the workplaces and work lives of advanced capitalism.

It should be clear: I am not offering an art reading or critique of street art but rather an argument about the branding of creativity. Street art provides a useful lens through which to rethink what is meant by creativity in the first place: the boundaries between art and commerce have arguably always been blurred, so what is it about contemporary creative culture that affords a different perspective? I have argued here that the increasing presence of brand cultures in the US helps to define street art as a deep, often ambivalent, interrelation of a variety of realms: the public and the private, the independent and the mainstream, the artistic self and the brand. The branding of "authentic" creativity needs to be interrogated not only for what it authorizes in terms of new understandings of culture and the individual but also for what other ambivalences these dynamics obscure. *Exit through the Gift Shop* shows clearly the ways in which contemporary street artists, as enterprising subjects endowed with shifting definitions of creativity, individualism, and entrepreneurialism, are logical distributors of this brand. Thierry Guetta becomes a brand simply by utilizing the resources afforded him by advanced capitalism, resources that enable him to "make his name sing" in a specific context.

Street art occupies different spaces within brand culture—and maintaining the difference in these spaces as oppositional is absolutely crucial to contemporary capitalist practices. Ambivalence within the space of culture, in other words, implies a relentless power struggle between emergent modes of creativity and the dominant modes of the market; that power dynamic authorizes the branding of authentic creativity itself. The branding of the authentic is, in this context, not a misnomer, an oxymoron, or an example of capitalist hypocrisy but rather a defining feature of the contemporary cultural economy in the US.

4

BRANDING POLITICS

People seek authenticity because no one wants to be a means to someone else's end. Yet marketing is all about a means to an end. And in a world where manipulation is omnipresent—on our cell phones, our email in-boxes, our shopping carts, our kids' schools and so forth—the immutable law of supply and demand makes authenticity increasingly precious. However, if your enterprise is part of the culture of social responsibility, then authenticity is something you get free with the price of admission (i.e., your commitment).

—Jerry Stifelman, Treehugger.com

In the fall of 2010, the nonprofit company Free2Work.org launched a new iPhone application. The phone app, Free2Work, grades companies based on their commitment to offering a living wage for workers and a democratic work environment. The press release for the new app reads:

> Become a conscious consumer. This holiday season, you can support companies working to end slave labor in supply chains as you shop your favorite brands. See how apparel companies like Gap and Levi's compare. Check out hot toy companies like Fisher Price, Lego, LeapFrog and Pillow Pets. Use the information on chocolate and other ingredients to help ensure your holiday meal is slave-free.[1]

The connection Free2Work makes between the use of an iPhone application (which can only be used on an iPhone) and the promise that one's holiday meal will be "slave-free" is fairly easy to characterize as ludicrous or, at the least, hypocritical. It is tempting to say, that is, that this iPhone app is an obvious example of a manipulative attempt by corporations such as the Gap and Levi's to attach their products to progressive politics. It is hard to miss the irony of an Apple iPhone app that promotes "slave-free" politics given the recent publicity over Apple's deplorable sweatshop labor practices overseas.[2] It is also easy to critique the reductive idea that "authenticity" is a kind of product, "free with the price of admission" through one's commitment. Throughout this book, however, I have argued against this temptation, and against thinking about today's capitalist culture as merely an ever-richer context for traditional and emergent forms of corporate appropriation. The notion that we can fight against global slave labor by using an iPhone app (to help us shop, no less!) surely makes that temptation all the more, well, tempting.

Yet, it remains important to not settle for this kind of critique, for yet another binary that opposes corporate appropriation and some vague ideal of progressive politics. Rather, we must think more deeply about how this iPhone app is representative of a branded politics. In the 21st-century US, it is clear that social and political action, cultural resistance, and political identities are often attached to merchandising practices, market incentives, and corporate profits. Within this context, Free2Work makes logical sense as an "authentic" form of politics. More significantly, this iPhone app is but one example of political practice in a transformative moment: the US is witnessing, and participating in, a shift from "authentic" politics to the branding of politics *as* authentic.

We can see the branding of politics perhaps most vividly on the stage of electoral politics. The early 21st century, after all, is the era of the "Obama brand"; many argue that the first "digital president" was elected due to the complex branding of Obama, achieved primarily through social media and new technologies. This is also the historical moment where former Alaskan governor Sarah Palin has a reality television show that promises to reimagine and revitalize the "Republican brand" (also framed as "the American spirit"). Branding politics has likewise become increasingly common in the corporate world, particularly through the practice of corporate social responsibility, in which corporations use a social issue (such as environmental concern or poverty) as a platform not only to sell products but also to further their brand. Dove's clever use of soap as a vehicle to talk about positive body image and negative beauty culture (and, implicitly, about how its products can enhance the former and reduce the latter) is just one of innumerable examples. Arguably, in order to be a viable political presence in contemporary US culture, one must craft a successful political brand.

It has been my argument throughout *Authentic*™ that the emergence of brand culture in the contemporary moment means that realms of culture and society once considered outside the official economy—like politics—are harnessed, reshaped, and made legible in economic terms. In the specific case of political branding, this indicates a need to pay close attention to three areas of analysis: historical and current struggles over what political activism means; who takes shape as activists in contemporary society; and whom such activism is imagined to serve. To that end, in this chapter, I examine the histories of political consumption and a politicized consumer movement as a way to set the stage for today's political brand cultures. These brand cultures are supported in part by a broader context of corporate social responsibility campaigns, which then in turn continue to blur citizenship distinctions between individual consumers and corporations. I then turn my attention to the individual within these cultures to examine how consumer citizens are organized and crafted as political activists in the era of the brand. Consumer activists are authorized as citizens to "do good" by "buying good," and within the context of shifting conceptions of citizens (aided in no small part by technologies that allow for new subject positions such as the "citizen journalist" and the "prosumer"), brand cultures are "coproduced" along the contours of specific political practices and ideologies, such as environmentalism. My focus on the "branded activist" here is on the ways in which corporate-organized branding campaigns position individual consumers in their campaigns (not necessarily how politically progressive activists use branding strategies themselves).[3] In the final section of the chapter, I analyze two specific "green" brand cultures for their potential possibilities as initiators of social change: the brand culture of bottled water in the US, and the emergence of urban farming as a brand culture amid the post-2008 economic crisis.

Nostalgia for What? Branding Politics

In 2010, Adam Silver, a marketing strategist for the design company frog design New York, commented that "[if] the last decade was defined by the lifestyle brand, perhaps this decade will be defined by a related, yet distinct identity: the political brand."[4] Even if—and especially if—the political brand will define the second decade of the 21st century, the increasing presence of political branding requires critique. The problem, however, is that much criticism against the branding of politics is steeped in nostalgia for a different, presumably more genuine, kind of politics. As reporter Sally Kohn wrote (in an article for a progressive audience) about the recent problems progressives have had building coalitions and fomenting social movements, "The progressive field is too focused on branding. In the case of movement building, not only is branding not the same as identity but organizational branding actually undermines movement identity."[5] Malcolm Gladwell, in "Small Change: Why the Revolution Will Not Be Tweeted," a 2010 essay in the *New Yorker*, while not commenting specifically on branding, makes the claim that, despite the hype about the revolutionary powers of commercial social media such as Facebook and Twitter, social movements and political activism need face-to-face commitment and a kind of loyalty and affiliation that presumably existed, especially in the civil rights era (apparently a moment before the convergence of politics with entertainment, or activism with consumerism). Citing civil rights activism as "high risk activism," and subsequently deriding new media technologies such as Twitter as overhyped, Gladwell makes a case for hierarchy and discipline in social movements as the most effective way to challenge racism and other discriminatory practices.[6] Both Kohn and Gladwell nostalgically reference earlier eras, where they imagine an apparently clear "movement identity" and real, face-to-face politics. It is important to examine the danger of being nostalgic for a previous (and fictitious) era in which commercial branding and politics were clearly separated.

As I have argued throughout this book, there are key differences between branding and commodification. Branded politics are foundationally structured by brand logic and strategy, so that politics are defined in terms of the brand from the ground up, originating within and related to branding. A branded politics by definition also involves coproduction with consumer activists, where people act politically by consuming. To assert that today's politics are commodified, on the other hand, as Kohn and Gladwell and other progressives do, assumes a more top-down act of appropriation and references an imaginary history in which politics existed in a noncommercial, authentic space before they were redirected and distorted by commercialism. Analyzing contemporary politics as branded means I will not linger in rehashing the various ways in which the cultural lines between "authentic" politics and consumerism have blurred; nor will I contribute to a nostalgia for a time when evidently politics were politics and consumption meant buying *things*, not identities, ideologies, or movements. However, the role nostalgia plays in the contemporary era does tell us something important about the branding of politics. Nostalgia often becomes a normative trope in political discourse as a way to mask or cope with anxiety about change; a close cousin to fear, nostalgia represents a longing for a time (which likely never existed) when it was easier and simpler to decipher a constantly changing world.

While the two examples just cited reference a left-leaning nostalgia for the politics of the 1960s, it is clear that nostalgia functions effectively on all parts of the political continuum. Conservative political groups in the US have for at least the last four decades brilliantly, and strategically, used nostalgia for a more harmonious and prosperous society to mobilize their political base. Ronald Reagan's 1984 "Morning in America" campaign film relies on a simplified but picturesque notion of hardworking, patriotic Americans longing for a return to the good life (not surprisingly, the overwhelming majority of people depicted in this campaign film are white and middle-class). Similarly, Sarah Palin's reality television show, *Sarah Palin's Alaska,* which aired on the cable channel TLC in the fall of 2010, promised an insider's look into the country's "final frontier" by portraying Palin engaged in "real" activities such as hunting, fishing, and camping. *Sarah Palin's Alaska* also represents a conservative's branded claim on environmentalism, part of Republicans' answer to the "progressive" tendencies of the green movement. By leveraging nostalgia for a more "authentic" sort of politics as part of brand strategy, political brand cultures tap into emotion, affect, and individualism as important conduits for political activism. The reliance on nostalgia for political branding supports the notion of the ethical consumer, an "authentic" political activist who is committed to political action. Yet, within political brand cultures, "authenticity," or political commitment, is, again, often "free with the price of admission." Political brand cultures are thus ambivalent spaces, where "authenticity" can be not only (often nostalgically) experienced but also purchased.

That is, the branding of politics—represented in the Obama brand, Republican brands, the Free2Work iPhone app, corporate social responsibility, and green branding, among others—is both an extension of and a response to nostalgia about "authenticity." The US has a long history of citizens consuming products as a means of comfort and security, especially in moments of national crisis. In contemporary US culture, mollifying anxiety through consumption is even seen as proof of the country's healthy status. As Marita Sturken writes, "The terrorist attacks of 9/11 produced a frenzied consumer response to the fear of terrorism, enabling a widespread consumerism of security," animating what Sturken calls a "broad range of consumer practices of security and comfort."[7] Unlike the consumer objects purchased by Americans after 9/11 that Sturken details, such as American flags, kitschy souvenirs like teddy bears and snow globes, and "security vehicles" such as the Hummer, contemporary branded politics offer a different sort of security: that one can be an ethical, virtuous consumer through affiliation with a brand and through the building of political brand cultures. Global shifts in the 21st century have led to a premium on ethical consumer citizenship and the security such citizenship produces.

The first decades of the 21st century are rife with anxiety and fear: continuing global violence, the "war on terror," the global economic collapse since 2008, and other international crises all signal fragility and instability, and all construct a context that is rich for branding and interpellating consumer citizens as activists. Nostalgia within the contemporary era for a different, less tumultuous time marks an ongoing transition from the commercialization of politics to the branding of politics, where branded politics are animated and given heightened significance because of widespread anxiety about social change and a need for security and comfort in times of crisis. First, though, what do politics *mean* within brand culture?

As several scholars have argued, the shifts in the political and cultural economies that have come to characterize neoliberalism point to a powerful turn in the modes and meanings of politics itself.[8] Within the contemporary cultural economy in the US, politics is becoming a marketable commodity. Again, however, the commodification of politics is not the same thing as the branding of politics. What might be termed "political consumerism"—ranging from boycotts to "buycotts" to investing in "socially responsible" corporations—is certainly part of, but not collapsible with, a political brand culture. In previous chapters, I argued that the technological environment of Web 2.0 and the expectations of participatory culture has made self-branding a normative personal pursuit. I also discussed the emergence of the creative city and the public-private partnerships between the state and corporations that facilitate that emergence, which need to be in place for the branding of creativity as a cultural formation. These cultural formations—self-branding, creative cities, and political branding discussed in this chapter—work as an entwined set of relationships to form brand cultures as the space in which individual identities, citizenship, and social action are crafted, experienced, and made normative. Thus, while I discuss specific practices of branding politics in this chapter, it is clear that the dynamics theorized are one element of a life today lived through the brand.

Politics, within the transitions and historical contingencies of advanced capitalism, is indeed slippery to define. As Wendy Brown asks: "When fundamental premises of an order begin to erode, or simply begin to be exposed as fundamental premises, what reactive political formations emerge—and what anxieties, tensions, or binds do they carry?"[9] The politics of the state, of sovereign individuals, even of the practices of everyday life, have all been put to question within the global neoliberal capitalism that has dominated Western culture since the 1980s. As I state in the introduction to this book, advanced capitalism not only is a political economic condition but also functions as a political rationality, one that works as a system of governmentality and management that not only builds culture but also reimagines definitions of the state and the individual. The anxieties, tensions, and binds referenced by Brown are not resolved within the contemporary political economy of the West, but they are addressed through a number of practices, including the continuing destruction of the welfare state, the increasing marketization of intellectual and cultural life, and the intensifying blurring of boundaries between the corporation and the citizen. As Brown asks further, when discussing the history and legacies of liberalism in the present political moment, "What happens to liberalism's organizing terms and legitimacy when its boundary terms change—when its constitutive past and future, as well as its constitutive others, lose their definitive difference from liberalism's present and identity?"[10] While surely the branding of politics is not the only thing that "happens" to these organizing terms of liberalism, the dominance of the brand has reimagined politics and political activism.

As a way to analyze neoliberal political dynamics, Nick Couldry distinguishes between "neoliberalism proper," which is the principle that installs "market functioning as the dominant reference-point of economics and, bizarrely as it might once have seemed, political and social order as well," and "neoliberal doctrine," which includes the wider set of "metaphors, languages, techniques and organizational principles that have served to implement neoliberalism proper as the working doctrine of many contemporary democracies."[11] When thinking about the shape and operation of political brand cultures, both of these levels of meaning are implied (and, indeed, are mutually constitutive), but when trying to parse the contradictions that structure the relationship between consumer citizens and political brand cultures, neoliberal doctrine more clearly informs its logics and vocabulary. Thus, as neoliberalism emerged in nations such as the UK and the US as a response to the 1970s global economic crisis, as Couldry points out, politics, and the citizens who acted politically, were organized around and within market logic, expressed through brand designs, logos, symbols, and metaphors.[12]

Branded politics are thus part of the contemporary era's structure of feeling.[13] Raymond Williams describes structures of feeling as "social experiences in solution,"[14] which seems a particularly apt explanatory mechanism for understanding branded politics. Williams borrows the concept of solution from chemistry: a structure of feeling is like a mix, a chemical solution, in which everyday life is lived.[15] Embedded in this solution, with different social experiences mixed together, there are no distinct boundaries or divisions between the authentic and the commercial, affect and the market. If politics is the space "where struggle and debate over 'the authoritative allocation of goods, services, and values' takes place," then branded politics reimagines these struggles and debates: goods, services, affect and desires interact as an everyday mix, a solution, so that their definition is transformed to make sense for ordinary consumer citizens.[16] A reimagining, of course, is necessarily embedded in history. In order to understand a shifted, emergent form of activism, we need to examine historical contexts that not only provide residual understandings of politics for consumers but also pave the way for new forms.

From the Right to Buy to Buying Right

In April 2010, the snack brand Sun Chips introduced its first "100% compostable bag." Not surprisingly, the marketing strategies to get the word out were multiple, including partnerships with environmental organizations, such as Green Current, and a new television ad that was also posted on YouTube. The ad opens with an empty bag of Sun Chips in a pile of dirt, accompanied by singer-songwriter Marc Robillard's "So Much More"; using time-lapse technology, the bag slowly decomposes (over a period of fourteen weeks, according to the textual timetable onscreen) and becomes indistinguishable from the dirt. The camera pans to a blue sky (time-lapsed clouds racing by) and a slowly budding yellow flower. The text reads: "Introducing a chip bag made with plants, so it is 100% compostable." The closing shot shows the yellow flower in full bloom against a blue sky, above the tagline "Change is Irresistible."

While a "chip bag made with plants" may be a new product, the ad, as well as its environmental rhetoric, is certainly not new—it joins hundreds of television and online ads from a variety of companies eager to announce their commitment to the environment as a platform for selling products.[17] Oil and energy companies like Chevron and Exxon have a slate of advertisements offering testimony to the efforts each company has made to combat global warming; manufacturers of household products from dish soap to diapers have embraced a green ideology so that individuals can practice environmental politics when performing mundane domestic duties; technology companies routinely tout their commitment to the environment in their marketing, perhaps so that consumers will not focus on the environmental damage that often occurs with the manufacturing of their products. To wit, and in the postmodern spirit of ironic advertising, IBM created an ad in 2010 that initially mocks "tree huggers" by first depicting a white male corporate executive challenging an environmentally aware proposal from a young white woman, saying, "See, the folks that I report to—they don't eat granola." When the woman points out that her proposal will save IBM 40 percent in energy costs, the man immediately changes his tune. "Where do I sign?" he asks as the background music brightens from a somber piano solo to a song from *The Wizard of Oz* (when Dorothy and her entourage emerge from the woods to see the Emerald Palace): "We're out of the woods, we're out of the dark, we're out of the night." Sweet animated forest creatures surround the executive, and the ad ends with the text "Stop Talking. Start Saving. IBM— Go Green."

The IBM ad is particularly instructive in its gesture toward a generational difference when it comes to "going green." It taps into a discourse about an old-fashioned resistance to change, signaled by the contrast between the stodgy corporate executive and the young upstart employee, a discourse picked up on by the Sun Chips tagline "Change is irresistible." Green branding strategies such as these are certainly not new to the 21st century but rather mark a space on a historical continuum between niche marketing and advanced capitalism that has capitalized on a growing public awareness of environmental damage over the past fifty years.

Recent scholarship by historians of consumer culture intervenes in a deeply held popular belief that there is an analytical and subjective distinction between the consumer and the citizen in the US. While some, notably Lawrence Glickman, Gary Cross, Lizabeth Cohen, Matthew Hilton, and Robert Weems,[18] have offered compelling historical evidence that these two subject positions have always been mutually constitutive as part of the makeup of American democracy, there remains a residual ethos (in the popular, political, and academic spheres) that, as Glickman points out, Americans acted first as virtuous citizens before *transforming*, or from a more critical vantage point, *disintegrating*, into consumers (a transformation aided by, depending on one's theoretical point of entry, whether you see the buying of goods as conspicuous consumption, patriotic duty, or evidence of mass deception).[19] Consumption is often positioned as detrimental to citizenship, in that it is largely seen as motivated by emotion, impulse, and irrationality, whereas politics is ostensibly about rational thinking and reasonable deliberation. As social theorists ranging from Habermas to Adorno to Benjamin have long argued, consumerism distracts a public from true deliberation and contemplation; in addition, a consumer context (or a "culture industry") makes for an electorate that is "too passive, too ill-informed, too ready to be moved by symbolic (i.e. emotional) appeals, too disinclined to listen to real policy discussion, too ready to be distracted by the drama of personality and the politics of slash and burn."[20]

This residual division between consumption and politics is yet another nostalgic trope, harkening back to an imagined time when this distinction was ostensibly clear and well-defined. Yet the rights of US citizens have always been understood and experienced most clearly, despite nostalgic denials, through the lens of consumption and consumer access. From challenging taxation to buying war bonds to boycotting to lunch counter sit-ins to property ownership to understanding the rights of free speech within "a marketplace of ideas," citizenship in the US is inherently bound with consumption practices.

However, there is a theoretical—and, indeed, a moral—stake in keeping citizenship and consumerism as separate ideological and cultural realms, precisely because citizens are expected to act rationally, and consumption is so often positioned as emotional, escapist, desirous. Consider, for instance, the reductive and nostalgic historicizing about consumption often expressed by the US media. Coverage of economic crises, ranging from the savings and loan scandals of the 1980s to the dot-com crash in the early 1990s to the catastrophic global financial crisis of the first decade of the 21st century, has often featured a narrative of irresponsible consumers. The media focus on the individual victims of these various financial bubbles and the rhetoric of irresponsible consumption obscure how these dynamics continue to facilitate an ever-increasing socioeconomic class division.[21] Indeed, the emphasis on a kind of pathological consumption paints those consumers at the bottom of the socioeconomic hierarchy as the *most* irresponsible—even while the vast gaps between rich and poor are obfuscated by the celebration of enterprising individuals bent on neoliberal definitions of innovation and entrepreneurship. This media frame maintains an ideology in which citizenship and consumption are two distinct experiential realms, with the pathological tendencies of the latter always in danger of corrupting the purity of the former.

Of course, certain consumer behaviors are exempt from this moralizing frame. So, for example, the state's encouragement to consume during times of war as a patriotic "obligation"—ranging from buying war bonds in the mid-20th century to George Bush's plea for Americans to "go shopping" after the attacks on the World Trade Center on September 11, 2001, as a way to demonstrate loyalty—is not criticized by the mainstream media as detrimental to citizenship. Nor is the widespread deregulation of the communication and media industries enabled by Reaganite and Clintonite economics that privilege the "free" market. Indeed, these practices are located as the opposite: they are discursively framed as "protecting," and perhaps even liberating, American citizenship.[22]

Needless to say, consumerism and citizenship are deeply related realms of individual experience, but they are also fraught with contradiction. When we acknowledge the long-standing merger of these two categories, and speak of a "citizen consumer," the questions are no less tricky. Is being a "good" consumer part of being an overall "good" citizen? In contemporary advanced capitalism, can one still be a "good" citizen without being a "good" consumer? These questions bring to bear the fact that financial transitions and crises describe and enable a nation of consumers as what Lizabeth Cohen calls "purchaser" citizens.[23] They also highlight the ways in which a "logical" ideological shift from a collective sensibility to an individualist entrepreneurship has been normalized in contemporary culture. Further, these questions point to the fact that it is precisely the context of consumer capitalism that not only resolves inconsistencies within consumer citizenship but also animates and enables emergent consumer practices. This is the context in which brand culture becomes legible and normalized. The US (as well as other advanced capitalist societies) has been in a period of transition in terms of how this relationship of politics and consumption has been configured. Within the current moment of advanced capitalism, the relationship between politics and consumption has deepened even more, when the ways in which politics, the state, and consumption are imbricated (including corporate social responsibility and new forms of commodity activism) are made possible by the concurrent intertwining of advanced capitalism and brand culture.

As I discuss in the introduction to this book, the industry of branding, like advertising, is key for the continual workings of a global capitalist economy: the competitive landscape of brands; the subindustries sustained by brands such as the practice of self-branding, creative city planning, corporate social responsibility, and so on; and the increasing transnational flows of global brands, among other things, are crucial for capitalism to continue its efficient embrace of more and more of the world.[24] The individual-as-commodity is validated within these dynamics, complete with a politicized "voice" that is reimagined within the expansion of advanced capitalism and its adoption of cultural characteristics that *feel* distinctly noncapitalist, such as advocating for an environmentally sound planet.[25]

The shape of consumer citizenship, then, whether formed as a kind of social activism or an individual praxis, crucially depends on the varied historical moments in which it takes shape and becomes legible. This legibility, in turn, relies on not simply the political economic context—that is, how consumerism is defined and reimagined in different eras—but also on how activism, or more specifically the activist, is simultaneously defined and reimagined. Historian Lawrence Glickman argues that the history of consumer activism must be understood in the framework of a *longue durée,* that is, as a two-centuries-long trajectory that is characterized as a perpetual push and pull, as individuals vacillate between acceptance and rejection of consumer activism, rather than distinct periods of acceleration or decline. As Glickman points out:

Consumer activism...is a protean form of protest reflecting important shifts in self-understandings and strategies....the history of consumer activism is marked by debates about whether consumers should embrace or reject fashion, eschew immoral products or promote the consumption of alternatives, and employ or reject the techniques of consumer society. Rather than a linear progression, these competing conceptions have existed as tensions within particular consumer movements and across time.[26]

I argue here that the current reimagination of consumer activism moves from a 20th-century focus on the consumer movement to an everyday, routine, and individual participation in brand culture. Brand culture is, then, a useful optic through which to understand not simply the ways in which politics itself becomes branded but also how consumers who act politically within political brand cultures are encouraged to see themselves as activists. Brand culture provides a kind of index for supporting and legitimating specific political consumptive acts, such as ethical or moral consumption, as well as a context in which "ethical" consumers emerge.

In order for political brand cultures to emerge as normative, the place of the consumer citizen, or, more accurately, the consumer activist, had to be assured. In the consumer movements and organizations of the 19th and early 20th centuries, such as the National Consumers League, Consumers' Research, and Consumers Union, the emphasis of political mobilization was focused not on the actual identities of consumers themselves but rather on redefining the market so that it functioned more efficiently for all kinds of consumers.[27] So consumer activism in earlier historical moments mobilized around issues of broad access—access for the poor, the marginalized, or the disenfranchised. In Robert Weems's work on African American consumer politics in the 20th century, he argues that African Americans had long been targeted as consumers marked by racial identity and difference, and were thus considered a "niche" market well before that term characterized mainstream marketing.[28] Yet the construction of the African American market was not simply a mechanism of mid-20th-century mass consumption, where African Americans were strategically cultivated by advertisers as potentially lucrative consumers through the rhetorical use of political ideals of equality and freedom. As discussed in chapter 1, these practices certainly were characteristic of mass consumption, but to limit a focus to only those practices of consumption renders invisible some of the ways in which consumer culture and political ideals were connected beyond profit motive or added value. For instance, as Weems has shown, the US consumer economy of the 1950s and 1960s contained contradictory messages for African Americans. Consumption is not simply about buying products. Rather, consumer culture became one site for the struggle over political enfranchisement and citizenship rights. Clearly, economic empowerment and justice were primary elements of Martin Luther King's political platform in the late fifties and early sixties, and political acts such as the Montgomery bus boycott of 1955–1956 and sit-ins in Greensboro, North Carolina, in 1960 not only disrupted white business operations but also worked as a platform to point out the economic *and* political inequalities of African Americans. Indeed, as Weems, Cohen, and others have documented, despite the vast rhetoric of freedom and justice, the civil rights movement in the mid-20th century was largely organized around issues of consumption and access; the goal was to enfranchise African Americans whose options to consume were denied (be it within retail shops, lunch counters, or public transportation systems).[29] In these movements, consumer citizenship was largely understood as the conduit between social justice, equity, and community building. The consumer market—what it was and what it could be—was the focus of the consumer movement. These consumer movements, then, were often about collective action and forming consumer communities around political goals. Though obviously neither antimarket nor anticapitalist, the consumer movement in the early and mid-20th-century US waged its politics inside the market, according to its protocols, with the belief that the market was flexible enough to change and thereby improve conditions for all consumers.

However, shifts not only in consumer capitalism in the later half of the 20th century but also in the social construction of citizenship reshaped what is invoked by the concept of a "consumer movement." Critically, what distinguishes the contemporary consumer movement is that its emphasis has shifted from larger, communal political goals to consumers themselves "as the chief beneficiaries of political activism."[30] The impulse to construct consumers as individuals, rather than a collective body, stretches back to at least the 1970s. As Ralph Nader fought for "consumer rights," and as bohemians and hippies demonstrated against materialism, conservatives countered the very notion of a "consumer" movement. Their tactic, ironically, was to insist on the cultural values of diversity and pluralism: each consumer was *different* and should be allowed to make her or his own choices. By their definition, the notion of a collective movement was therefore a constraint of individual freedom. As discussed in chapter 1, the marketing world engaged in a parallel development, cultivating "niche" markets appealing to specific cultural and identity affinities, where consumers were no longer addressed as part of a monolithic, national group but instead targeted as "you," as a specific, unique individual. Ironically, the political organizing of consumers coalesced around this individualism, thus rendering obsolete the politicized collective bodies that had for decades challenged unequal divisions within the consumer world.[31]

In the 21st century, traditional consumer movements, though surely still alive and thriving in some realms of culture, have also emerged in another manifestation. Consumer movements are now often branded movements, with connections and intersections with the corporate world and a focus on the individual consumer who "does good by buying good" rather than on community politics such as equal access to the market or labor concerns. So while historically we can broadly trace the shift in the US consumer movement from an emphasis on consumer communities to individual consumers, in the first decade of the 21st century this emphasis shifted further, to brand culture. Contemporary brand culture is not as concerned with individual shoppers (though the importance of the moment of commodity purchase should not be underestimated), as it is with cultivating authentic relationships with consumers and communities that work to further extend and build upon the brand. Thus, individual entrepreneurs are the privileged subject positions of the contemporary moment. This is not a mere semantic difference but one that profoundly reconfigures the way in which individual identity is crafted and experienced within neoliberal brand culture.

Part of this reconfiguration is about political identity. As Glickman, Lisa Duggan, Wendy Brown, and others have documented, the global economic crisis of the 1970s demonized "liberalism," as new political economic practices began to emerge and take hold that challenged (and, indeed, often erased) earlier dynamics between the state and the citizen.[32] As Milton Friedman and other neoliberal economists have made clear, part of the imperative of neoliberal doctrine is an explicit challenge to the role of the state in politics and social life, as well as state intervention in the market. Indeed, in the US, the economic crisis of the 1970s (tied to rising oil prices, high inflation, labor strikes, etc.) was seen as a failure of liberal Keynesian policy, with its apparent emphasis on big government and its apparent "lack of faith in ordinary people, and a corresponding desire to limit individual freedom."[33] Thus, neoliberal capitalism involves, among other things, the reimagining of not just economic transactions and resources but also practices and institutions such as social relations, individual relations, emotion, social action, and culture itself. Importantly, it is not simply that capitalist ideologies and practices have "taken over" these realms of life hitherto understood in non-capitalist terms or spaces, but that society and culture have been reorganized such that "the social good will be maximized by maximizing the reach and frequency of market transactions, and it seeks to bring all human action into the domain of the market."[34] As Duggan has pointed out, the marketization of "human action" does not simply *describe* new configurations and relationships between the state and the market, such as the increasing normativity of public-private partnerships as ways to revitalize urban cities, but through that description these terms also "create or remake institutions and practices according to their precepts."[35] In other words, the term "neoliberalism" is often used as a "neutral" descriptive, one that simply maps out the contours of a market norm, when in reality it re-creates and reframes culture, cultural practices, and institutions. As such, neoliberalism positioned itself as a kind of savior for US democracy, thus paving the way for a new kind of relationship between private corporate culture and the individual to form, allowing for the emergence of brand culture.

These politics also reconfigured how the consumer citizen operated and, as important, was expected to operate, within the political realm. The redefinition of the free market likewise meant that its logics could shape not just economics but also politics and culture. As economics bled into politics and culture, the consumer citizen became a key *player* in this "free" market, rather than someone who was *protected* from its uneven and unequal practices. Consumption was the mechanism through which politics were realized, so that the focus of consumer movements shifted from a fight for the right to enter the market to one that privileged individual options within the market.[36] The consumer citizen is now an individual who coproduces political brand culture and is not merely protected from or inhibited by market ideology (again marking the distinction between commodification and branding).[37]

The historical ideals of the consumer movement—specifically that consumers should act politically to challenge the ways in which capitalist markets constrain particular constituencies—were increasingly rendered hostile and irrelevant to a "free" market that gives options to all consumers. As I argued in chapter 1, widespread policies in advanced capitalism, from Reagan's "trickle-down" economics, to massive deregulation of the communication and technological industries, to the passage of the North American Free Trade Agreement, helped organize and normalize political and cultural life as explicit functions of the market. As Couldry argues, "Neoliberal rationality provides principles for organizing action (in workplaces, public services, fields of competition, public discussion) which are internalized as norms and values (for example, the value of entrepreneurial 'freedom') by individuals, groups, and institutions: in short, they become 'culture.'"[38] But this culture has a specific form and shape in the 21st-century US: it is organized around, and embedded within, the ideologies, rationales, and practices of brands and branding. And, within this brand culture, the individual entrepreneur is both privileged and rationalized. This subject position is not only, as I discussed in chapter 3, part of the creative economy, but also an important factor in political brand cultures.

The Branded Political Activist

The emphasis on the individual political activist within advanced capitalism—*everyone can be an activist*—comes along with the retreat (both ideologically and in practice) from a sense of the "public." Delving further into this context, this twinning is supported by another pair: not just by a newly emerging technoscape that embraces a kind of individual agency (*everyone can be a producer*) but also by a reorganization of creative industries that idealize the individual entrepreneur (*everyone can be creative*). Rhetorically, the freedom that "everyone can be" what they want to be sounds like a challenge to liberal exceptionalism, but materially this ideology functions through the exclusion of others. The contemporary idea that "everyone can be" an activist, a producer, or a creator relies on a basic tenet of advanced capitalism, in which advertising, marketing, digital technology platforms, and political movements all encourage consumers to think of themselves foremost as individuals. Additionally, this infrastructure primarily recognizes those individuals who have market value in what they do. Not everyone can make a living out of being creative, a political activist, or a producer, but the neoliberal ideal that "what one is = what one makes money doing" obscures the fact that not everybody has the same opportunities. Privileging the "free" individual masks the exclusion that undergirds this illusion, and the material reality that not everyone is free.

It is easy to see the emphasis on the "free" individual consumer, rather than a consumer collective, as a kind of corporate appropriation of politics, where the "real" politics of a movement are commodified, leading only to an "inauthentic" and vacuous political *expression*, but not action. But the reality is more complex. Rather, neoliberal brand culture situates political actors as political, but in a way that is removed from collective action or social justice. If politics themselves are organized by the market, then acting politically means acting within the protocols of that same market: to be a political—or social—activist means constructing one's political identity using the terms, ideologies, and vocabularies of the market. This means, according to Glickman, that we witness a shift in identity construction—from individuals who participate in a *consumer movement* (such as the civil rights movement) in order to gain access to the market, to those who identify as *consumer activists,* in which not only the ideals, principles, and rationalities of the market are normative and assumed to be valid but indeed politics themselves are understood through the language of the market (recalling Foucault's *Homo economicus*). The key distinction between individuals who act in a consumer movement and the acts of individual consumer activists is the emphasis on individual consumer choices as the literal stuff of politics. If the market organizes politics and cultural life, so that it no longer makes sense to consider ontological boundaries between these realms, then political goals such as collective justice in turn are often characterized as old-fashioned and ineffective.

Enter the branded political activist. Retooled capitalist practices enable a new social and cultural arrangement of not only political consumption but also the political activist, and both take shape within brand culture. The object of political analysis changes in this shift; as Glickman points out, in an advanced capitalist landscape of political consumption, the question of what "ethical" consumption means has transformed "from the ethics of consumption (how do my actions impinge on other people, ecosystems, and nations?) to the personal effects of consumption (how does what I buy change me?)."[39] This is a logical transition in the era of the branded cultural entrepreneur.[40]

Samantha King, writing about breast cancer philanthropy, and the "active citizens" who participate in such philanthropic activities, ranging from buying pink ribbon apparel to breast cancer research "walk-a-thons," argues:

> The assumption that quick, convenient, and relatively inexpensive acts of giving have nonetheless powerful effects and deep spiritual meaning constitutes a common theme in contemporary discourse on philanthropy. The significance attributed to such acts stems in large part from their association with ideals of active citizenship, or from the notion that citizenship in the contemporary moment should be less about the exercising of rights and the fulfillment of obligations and more about fulfilling one's political responsibilities through socially sanctioned consumption and responsible choice. In this new configuration, the government is seen to be at its best when playing the role of the facilitating state; that is, the state that enables Americans to pursue self-fulfillment through acts of generosity.[41]

Politicized brand cultures are one common way the active citizen participates in contemporary culture. These cultures are not always bound by a specific product and its attached politics—say, purchasing Starbucks coffee to support fair trade, or buying American Apparel to support antisweatshop labor—but rather operate in a more diffused way, where the logic of brand management in turn forms the logic for political activism. This brand logic appeals to consumers through emotive and affective relationships that structure privatized management and state deregulation and privilege the consumer citizen. Politics, in this context, are branded commodities, and the consumers who invest in them are "free" to make choices that are facilitated, but not governed, by the state.

How do these affective relationships inform and shape the contemporary political activist within brand culture? The branded political activist is legible within a number of entangled discourses: the expanded reach of advanced capitalism; a redefined sense of morality, virtue, and ethics; and the reimagination of social activism as an individual, rather than a collective, act. To take a recent example, the clothing company Levi's created a $55 million multimedia ad campaign in 2010 that featured the struggling steel mill town of Braddock, Pennsylvania. The press release for the campaign—which was titled "We Are All Workers"—began:

> Amid today's widespread need for revitalization and recovery, a new generation of "real workers" has emerged, those who see challenges around them and are inspired to drive positive, meaningful change. This fall, with the introduction of Go Forth "Ready to Work," the Levi's® brand will empower and inspire workers everywhere through Levi's® crafted product and stories of the new American Worker.[42]

The campaign featured eleven short video episodes (posted on YouTube and various social media sites), created in conjunction with the Independent Film Channel and the Sundance Film Festival, and clearly meant to tap into the trope of the "authentic" American, long a staple of both narrative and documentary films, as well as align the Levi's videos with a tradition of media activism. Not surprisingly, while the global economic crisis of the 21st century is referenced through vague acknowledgments that the US needs "widespread revitalization and recovery," the actual reasons for the crisis, the collapse of capitalist practices in banking and trade, go unmentioned; rather, the individual "authentic" worker is the one responsible for the country's recovery. (Indeed, the campaign even states, with clichés that would make Horatio Alger proud, that Braddock is a town of real workers who—with Levi's help—are "rolling up their sleeves to make real change happen.")

The eleven episodes feature individuals who "tell the story of Braddock" through their efforts, funded by Levi's, to revitalize the town: a new community center, the development of a Braddock urban farm, the efforts of

Mayor John Fetterman to enlist the help of what Levi's calls "modern pioneers"—artists, musicians, craftsmen—to rebuild the town.[43] The videos are
moving, a clichéd but effective pastiche of dilapidated buildings, hollowed-
out schools, boarded-up businesses, all set to stirring soundtracks. As the
viewer moves through the episodes, the town is slowly built up through the
efforts of these "pioneers," who become central citizens in the Levi's brand
community.

The videos and the ancillary print and billboard ads that are part of
the same campaign were created by the ad firm Wieden + Kennedy. The
campaign, according to Levi's, is targeted toward Americans who are living through the "jobless recovery" of the post-2008 global economic crisis
(though Braddock had been a town in recession for years before 2008) and
uses actual Braddock citizens as models in the ads. Fetterman is the "face"
of the campaign and has been adamant that the Levi's partnership is an
opportunity to rebuild his town. As he said in an interview, "If someone
wants to give me $100 million, I'll kiss their ass and call it ice cream....It's
not about kissing anyone's ring—it's about folks in the business community that are enjoying a high level of success looking at communities that
are struggling."[44] Indeed, the branded efforts of companies like Levi's are
often positioned by economically struggling towns as not simply the best,
but the only, way to fund public spaces. As Fetterman continued, "I think
that this kind of private philanthropy—I'd like to see it continue....It really
does deliver benefit in a way that government assistance and foundation
assistance can't."[45]

Without diminishing the potential rewards of a collaboration of Levi's, I
want to point out how the company uses authenticity and "real" individuals, and the goal of building community, to form a politicized brand. A corporate business model is framed as the logical means to revitalize a community, and the individual entrepreneur—here celebrated as the "modern
pioneer"—is positioned in this political brand culture as an activist. The
use of "emotional capitalism" as a way to build Levi's political brand culture and the use of multiple spaces (from conventional print and television
advertising, to YouTube and social media sites, to blogs, DIY production,
and consumer-generated content) are characteristic of advanced capitalist practices, which seek to expand market logic and strategies far beyond
simply selling a particular product.[46] Indeed, through this ingenious campaign, when we buy a pair of jeans, not only are we making a political
statement by aiding in America's recovery, but each of us becomes a more
authentic individual. The personal, in this case, is explicitly and reward-
ingly (but nonthreateningly) political.

Putting the Corporate in Social Responsibility

If advanced capitalism is the political-economic context for political brand cultures, and the branded consumer activist is one embodiment of the larger category of individual entrepreneur, then the increasingly normative practice of corporate social responsibility is perhaps its quintessential expression. The infamous op-ed that Milton Friedman wrote for the *New York Times Magazine* in 1970 is often cited as one of the hallmarks of the emergence of the neoliberal economy in the US.[47] "The Social Responsibility of Business Is to Increase Its Profits" offered Friedman's argument that business should be about business—period. He clearly had no patience for those who claimed that "business is not concerned 'merely' with profit but also with promoting desirable 'social' ends; that business has a 'social conscience' and takes seriously its responsibilities for providing employment, eliminating discrimination, avoiding pollution and whatever else may be the catchwords of the contemporary crop of reformers."[48] Friedman captured an emerging cultural current in the US and elsewhere, as "business for business" eventually became the dominant way of understanding the relationship between corporations and social life. As I have discussed, in the consumer movements of the 1960s and early 1970s, some corporations did participate, and did attend to discrimination, inequities, and labor issues. However, the response to the global economic crisis of the 1970s was largely to prioritize the market as the central organizing feature in US society, so that the earlier political interests of corporations were rendered obsolete, without value in a business-oriented culture.

Yet, despite Friedman's imperative that the social responsibility of business is only to increase profits, the emergence of advanced capitalism did not result in the elimination of business' relationship with social and political causes; instead, the corporate world translated political and social causes *into business logic.* The practice of contemporary "corporate social responsibility" (CSR) is the embodiment of this logic. It is not the logic of social justice, or what a corporation might do beyond the confines of its own bottom line to create a more equitable market. Rather, the logic of CSR is about the various ways in which a corporation's support of social issues—be they sweat-free labor, the environment, or funding for AIDS or breast cancer research—can build the corporation's brand and thus bring in more revenue and profit. The attention to social issues is a "value add"; saving the world, in the language of the corporation, can be profitable. As Inger Stole puts it, "The practice of cause marketing suggests that businesses may leverage the existence of dire social problems to improve their public images and profits while distracting attention from their connections as to why these social problems continue to exist."[49] CSR, in other words, is good for business, and within the context of contemporary advanced capitalism—a more heightened capitalist economy than the one in which Friedman was writing about in 1970—this means exploiting what David Vogel calls "the market for virtue."[50]

Vogel highlights this historical shift in the logic of CSR with a compelling example about the consumer activists who, in the 1960s and 1970s, protested Dow Chemical because the company was producing napalm that was being used in the Vietnam War: "The antiwar activists who, during the 1960s, pressured Dow Chemical to stop producing napalm, framed their argument exclusively in moral terms: they neither knew nor cared whether producing napalm would affect Dow's earnings. In contrast, the contemporary environmental activists who are working with Dow to reduce its carbon emissions argue that doing so will make Dow more profitable by lowering its costs."[51] Vogel astutely points out the differing logics that motivate activists in these very different historical moments, but he misses the opportunity to theorize how neoliberal corporate responsibility—and consumer activists—are, in fact, working within a very specific moralist framework. Moralism, or virtue, has been reframed in this moment to be a specific *product* of capitalism; consumer citizens in late capitalism produce, accumulate, spend, and trade *moral capital*, just as they do social capital and economic capital.

Political virtue, emotions, affect, and morality did not, then, disappear from the corporate landscape as a consequence of neoliberal doctrine and practice (as Friedman suggested they must in order to do the actual work of advanced capitalism). Rather, these dynamics have been reimagined and made legible from the perspective of individualized politics. This reimagining takes place in the context of a contradiction: the rise of advanced capitalism, with its blurring between state and corporate interests, and the marketization of individuals and the normalization (in the US, at least) of self-branding are accompanied by what seems to be an oppositional discourse, an increasingly public lament about the loss of morals, ethics, community, and meaning in the lives of individuals.[52]

Corporate social responsibility campaigns attempt, in part, to "resolve" this contradiction. The contemporary creation and expansion of a "market for virtue" reframes the subject position of the consumer activist as an individual who behaves rationally according to market values and logic—indeed, the values and logic of the market become subsumed by the values and logic of individual subjectivity. As Vogel points out, significant numbers of consumers claim that they are invested in doing business with "more virtuous" companies. (The standard logic goes that these consumers are willing to pay a higher premium for such products; the "virtuous" consumer, by definition, therefore belongs to a specific socioeconomic class. The person who takes advantage of the Free2Work app, in other words, has to be able to afford an iPhone in the first place.) Interestingly, there is very little evidence that corporations that practice "social responsibility" reap a profit from their activities, or that consumers do, in fact, conduct more business with "virtuous" companies—even if they say they do.[53] Politics here exists more as an idea, or an ideal; CSR, that is, does not seem to always be profitable, and consumers seem to like the idea of a virtuous company more than they actually spend money to support these companies.

Ultimately, I believe, the political consumer activist participates in corporate social responsibility as a way to "govern the self" through a new form of ethics. Typically, such participation revolves around a brand community, created by a corporation to promote a specific cause, but then developed as a context for a relationship between consumers and corporations. Political brand communities offer something different from (though of course related to) the practice of self-branding; brand communities offer an ethical and moral context in which one can "take care of the self" in terms of consumer activism. This kind of care of the self, unlike maintaining the self-brand, is about the maintenance of a politically virtuous self, one who participates as a kind of activist within brand culture. Laurie Ouellette, discussing the branded politics of commercial television, points out that "under neoliberal conditions, the imperative to govern ourselves through our own choices and initiatives has intensified—as have dispersed technologies (such as do good campaigns) for activating our capacities and steering them toward desired outcomes (such as community)."[54] This is important, as it challenges a more reductive perspective that assumes that consumers who vote with their pocketbook or participate in corporate socially responsible campaigns are somehow without knowledge that the political work they are doing is, in fact, about corporations making a profit. Ouellette continues, "Contrary to theories of false consciousness...brands [are] productive 'platforms for action' that are increasingly 'inserted into the social' in order to 'program the freedom of consumers to evolve in particular directions.'"[55] Political brand communities "insert the social" by appealing to consumers' freedom and desire for social justice and democratic communities. Through such an appeal, political brand communities resolve the potential contradictions of using the logic of business to help social causes.

In this sense, it is not helpful to focus on whether or not CSR campaigns are "authentic" forms of democratic participation. These campaigns are branded as authentic. Political brand cultures are not less real or authentic than the consumer movements of the early and mid-20th century; as with all sociopolitical movements, both are fraught with contradictions. What is different about the current moment is not the use of authenticity—the allure and the flexibility of authenticity mean that it is always invoked in one way or another; rather, the transformation I am charting here is the movement from an "authentic" politics to a politics of authenticity, realized through branding.

While the ideologies of corporate social responsibility programs claim to offer access to authentic democratic political participation through corporate culture, it is also clear that not all politics are useful for corporations. If the credo is "buying good is doing good," it is evident that what constitutes "good" politics is clearly dependent on dominant hegemonies. In other words, some politics lend themselves easily to branding, such as environmental politics, and in these cases it is easy to think of CSR as a kind of slick corporate ruse. Indeed, corporate watchdog groups routinely identify companies as "whitewashing" or "greenwashing" their brand names so as to seem socially aware. The multilayered cultural and economic contexts that authorize the emergence of CSR as a strategy cannot be explained away as corporate appropriation or a con job (especially, as Jo Littler and others point out, since most CSR campaigns indirectly contradict Friedman's insistence that corporations have no social responsibility except to make a profit).[56] This progressive critique of CSR assumes that politics and the market are discrete realms of experience. Since the market is driven by profit, and since profit motive is assumed to be antithetical to politics, working politically for social good is seen as "structurally impossible" within this critical frame.

Yet, again, this assumes a simple binary. Corporations will insist that their campaigns are authentic, that their motives are sincere. Watchdog groups, progressives, and some consumer activists will insist the opposite. But more crucial than whether or not CSR is authentic is the fact that "buying good is doing good" is qualified by what counts, culturally and politically, as good. This calls into question the ability of CSR to truly form democratic political communities. If the market structures and determines what is defined as political, then market logic applies to politics: if an issue does not have a large enough consumer base, or is seen as too alienating or offensive to consumers, then it will not become a branded political culture. Thus, some issues cannot readily be made into a brand—things like pro-choice politics, queer issues, immigration rights, or health care reforms—because branding logic cannot be easily integrated or applied. If certain politics do not add value to a brand, and thus are not "brandable," a brand community will not form around and within these politics.[57] Narratives coded as rants, opinions, or conspiracies are not integrated as easily into business because they are not readily brandable.[58] CSR campaigns tend to attach to politics that are legible in brand vocabulary, are palatable to an audience of consumer citizens, and are uncontested as socially important issues (who is going to argue with the need to fight poverty or child abuse?). In other words, CSR politics are safe politics. CSR politics do not actually reimagine corporate power. If, as I argued earlier, political brand cultures are about offering security to consumer citizens in terms of their political convictions, then the political goals of CSR must be uncontested and stable. When a political issue becomes mainstream, it has the potential to become part of a brand. This is a key dynamic: if politics are increasingly understood only through the logic and the vocabulary of the brand, and this logic and vocabulary necessarily exclude some politics because they simply do not make sense as market commodities (they cannot, in other words, be efficiently branded), then only specific political issues can be understood as political and democratic.

Political brand culture therefore requires a contrasting process, in which nonbranded politics are rendered invisible. As certain political narratives are rendered audible—indeed, are rendered larger than life, in full color, with gripping soundtracks, and through the narratives of individuals who are beautiful but still "real"—then other politics are silenced or simply cannot compete. This contrast does not mean that the politics that are branded are by definition inauthentic or anemic, but rather that, like all brand cultures, political brand cultures are structured by ambivalence.

Consider the RED campaign, launched in 2006 by global pop star Bono and California politician and activist Bobby Shriver, as an embodiment of the logic of CSR. It is a cause-related marketing campaign that donates a portion of profits made from the sale of consumer goods such as iPods, Dell computers, and Gap clothing to the Global Fund to Fight AIDS, Tuberculosis, and Malaria, a nongovernmental organization that supports treatment for women and children in Africa. While resembling other "cause marketing" campaigns that tap into consumers' desires to be charitable, the RED campaign also operates under a contemporary economic and cultural model, which is explicit and unapologetic about the profit potentials for its clients. Rather than euphemistically framing itself as a morally upright, lofty, and philanthropic endeavor, the RED campaign does not hide its purpose—it is about making money. It is crafted as a straightforward business model, and it promises that this kind of campaign will initiate a new "consumer revolution."[59]

The RED campaign is an example of how profit motive can coexist logically alongside philanthropy in neoliberal brand cultures, as well as an example of the way ambivalence structures brand cultures. That is, the RED campaign appeals to consumers' desire to "do good," but it also is unapologetic about how this "doing good" will add to corporate profit; doing good and capital accumulation sit side by side in this campaign. This means that within the context of political brand cultures, we need to rethink those practices that historically have been considered "progressive" or even "anticapitalist." Indeed, Wendy Brown argues that the subject position of the "progressive" cannot exist within the framework of neoliberalism, as citizenship itself is now measured by the citizen's ability to be an entrepreneur and to help her- or himself rather than work toward a larger collective goal.[60] The unabashed consumerism of the RED campaign echoes the ethos of entrepreneurship, in which profitability, not ethical or collective ideals, forms the moral framework, and consumerism is an efficient route to social change, best achieved through "free" market forces. The RED campaign aims to cultivate consumers through what Brown calls a "raw market approach to political problem solving."[61] Within this new model of activism, the individual, rather than the state or the nation, bears the responsibility for social change.

Branding the Environment: The New Green Order

In the first decade of the 21st century, assisted by mainstream media efforts like Al Gore's film *An Inconvenient Truth* and a global push to engage in everyday practices that are good for the environment, environmental issues became particularly supple for branding. "Going green" as an explicit response to a global environmental crisis has become, at least in the US, a fairly mainstream stance. Surely, debates continue over whether or not global warming is a conspiracy of the left.[62] But generally, by 2010 mainstream communities all over the US saw "going green" as a positive goal, expressed through public and private education, CSR campaigns, state and federal policies, and individual consumption habits. As Alison Hearn has written in her analysis of "green" websites, in the current moment it is difficult to see an "environmental cause that cannot be addressed *through* consumption."[63] One consequence of this mainstreaming of green practices has been that the potential for corporations to attach their practices to environmental issues as a demonstration of social awareness grew exponentially with each recycled bottle or bag. "Going green" became the political goal of companies from Exxon Oil to Wal-Mart to Harvard University (which advertised its environmental awareness with banners in Harvard Yard that proclaimed "Green Is the New Crimson").

The notion that through everyday living humans are destroying the environment is a frightening one, highlighting the vulnerability of the planet.

Though strategies to address these issues vary widely, one particularly effective strategy in offering security to citizens about the fate of the planet has been to brand environmental politics. By constructing eco-friendly habits through the familiar elements of a brand, the historically radical politics of environmentalism can be transformed into the mundane, everyday practices of middle-class Americans. As Hearn points out, in the current cultural context of self-branding and celebrity philanthropists, "environmentalism becomes a chic, branded cause célèbre."[64]

Consider in this regard the 2004 speech given by the then Sierra Club president Adam Werbach (the youngest president in the nature conservation club's history) to the Commonwealth Club in San Francisco titled "The Death of Environmentalism." He argued for changing the language in which citizens were speaking of global warming—to change the discourse altogether, not simply make more rhetorically skillful arguments or speak louder. Rather, Werbach said, "What if we stopped defining global warming as an environmental problem and instead spoke of the economic opportunities it will create?" He and his peers in the environmental movement, he argued, "have tried to define a vision around the values of prosperity, freedom and opportunity—as well as ecological restoration and interdependence—out of the belief that this vision is more welcoming of the American people, businesses and labor unions than more talk of 'polluter pays,' 'fuel efficiency,' and 'carbon caps.'"[65]

This speech is impressive (not least because Werbach relied on social theorists such as Walter Benjamin and Michel Foucault to make some of his points) because Werbach argued for an interdependent, interconnected narrative for environmentalism, one that is not simply understood as a discrete "issue" but rather something that informs the economy, culture, and politics alike. Such interconnection is exactly the rhetoric needed to build a brand community; this interdependent narrative is the structure of feeling that describes contemporary green brand cultures. The shift in conversation Werbach advocates is precisely the shift—already occurring—from conventional political activism to political brand communities, where a central issue is organized, charted, and experienced based on its brand appeal, not its political valence: "the values of freedom, prosperity, and opportunity" should be the mobilizing discourses in the environmentalist brand, not, say, "fuel efficiency."

Werbach is especially interesting as an activist because of the way his own trajectory maps a similar shift, from conventional activist to a marketing consultant and brand builder. He was elected president of the Sierra Club at twenty-three and then left the organization to work on sustainability with some of the largest corporations in the world. In 2005, in a controversial move (at least for environmental activists), he headed the sustainability initiative at Wal-Mart; currently, he is chief sustainability officer at the global agency Saatchi & Saatchi, where, among other things, he has created the "Blue" environmental campaign.[66] His career thus mirrors the contemporary shift to political brand cultures that are authorized by an advanced capitalist market and the concurrent focus on individual consumer choices rather than a historically informed form of collective action. Changing the discourse or the narrative of environmentalism to something that not only interconnects with everyday practices but also is structured by discourses of prosperity and opportunity is more than a simple shift in vocabulary. It is a re-creation of environmentalism into a good business plan, a transformation from ethical necessity to economic opportunity. The logical end point of this shift, of course, is the branding of the environment, or green branding.

Green branding is a form of consumer politics that has caught the attention of not only corporations but also the mass media, not surprisingly amid the anxiety over global warming. Al Gore's film *An Inconvenient Truth* was lauded not only as ethically and environmentally important but also as a way to make "boring" issues such as global warming exciting for a mass audience. Each year between 2006 and 2009, the magazine *Vanity Fair* published a special green issue, with celebrities such as Gore, George Clooney, Julia Roberts, and Madonna gracing the cover as part of an effort that Amy Gajda calls "sexing up sustainability."[67] While "sexing up" the environment emerges from a variety of cultural factors in the late 20th and early 21st centuries (including postfeminism and the normalization of celebrity activism), the broader category of "environmental capitalism" has had a longer history. To name just a few stops along the way: Stewart Brand's *Whole Earth* catalog in the late 1960s and 1970s offered tools for reimagining a more socially and ecologically just world;[68] in the 1970s, craft, bohemian, and organic food cottage industries emerged from the US hippie movement that rejected materialism in the form of homemade clothing, communes, and farmer's markets;[69] and Anita Roddick founded the Body Shop in the 1980s as a green alternative to conventional cosmetics, infusing the company with social activism. These and other alternative consumer movements provide an important historical framework to contemporary green branding; Littler points out that "'alternative' and bohemian values came to fuel important elements of the culture of late capitalism. Such fusions of bohemia, environmentalism and the niche markets of late capitalism provide a key backdrop to any contemporary story of green consumption."[70]

Indeed, I would add to Littler's list of bohemia, environmentalism, and niche markets the ubiquity of the brand as crucial to the current story of green consumption. "Go Green!" is *the* political brand slogan of the 21st century, a telling signal that indicates the ways corporations express their environmental commitment through the language and design of the brand, with trademarked logos, slogans, and snappy jingles. Environmentalism itself has become a trademarked branded product, with websites and marketing books devoted to how to market and trademark green products, such as A Shared Planet™, created by the Starbucks corporation (with a tagline that reads, "You and Starbucks. It's bigger than coffee"). In 2010, the auction house Christie's held the Green Auction: A Bid to Save the Earth to "raise awareness and funds for the protection of our planet." Green branding, like political branding in general, cannot be reduced to a gimmick. The environmentally aware website Treehugger.com for instance, which often features exposés on corporations that fall short of their claims to be environmentally conscious, is a brand itself, complete with a green leaf design logo and the words "A Discovery Company" as a tagline. Green branding is now a process that occurs around and within any products that are marked as "green"—whether through their materials, packaging, strategy, or political commitment.

But importantly, green branding does not just refer to a company's efforts or strategies to address environmental issues. Here, the "greenness" of the brand, while intangible, is as much a crucial element to the brand as the actual product, whether that is the bag of chips described earlier in this chapter, a bottle of water, or a hybrid car. Brand culture is about, among other things, transforming quantitative exchanges and interactions (represented most obviously through the purchase of products, but also more generally, as in the overall workings of the market) into qualitative (read: affective) social relations, relations that are structured and made legible within the same assumptions that underpin the quantitative interactions. Celia Lury's argument that this process forms the "logos"—or the logic and rationality—of the contemporary economy is very useful, and part of this "logos," in 21st-century US culture, involves consumer interactivity.[71] Whether it is the practice of self-branding, the brand culture of creativity, or green branding, brand cultures are structured around and often legitimated by their interactions with consumers, especially as consumers use new technologies and spaces to reimagine and further—and therefore validate—the brand. This interaction takes place between consumers and media, but also between producers (in the case of green branding, corporations) and consumers.

Thus, political brand cultures are not merely formed from the top down but rather require feedback from consumers. As with all other contemporary branding, this implies not merely a strategy of commodification but, more broadly, a building of culture. Because the meanings of culture are constructed and taken up by individuals, these meanings are often ambivalent, and not always interpreted as intended by corporate producers. Not surprisingly, green branding has resulted in a robust critique of green branding as "greenwashing," a strategy whereby corporations do a kind of lip service to environmental issues by simply attaching their names to practices and policies that are required by law in the first place. So, Treehugger.com and other environmentally conscious websites like GreenPlanet.com have regular features on "how to spot greenwashing." The most egregious greenwashing ads are compiled on EnviroMedia's greenwashingindex.com, where companies and advertisements are ranked on a "greenwashing index scale" that ranges from 5 (Bogus) to 3 (Suspect) to 1 (Authentic). Many of the critiques have come from green branders themselves, as a way to distinguish their own practices from those that are deemed inauthentic. The aforementioned Adam Werbach, for instance, wrote a critique of Chevron's "We Agree" campaign, in which the oil company attempts to persuade the American public that it accepts responsibility for the damage it has done to the environment, and that the corporation has "fixed" the problems (such as damage in Ecuador caused by oilfields).

In this critique, Werbach claims that in the current historical moment, US consumers are too savvy in both their political awareness and their technological acuity with tools like social media for "greenwashing" to be effective. As Werbach states, Chevron's splashy "We Agree" ad campaign was "hardly the first time that a global energy company has spent millions of dollars trying to enhance positive perceptions of their brand by pivoting away from public opposition. But it may be one of the last times that we see energy companies trying to saddle up to members of the public as if they were a potential date at a Georgetown bar."[72] Citing other greenwashing attempts—like Kentucky Fried Chicken's Pink Bucket for breast cancer research—as ridiculous, Werbach contends that "the era of greenwashing is over for the simple reason that it doesn't work. For the price of a URL and a little wit, a campaign that is out of step with reality can be hacked and become more of a liability than a potential benefit."[73] Werbach's argument is important here because political brand cultures do not work within a more traditional advertising model of persuading the consumer to believe in something through campaigns that are "out of step with reality," and the brand that organizes the political brand culture does not even have to be overtly visible for the brand culture to signify to consumers. The savvy consumer Werbach mentions is a key threat to successful green branding strategies, so marketers go to great lengths to respect this consumer rather than manipulate her.

While I agree with Werbach's sentiment about the futility of greenwashing in an era of savvy consumers, I also think that his optimism about consumers misses a larger idea: green branding accomplishes something for the consumer as well as the corporation. While some consumers will doubtless act as watchdogs and expose instances of greenwashing, others might want to participate in these very brand cultures because they want to believe that they are acting politically to help the environment, since the notion of changing the environment via consumption is a satisfying practice. Thus, even when greenwashing does occur, consumers still may feel as if they are "doing good" and operating as virtuous selves by participating in green brand cultures.

Green Water

To grapple with the intricacies of green branding, and through these intricacies the work and the consequences of political branding in general, consider one particularly successful manifestation of green branding: bottled water. As I have argued throughout this book, brand cultures are a context for what Foucault theorized as practices of governmentality.[74] A crucial way in which contemporary governmentality is validated is through the discourse of "freedom," where individuals are not coerced, but rather "freely" engage in everyday practices that work to secure dominant hegemonies. These actions are understood not as effects of power but rather as ethical, moral, or self-reflexive choices, made by individuals acting "freely."[75] Brand culture provides a context for these everyday actions, so that the act of, say, drinking water, is part of a much broader set of habits that fulfills the obligation to take care of oneself, habits that are in turn capitalized on by corporations. As Gay Hawkins points out, "Drinking as an everyday practice is problematized and medicalized with a campaign that relies heavily on the authority of medical expertise and popular concerns about health."[76] Brands of bottled water that emphasize health or nature or origin are critical to these campaigns, giving brands an authoritative voice, one that guides us (and celebrates us) in our ethical behavior, in our ability for self-governance.

Like other brand communities, individuals who drink specific brands of bottled water share characteristics with each other: an affiliation with common political goals, such as recycling and environmental awareness, a loyalty and identification with a product, the creation of specific cultures (e.g., "Perrier drinkers") through the use of a product. Various brands of bottled water capitalize on consumers' growing environmental awareness by building a rhetoric of their brand's "natural" and environmentally friendly elements: Dasani (a subsidiary of Coca-Cola) cites its water conservation efforts by informing customers that Coca-Cola has made a $20 million investment in the World Wildlife Fund to conserve freshwater river basins; Calistoga claims its bottling techniques help to restore a fluid base in the earth; Aquafina, which claims to be "always looking for ways to make our world a little better," developed an "Ecofina" bottle that uses less plastic than the Aquafina bottles of previous years.[77]

Not surprisingly, the story behind these claims—like the larger history of the bottled water industry in the US—is far less transparent. While on the face of it, bottled water branding is not always about green branding, the rhetoric of the industry increasingly revolves around environmental awareness—especially in terms of individual safety. Tap water in the US is largely safe (by some counts, 94 percent of the water in the US is safe to drink from the tap).[78] In order for a bottled water brand to develop and expand, the safety of tap water had to be challenged, as a way to manufacture a need for bottled water. What better way than a culture of fear about the inefficiency of public services to provide potable water for its citizens?[79]

In 1974, after organic contaminants were found in drinking water across the US, Congress passed the Safe Drinking Water Act.[80] Around this time, while some consumers prided themselves on consuming imported water— namely, Perrier, which, using the cultural capital of the French, dominated the boutique American market—the overall public sentiment was: Why buy water when it is free? However, the development of the bottled water market exploded after the passage of the Safe Drinking Water Act, with companies such as Pepsi and Coca-Cola wanting not only to break the market share held by Perrier but also to create a brand culture around bottled water: not as the preference of the elite but rather as the choice of ordinary Americans concerned about health and safety. As a way to create a market, advertisers promoted the need to drink "healthy" bottled water rather than tap water. Exploiting the public's fears of contaminants in tap water (the reason for the creation of the Safe Drinking Water Act in the first place), corporations such as Pepsi and Coca-Cola expanded their beverage market to bottled water, touted bottled water as the safest water to drink, and in the process stoked consumer fears about drinking tap water by devaluing it.

An ad for Nestlé Pure Life bottled water reads: "Bottled water is the most environmentally responsible consumer product in the world." In fact, bottled water is *not* the most environmentally responsible product "in the world," but it is hard to know this upon examining its exponential growth. It seems that the message that bottled water is "environmentally responsible" has been received by consumers: bottled water is often noted as one of the fastest-growing industries in the world, and, according to a report from the Beverage Marketing Corporation, sales of bottled water in the US continue to grow dramatically each year. The global rate of consumption of bottled water has more than quadrupled between 1990 and 2005, and the projected value of the bottled water industry in 2011 is more than $86 million, an increase of 41.8 percent since 2006.[81] Since 2003, bottled water has been the second most popular drink in the US, after carbonated sodas. The hyperbole of the Nestlé ad cited earlier has registered.

As the branded bottle water industry exploded, so too did the unavoidable side effect of the industry's success: millions and millions of plastic bottles. The irony here is hard to miss, and the industry has faced severe criticism from environmentalists. To maintain the integrity of the brand, the bottled water industry responded by framing the choice to drink bottled water as an environmentally sound one. In response to critics who cited the waste caused by bottled water, companies directed attention to recycling as a politicized consumer act for environmentally aware individuals. Indeed, obfuscating the *industry* of bottled water is central to the successful branding of bottled water. Unless, of course, a corporation's industrial practices can be incorporated into a compelling origin story, such as FIJI Water. Anna Lenzer writes about the FIJI Water brand:

> Even though it's shipped from the opposite end of the globe, even though it retails for nearly three times as much as your basic supermarket water, Fiji is now America's leading imported water, beating out Evian. It has spent millions pushing not only the seemingly life-changing properties of the product itself, but also the company's green cred and its charity work. Put all that together in an iconic bottle emblazoned with a cheerful hibiscus, and everybody, from the Obamas to Paris and Nicole to Diddy and Kimora, is seen sipping Fiji.[82]

As Lenzer illuminates, Fiji the country has been obfuscated by FIJI the brand, so that the nationwide environmental hazards, military juntas, and realities of poverty for inhabitants of Fiji are buried underneath the narrative of the water brand, which is situated "squarely at the nexus between green and glamour."

In many ways, the bottled water brand is the quintessential brand success story; after all, corporations such as Coca-Cola and Pepsi have been able to make enormous profits on a product that is more or less free to produce.

Multinational companies make billions of dollars on water they simply extract from the ground, label with a brand, and sell at competitive prices. As a further bonus, it was quickly clear that bottled water was a somewhat easy way to make a profit: there were very loose restrictions on water withdrawal, so that selling "free" water was relatively uncontested. In areas with few to no restrictions, companies are able to build high-capacity withdrawal wells and construct bottled water plants without governmental or environmental oversight.[83]

More than that, companies such as Pepsi (which owns Aquafina, Smart-Water, and vitaminwater), Coke (Dasani), Nestlé (Perrier), Evian, and FIJI have created robust brand communities where consumers pledge their loyalty to one water or another, and where nostalgic origin stories about mountain springs and good health give a narrative to the brand. Many brands offer a history of the water, usually beginning hundreds of years in the past, and connect their products to water's many purported medicinal purposes and miracle cures. If an individual cannot afford the miracle cure, or if city life means that individuals are removed from nature and all that is "natural," they can still drink the water for a similar effect.[84] The contemporary bottled water industry capitalizes on this history and has literally created its own water culture, with origin stories, a romanticized individualism of the founders of these companies, and the public need for water—all centered around the brand and brand logic. Calistoga Water, for example, cites its history as 500 years old, tied to the Wappo Indians and the health benefits they enjoyed from the geyser springs of the region. Perrier's water is said to come from a spring in Vergeze, France, which has been used as a spa "since Roman times."[85]

When examining bottled water, the ironies extend far beyond the wasteful packaging: bottled water is much less likely to be found in developing countries, where public water is least safe to drink; there are relatively few regulations on what bottled water can contain (it is regulated by the Food and Drug Administration in the US, in the same category as cosmetics); and many bottled water brands are simply refiltered tap water. Clearly, the success of bottled water brands required that ideal of advanced capitalism: the individual consumer citizen who takes care of her- or himself. This ideal, in conjunction with the expansion of the advanced capitalist market, and especially the shifting of responsibility from public services (like providing clean water for citizens) to private corporations (like Pepsi and Coca-Cola, which could bottle water), helped to create a brand culture around water. In the US today, safe drinking water (tap water) is underfunded by $24 billion: there is little new investment in public water infrastructure because so much is privatized and, as important, because contemporary consumers accept such privatization as natural.[86] In short, US citizens' basic perception of water has changed as a result of bottled water brands; a brand culture was created, and then continuously remade, by corporations and consumers.

Branding has been crucial as a conduit not only for giving branded bottled water an authoritative voice but also for the simultaneous devaluing of tap water and "rendering it both ordinary and suspect."[87] Again, green branding in the current historical moment cannot be separated from the concurrent privatization of state economies and services. The need for this strategy is particularly acute with green branding, as the problem of the environment is not, by any means, a private, individual problem but rather one of the planet. Yet the problem is theorized, addressed, and, at least in the minds of some, "resolved" through private choices and acts, such as drinking bottled water.

A Green Alternative: Urban Farming

Unlike the booming industry of bottled water, contemporary practices of urban farming did not grow out of manufactured demand as a deliberate marketing strategy but rather are a consequence of economic collapse. The global economic crisis that emerged in force in 2008 has allowed for a reimagination of the practice of urban farming in at least two ways. One is geographic: the housing and loan crisis in the US has left thousands of homes abandoned, and thousands of lots unbuilt, particularly in cities such as Detroit, Michigan; these unused public and semipublic spaces have become a bounty for urban gardeners. Another is cultural: amid the growing popularity of organic and locally grown food, urban farming has been renovated from its earlier manifestations and has become an emergent 21st century industry. In the process, the urban farmer has risen to prominence as another manifestation of the individual entrepreneur.

As governments, pundits, and ordinary citizens know, in the wake of the ongoing global economic crisis, capitalism's stability is uncertain. As urban centers around the world frantically try to figure out how to recover in the first decades of the 21st century, some individuals have capitalized on the already established logic and language of the brand to reframe, yet again, both consumer activism and social responsibility in the market. Though urban farming has a long history in the US, in the first decade of the 21st century, there has been a dramatic increase in the public visibility of community agricultural programs. The organic food movement, the proliferation of farmer's markets in urban areas all around the US, and the development of the urban farming movement have all featured prominently in the mainstream news media coverage of the economic crisis. While these "food politics" and consumers' efforts to "eat for change" are shaped by a variety of ideologies and discursive racialized and classed practices, as well as political goals, they are yet another manifestation of political brand cultures.

As Josée Johnston and Kate Cairns have argued, "Green and alternative consumption became enshrined in popular food discourse in the late 20th and early 21st century."[88] The discourse of "eating for change" became mainstream in the US during this time, with food corporations quickly hopping on the bandwagon to provide more expensive organic options for grocery stores, upscale restaurants offering sustainable, local food, and consumers shopping at organic and locally supported high-priced grocery stores such as Whole Foods. As Johnston and Cairns mention, documentary films such as Michael Pollan's *Food, Inc.* followed in the successful mainstream footsteps as *An Inconvenient Truth,* but food politics found an even more mainstream audience on organic cooking shows on niche cable channels such as the Food Channel, reality programs that featured "healthy lifestyles," and, most recently, celebrity chef's Jamie Oliver's *Food Revolution,* in which he enters US public schools and revamps the school lunch program to offer healthier and more local fare.[89] As yet another example of farming's new popularity, the Facebook game FarmVille, a product of the gaming company Zynga, is the world's biggest social media game, with almost 80 million players (almost 20 percent of all Facebook users); some 30 million players tend to their crops daily.[90] While clearly playing FarmVille is a different sort of activity from actual farming the land, the popularity of this game is telling in terms of the increasing visibility of farming as an activity for those who are not often considered farmers. Popular food discourse and the narrative of "eating for change" smoothly became part of the vocabulary and culture of branding in the 21st-century US, focusing on individual consumption choices and the idea that social change is best realized in the hands of individual consumers.

Individuals who consume differently and who find alternative sources of food are understood as the drivers of change in contemporary food activism, corroborating the neoliberal practice of abdicating the state's responsibility, in this case, for the provision of healthy food for its citizens. As Julie Guthman has pointed out, the contemporary focus on alternative food practices reflects a neoliberal conceit that individual consumer choices are easily conflated with political activism: "Food politics has become a progenitor of a neoliberal anti-politics that devolves regulatory responsibility to consumers via their dietary choices."[91]

As with all brand cultures, contemporary food politics vary greatly depending on class and race, even though a key ingredient in these politics is to ignore those differences and to imply food as a universal value. The popular sardonic renaming of Whole Foods as "Whole Paycheck" is but one demonstration of how the "choice" to consume organic foods is one that is available only to those who have the financial means to make this choice. Not only are organic foods expensive, but they are often not available in supermarkets in low-income areas (indeed, in certain urban areas even supermarkets themselves are hard to find).[92] The 21st-century expansion of farmer's markets is another manifestation of the choices made by individual consumers who wish to take part in food activism. And, while urban farming has been a source of food for varied communities for decades, in the current moment a specific version of urban farming is particularly brandable.

Urban farming is an offshoot of community-supported agriculture and is often signaled as an environmentally aware politics because it shortens the distance (both social and economic) between consumers and producers, it taps into a DIY ethos, and it challenges an increasingly globalized food industry; in short, it helps foster democratic participation in the area of food politics. The notion of growing one's own food as a kind of empowering morale booster, with federal and state support, has a history; the Victory Gardens that were planted during World Wars I and II were efforts to boost the public food supply, and public engagement, during wartime. Eleanor Roosevelt planted a Victory Garden on the White House lawn, and the National War Garden Commission issued posters during both wars that proclaimed, "Sow the Seeds of Victory! Plant and Raise Your Own Vegetables," and "Every Garden a Munition Plant."[93] During the global economic crisis of the 1970s, widespread urban decline in the US, including the foreclosure and abandonment of homes, and increasing numbers of vacant lots, mobilized urbanites to transform these urban spaces into gardens, flower beds, and playgrounds.[94] During this time, the National Urban Gardening Program provided five cities with financial support to sustain the new urban gardens.[95] Similarly, the recent global economic crisis has renewed interest in urban farming, and cities such as Detroit, hard hit by economic recession, have been the sites of what might be called an urban farming movement.

Despite urban farming's presence in the US for decades, even centuries, as the "movement" has been branded in the contemporary moment, urban farming has gained a heightened visibility and cultural validation as part of a reimagined "entrepreneurial spirit" of American citizens. Contemporary urban farming is a response, and even a challenge, to the instabilities of advanced capitalism. However, because it is easily branded, that is, uncontroversial, appealing to the upper and middle classes, and complete with the easy-to-valorize figure of the farmer, the problems that necessitate urban farming are buried beneath the promise it represents. In 21st-century neoliberal culture, the idea that there would be a National War Garden Commission or that a state or federal program would exist to sustain such gardens is no longer plausible; rather, the impetus is placed on the entrepreneurial individual, occasionally with corporate sponsorship. In 2010, First Lady Michele Obama planted the first garden on White House grounds since Eleanor Roosevelt's Victory Garden, as a way to demonstrate the benefit of organic food. Her effort was not about integrating healthy food as an issue of federal policy but a way to demonstrate to entrepreneurial individuals that they, too, can grow organic and healthy food.

In another example, episode 7 of Levi's "Ready to Work" campaign focuses on the urban farm. Levi's funded farmers such as Marshall, featured in the four-and-a-half-minute video, to build an urban farm in the economically depressed city of Braddock. The episode is an exercise in nostalgia. Bluegrass music plays in the background, Marshall walks down a street with a wheelbarrow, and the camera pans across green spaces and empty lots. In a clear reference to the Great Depression and Victory Gardens, Marshall invokes the individualist impulse behind much urban gardening: "Every empty lot is an opportunity."

I do not mean to diminish the social good that can emerge from urban farming. On the contrary, the recent renaissance of urban farming offers a startling vantage point on the ravages of advanced capitalism: when homes are abandoned because of foreclosure or defaulted loans in an economic crisis, opportunities arise for green spaces to be farmed.[96] Urban farming can be an important act of cultural resistance to the bullying powers of capitalism. As an expression of resistance, some forms of urban farming occupy (the now empty) space of private ownership differently, transforming these spaces from shrines of consumption into those of consumption *and* production. However, the public visibility of urban farming in the contemporary moment makes some urban farms far more brandable than others.

As an (admittedly extreme) example of how urban farm has been branded—and the privileged urban farmer who emerges from this branding—is the "new hot trend of urban farming": according to at least one website, you can now hire a "rent-a-gardener," where "for a fee, trained gardeners will come to your house, cultivate your backyard, and deliver the fruits of their labor straight to your fridge . . . it's the ultimate urban gardening trend, melding the urbanite existence with the constantly evolving food movement."[97] The assumptions about class and race that are behind the "ultimate urban gardening trend" are clear. Those who embody the "urbanite existence" own private homes with backyards and have the financial means to rent a gardener, in other words, to cultivate local, home-grown produce using others' labor.[98] The contemporary urban farmer is a privileged subject position and not an "ordinary gardener," who, in the American imagination, is often an immigrant laborer or a working-class person of color.

It is not only the extremes of the "rent-a-gardener" that perpetuate racial and class divides when it comes to this kind of green branding. The spaces of the contemporary farmer's market, community agricultural efforts, and urban farming are often bounded by discourses of whiteness, manifest in color-blind ideologies and assumptions of universalism. As Guthman points out, "Much alternative food discourse hails a white subject to these spaces of alternative food practice and thus codes them as white."[99] The individual entrepreneur, the DIY "pioneer" who works the contemporary urban farm, is often by default white and middle class (according to Guthman, 74% of people who shop at farmer's markets are white). The assumption of the subject of contemporary alternative food practices works not only to exclude much of the country, but, as Guthman points out, "it also colors the character of food politics more broadly."[100] Indeed, the media visibility of some urban farms, such as those in Braddock, and the focus on the individual entrepreneurs who work these farms erase the various ways in which underprivileged communities rendered invisible by capitalist practices have also made alternative consumer choices, such as urban farming. Once it is clear that this consumer choice can be levied into a brand, the cultural and media focus on urban farming emphasizes the individual farmer as cultural entrepreneur, one who sees every empty lot as "an opportunity," rejuvenating the subject position of the rugged masculine American individual as the enterprising subject in a contemporary economic crisis moment.

Key to food politics is an easily distorted notion of rights. Good food, according to conventional belief, is a universal right; following that right, healthy eating is a "lifestyle choice," positioned as something that anyone has the ability to do, regardless of cultural and social contingencies such as race or class. Like other constructions of rights, the conflation of healthy eating with a "lifestyle choice" ignores the significant disparities in the kinds of food that are available and affordable to different communities. Here, it is clear that advanced capitalism's transition from the obligations of the state to the responsibilities of the individual has dire consequences. If an upper-middle-class white person makes the "lifestyle choice" to eat locally sourced, organic food, with capitalism's contemporary emphasis on individual responsibility, it becomes far easier (and more politically acceptable) to judge and discipline a poor person of color who eats differently. Once again, the imbrication of social responsibility with the logic of the market hinders thinking in terms of community action, or broad cultural change, and instead encourages individuals to pursue niche, branded interests.

As George Lipsitz pointed out about housing policies, federal programs, and transportation systems in the mid-20th-century US, political brand cultures are also examples of the "possessive investment in whiteness," where not only the brands themselves cater to a racialized and class demographic but the subjects who are participants in these brand cultures are often white and middle-class.[101] Labor reform in immigrant and marginalized communities is a fraught national focus and does not often surface as part of contemporary green branding. As with other politics that are not appropriate for branding, immigrant and marginalized labor does not lend itself to the broader virtues of prosperity and opportunity needed to build a political brand culture. Unlike corporate imperatives to Go Green!, or auction houses that offer pricey goods as a way to raise funds to "protect our planet," or the urban "rent-a-gardener," the brutal reality of much farm labor, performed by immigrants and the poor, does not make a particularly catchy logo or tagline for a political brand culture.

The cultural politics of race and class inform political choices: they literally make some choices possible and others not. But this reality flies in the face of brand culture. Indeed, the legitimating discourse and fundamental structure of brand culture is that it is *a democracy*—the neoliberal strategies that validate and animate brand culture are based on the idea that "anyone can be an activist," just like "anyone can be creative." This discourse of inclusion is, as is borne out historically, based on exclusion and, more insidiously, on the cultural assumptions of color blindness and universalism. It is important, then, to think carefully about what kind of consumer the kind of branded activism I have discussed in this chapter is imagined to serve.

The context of political branding, that is, reframes "morality" and gives shape to Vogel's notion of "the market for virtue" as a kind of product, something that is available to everyone.[102] Political brand cultures reflect the change in a cultural definition of value; the environment, like many other social issues, is reframed as a discrete product that can be "resolved" through individual acts of consumption. Littler presents this as a "deep ecology," where the environment is separated out from other political issues so that, for instance, the fact that big oil is a significant contributor in global warming is not (and in some ways cannot be) addressed through the efforts of oil companies to green brand.[103] Rather than emphasize the interconnectedness of political issues, singular, discrete brand cultures are organized and enabled, and politics themselves shape-shift into tangible products. This shape-shifting corresponds to the transformation of "authentic" politics to the politics of authenticity, and charts the branding of politics.

5

BRANDING RELIGION

"I'M LIKE TOTALLY SAVED"

Genuine. Real. For You.
—Slogan for Jesus Christ TV

If there's one thing that trumps religion, it's capitalism.
—*The Easy A*

The Church of Latter-Day Saints launched a new ad campaign in August 2010. The ads, which were aired in nine cities around the US, featured young, energetic people surfing, skateboarding, and engaging in everyday—yet hip and cool—activities. In one ad, a young white woman spends almost the entire minute and a half of the video describing her life as the 2008 national longboard surfing champion. The ad ends with the woman saying, "My name is Joy Monahan, I'm a professional longboard surfer, and I'm a Mormon." Another ad features a young white skateboarder describing his love of the sport; he introduces the fact that he's a Mormon casually by saying, "People always wonder why I don't drink." The ads proclaim that Mormons are like everyone else, that Mormonism is not exotic or odd, but rather part of the vaguely defined, though ideologically powerful, "Middle America."[1] The campaign is intended to resonate with a broad, populist audience and obliquely addresses widely publicized stories of Mormons as both polygamists and antigay by positioning them as "normal" and depicting Mormons as everyday Americans doing everyday things, portraying them as "not weird."[2]

Mormons have been running ads on television since the 1980s. Creating television advertising to sell and promote a particular faith is by no means a new tactic in the commercialization of religion. Spiritual organizations such as Scientology have used TV ads to disseminate their messages, as have more formalized religions, such as Jehovah's Witnesses. This new ad campaign, however, is an example of the way in which the Mormon religion (as well as Mormons themselves) can be branded in everyday contemporary culture. In his work on promotional culture, Andrew Wernick explores a variety of ways in which the traditional components of branding—advertising, marketing, commodity signs—are only a part of a more general ethos wherein culture becomes brand culture, as I have discussed throughout this book.[3] The material presence of brands in everyday life is a significant part not only of the symbolic world but also of the communicative and ideological presence of brands—how branding becomes the way we tell stories to ourselves about ourselves and our identities—performs important work within what Stuart Hall would call circuits of culture.[4] One of the more lasting and powerful symbolic worlds in the US is the world of religion. In this chapter, I explore some of the ways religions are branded.

Religion has been largely positioned and experienced in modernism—by both individuals and social institutions—as a symbolic world. The symbolic world of religion provides a moral guide for individuals through formal institutions, iconography, and signs, and through the use of religious metaphors and themes. Despite deep historical relations with other social systems, especially political and economic structures (manifest in centuries of war and in economic practices such as tithing), religion has been powerfully, though not wholly, culturally defined by the content of its beliefs rather than its social, economic, or commercial purposes. As Vincent Miller describes, "We can readily list any number of Christian theological themes that run counter to the implicit anthropology of consumerism: creation, unmerited grace, the paschal mystery, charity, sacramentality, the preferential option for the poor, forgiveness, denial of the flesh, and so on."[5] The "authentic" values of religious beliefs are in contrast to the banal and base practices of consumerism—in fact, religion is often the place one turns to for escape from these materialist practices.

However, as Miller points out, religious values and themes are often incorporated within consumption practices, changing individuals' relationship with religious beliefs, narratives, and symbols. Miller, like Marx, sees the commodification of religion as a practice of corporate appropriation, one that manipulates consumers and religious individuals. Indeed, this is precisely the root of Marx's problem with religion, which he understood as a kind of illusion that alienated individuals just as capitalism did. Religion, for Marx, disguised "real" happiness; it is, in his words, "the sigh of the oppressed creature."[6] In this view, convincing individuals of the authenticity and uniqueness of religion is one of the triumphs of modernism: even if political and economic mechanisms play an obvious role, assisting in the religious life of some individuals, or constraining the religious life of others, these elements are seen as manipulative tools outside the "real" work of religious doctrine.

That religion has been defined in terms of the contents of its beliefs—spirituality, faith, otherworldliness—is, of course, central to its sacralization. As Viviana Zelizer argues, in order to marketize elements in culture that are seen as beyond, or more than, mere commodities (such as human life or religious faith), the material aims of capitalism are retooled as somehow not only about capital accumulation.[7] The result is a profound contradiction, which derives its power precisely because it is not seen as a contradiction: in most religious rhetoric, capitalist doctrine is disavowed, but at the same time, marketing strategies are used to evangelize, or bear witness to, religious beliefs. To claim authenticity, religious brands openly use the strategies of capitalism while denouncing the ethos of capitalism. Branded religions are encompassing of a critique of capitalism; indeed, it is this critique that provides a crucial gravitas to claims of authenticity within branded religions.

This chapter traces some of the ways the branding of religion is both a residual and an emergent formation through an examination of two branded religious cultures: Prosperity Christianity and New Age spirituality. It should be clear that, through this discussion of the branding of religion, I am not commenting upon or evaluating the desire or need for individuals to have faith in their lives or making an argument about religious purpose at all. Rather, I examine here the ways that religions shift within advanced capitalist brand cultures and argue that religious life in the US, like many other cultural practices that I have discussed, are increasingly experienced within and defined by the realm of the brand. Of course, there are many different religions and forms of spirituality, and this chapter does not attempt to be exhaustive in its scope. I do attempt, however, to bring to bear critical and theoretical questions about the ways in which these two forms of religion have been branded in the contemporary context. Specifically, these two brand cultures represent what I call a neoliberal religious divide. Prosperity Christianity relies on a residual ideology of Christian tradition, focusing on American heritage, conservative values, and Christian themes even as it reimagines these traditions within a materialist, consumerist framework.[8] New Age spirituality, on the other hand, takes religious branding in a new direction, one that relies on very different impulses of individual choice and avenues for self-fulfillment. The entangled discourses of tradition and heritage, and of choice and self-fulfillment, cohere in the early 21st century to authorize the religious branding of Prosperity Christianity and New Age spirituality. These discourses engage individual entrepreneurialism in ways that are more generally characteristic of advanced capitalism: the connection between economic prosperity and religious tradition (indeed, the symbiosis between the two);[9] the proliferation of privately organized institutions such as megachurches and "spirituality" franchises such as yoga centers; the burgeoning retail industry that promotes religious ideologies; the use of communication technologies to distribute information about religion to a mass audience; and an acute awareness of the power of youth culture. As I detail in chapter 4, some politics, such as environmentalism, are especially brandable, while others, such as immigrant rights, are not as easily encompassed by brand logic. Historical transformations in the commodification of religions play residual roles in the contemporary branding of religion, even as advanced capitalism ushers in other shifts that reimagine and reframe concepts of the individual, morality, and cultural value. The history of religion and business, of "faith and the market," is critical for understanding contemporary religious brand cultures, as the language and logic of the market have to be utilized for religion to be widely diffused to broad audiences of consumers.[10] The histories, ideologies, and connections to a broader capitalist market, and the fact that both Prosperity Christianity and New Age spirituality are non- or postdenominational, make these religious movements especially brandable.

Commodified Religion versus Branded Religion

In this chapter, I use cultural analysis to examine the processes by which two sets of religious and spiritual practices have been branded in contemporary US society, and what such branding "accomplishes" for religious consumers.[11] As Mara Einstein argues, within the contemporary marketplace and information economy, "religion must present itself as a valuable commodity, an activity that is worthwhile in an era of over-crowded schedules. To do this, religion must be packaged and promoted. It needs to be new and relevant. It needs to break through the clutter, and for that to happen, it needs to establish a brand identity."[12] However, establishing a brand identity for religion is not a simple matter of mapping a business model onto the organization of religious beliefs and institutions. It means something different than the commodification of religion, which implies this kind of linear mapping, where business strategies are applied to religion as a way to market it. Rather, through the process of establishing religious brand cultures, both religion and branding take on new meaning, changing the way individuals experience and affiliate with religions.[13]

Hanna Rosin, in a 2009 *Atlantic Monthly* article, states, "America's churches always reflect shifts in the broader culture."[14] It thus makes sense to look at religion as a productive (in the sense that it *produces* a particular definition of the brand) lens through which to understand how branding works in everyday practice. Religious brand cultures occupy a slightly different cultural position from, say, political brand cultures or creative brand cultures. In some ways, contemporary promotional culture enables the building of religious branding, as in the example of the new Mormon ad campaign (and in the same tradition as corporate social responsibility or building the "creative" city). But in other ways, religious brand cultures are positioned as a *response*—even a challenge—to advanced capitalism.

Popular culture in the 21st century is rife with moral panics about the isolation and alienation of individuals, with new digital media often targeted as the culprit. In 2000, political scientist Robert Putnam wrote *Bowling Alone: The Collapse and Revival of American Community,* in which he described the decline of "social capital" in the US in the last half of the 20th century.[15] This decline of social capital, defined as the "connections among individuals' social networks and the norms of reciprocity and trustworthiness that arise from them," has led, according to Putnam, to a similar decline in a robust civic culture and individual engagement within that culture, so that people in the US spend more of their lives alone, often isolated with media such as television, rather than in social and community groups.

Putnam's argument ignores nontraditional forms of social capital and also does not engage in an in-depth critique of how particular social institutions, like his idealized bowling league, are often defined by the exclusion of social groups, such as racialized constituencies (in a way similar to how civil society itself has worked in the US). Yet Putnam's work clearly struck a chord. After *Bowling Alone* was published in 2000, Putnam not only was interviewed across the news but also was named as President George W. Bush's "theocratic" adviser and speechwriter. According to Putnam, the idea that US citizens are spending their lives alone, alienated from social life, is connected with a decline in political participation, eroding union membership, the decline of civic and educational volunteering, and a general retreat from church attendance.

Putnam's emphasis on this last shift has endured. In his recent work (including his new book *American Grace*) he focuses more specifically on religion. At the Pew Forum on Faith and Public Life in 2009, he discussed the general absence of religious affiliation among young Americans, producing findings from his research that between 30 and 40 percent of young Americans (primarily those in their twenties) have no religious affiliation.[16] Putnam's data are selective, as he does not discuss the impact of social media on religion, which has clearly created social capital among traditional religions as well as new religious or spiritual affinity groups, especially with a younger demographic. But selective data aside, Putnam's nostalgic mourning for traditional religious participation also obscures the increasingly normative branding of religious cultures.

Though an integral element of advanced capitalist culture is the celebration of individualism, entrepreneurialism, and specific forms of "innovation," the other side of this neoliberal coin contains a lament about alienation, a longing for social communities—imprecisely represented by the supposed decline in Putnam's "social capital." That is, what Putnam does not interrogate is the way in which alienation is mutually constitutive with the drive for individualism. Though the deep interrelation between relentless entrepreneurial individualism and alienation is not always made explicit, it is clear that subjects in advanced capitalism enjoy the pleasures of being entrepreneurial individuals—even while this individualism leads to alienation (because it undermines emotional connection and affective relationships). This contradiction makes religious cultures particularly brandable. It thus seems appropriate for the last chapter of this book on brand culture to focus on religion and spirituality. After all, it is easy to see (as many branders of religion and spirituality insist) that these "timeless" practices are ostensibly responses to the alienating individualism that is a hallmark of advanced capitalism. Yet in a predictable dynamic, the contemporary environment is one in which the individual is centered at the expense of the social or collective. In response to this alienation, the branding of religion and spirituality ironically proceeds through the same logic of centering the individual. Branding religion is an integral part of advanced capitalism, not simply a reaction to it.

Indeed, in the contemporary moment, religion is expansively branded, ranging from existing practices, such as conventions and retreats, to traditional artifacts such as rosaries and crucifixes, to Christian stores for teens at suburban malls that sell ironic, kitschy merchandise such as T-shirts that proclaim "Jesus Is My Homeboy," to the booming industry of Christian rock, to Christian "Biblezines" for teenage girls, to the ever-more-burgeoning yoga industry, to the explosion of the New Age self-help market and its endless array of items for sale. Spiritual practices have been marketized not only as commodities but also as part of the infrastructure of the marketplace;

corporations offer yoga classes as a way for employees to relax, and "Christian free enterprise," taught in some business schools, forms the guiding principles for major corporations such as Wal-Mart and Pizza Hut.[17] Religious institutions, then, have used the language of the brand and principles of marketing as ways to communicate religious messages; simultaneously, corporate culture has used both explicit and implicit references to religion and spirituality as a way to extend markets and create a distinct niche in the contemporary economy.[18] This economy is one informed by advanced capitalist practices and doctrine, but the marketizing of religion also has a rich history.

Historically, the commodification of faith has proved a clever business strategy. In the contemporary political context of the US, where what used to be called the religious right is now mainstream business and politics, the commodification of religion has been especially embraced by business culture. But, as I have argued throughout each of the chapters in this book, regarding different brand cultures, the commodification of culture is not equivalent to the branding of culture. Branding religious lifestyles represents an open-ended marketing and business *opportunity*, where there are no discrete products to commodify but rather politically-diffused identities. These identities are reimagined and reframed not only within and as consumer items but also in the ways in which religion is organized, institutionalized, and experienced in everyday life. In an era of digital technologies and advanced capitalism, religious branding has both capitalized on existing marketing strategies and logics and invented new ones as a way to capture an increasingly hard-to-reach audience. Christian businesses have especially targeted the hard-to-reach youth demographic (particularly white and middle-class youth culture) through retail and media, by diffusing a vague Christian message through popular cultural products. If branding is, as Adam Arvidsson has argued, an ambience for everyday living in the US,[19] then religious habits and practices are part of this branding ambience; not simply a way of marketing products, branding religion represents a shifted understanding of what religion means in US culture.

Religion has been commodified in many ways, but I argue here that the contemporary political economy of advanced capitalism encourages a shift from commodification to the branding of religion, where brand strategies intersect with consumer activity and content to create a brand culture around religion, and where capitalist business practices merge with religious practices in an unproblematic, normative relationship.[20] Again, there are key differences between commodification and branding. The commodification of religion implies two separate realms: the commercial and the religious.

Commercialization is a process of determinism or appropriation, a mapping of one realm onto the other. Within the framework of commercialization, these two realms are intertwined, but even in their deep interrelation, they maintain a separate identity. The branding of religion is not a process or a mechanism; it is a broader structure of feeling or an ambience of culture. It also involves the coproduction of culture with consumers; branding is not only a top-down dynamic but one that utilizes consumer labor as part of its creation. As such, the branding of religion is not constituted within two separate realms of culture and commerce.

The Business of Religion: PR Men and Preachers

Historian T. J. Jackson Lears argues that the reliance of religion on what he calls the "therapeutic ethos" of the late 19th and early 20th centuries indicated larger cultural shifts. Specifically, he points out that "changes in material life bred changes in moral perception."[21] As contemporary culture privileges practices of branding (including self-branding) over historical processes of commercialization, religion is not exempt from these strategies. On the contrary, if religious beliefs continue to play a key role in defining an individual's sense of self, and if that self is increasingly understood within the logics of branding, then the changing material realities of the current moment of advanced capitalism breed changes in the moral perception of religion.

For the branding of religion to appear as logical in the late 20th and early 21st centuries, a normative historical relationship between the economy and spiritual life is necessary. As John M. Giggie and Diane Winston argue in their work on the presence of religion in US urban centers in the 19th and 20th centuries, there is a deep link between commercial life and religious practice. Importantly, the link has been an *enabling* one; as Giggie and Winston point out, "The rapid advance of industrial capitalism in North American cities from the late nineteenth century onward did not fuel a declension in religious devotion and practice, as many historians suggest, but rather a profound transformation, even flowering, of it."[22] The relationship between religion and capitalism thus had far greater depth than the more superficial manifestation of tithing, or of church funding; rather, the logic and norms of capitalism enabled the dissemination of religious values in broader culture and facilitated the increasingly blurred boundaries between the secular and the sacred. Churches and religious institutions were geographically positioned side by side with groceries, retail shops, and schools in the industrial landscape of the city.[23] Indeed, capitalist logic and norms structured urban religious practices.[24]

Yet, despite the increasingly blurred boundaries between secular and religious life, dominant ideologies maintained a separation between the two. Religion represented "authentic" sentiment and moral value, whereas commercial life represented the spurious, superficial, and often the immoral (or, at the least, the amoral).[25] The entwined relations between urban capitalism and religion *and* the cultural notion that these were separate and distinct realms allowed for what Giggie and Winston see as the nurturing of new spiritual identities in the early 20th century from a range of religious ideologies, including Orthodox Jews, Christian Scientists, Black Muslims, and Salvation Army "slum angels."[26] Even as religions were criticizing the market as amoral, they were incorporating its principles to form new kinds of identities and institutions.

In the US, where religion is disestablished from official state politics, religion has "had to 'sell' itself in order to survive," as Laurence Moore, Heather Hendershot, and others have pointed out.[27] The history of religious practices in the 19th and 20th centuries in the US reveals a kind of recoding of the social and cultural context of religion into an economic context, without seeming to wholly create religion, or spirituality, as a simple product that moves through the circuit of economic exchange (a recoding that goes through yet another shift in the political economic context of 21st-century neoliberal brand culture). In the US, the freedom to practice religion is a constitutionally guaranteed right provided in the religion clauses of the First Amendment to the Constitution. Despite the noted religious affiliation of conservative political communities in the US, the separation of church and state appeals to a hegemonic nationalist ideology, one that conjures American heritage and tradition. At the same time, the idea that religion is not determined by the state but is constitutionally protected in the same way markets are, as a "freedom," resonates with a neoliberal presumption that all markets, including the marketplace of religion, should be unregulated.

In her work on the commercialization of Christianity in the US, Heather Hendershot points out that the US Constitution has been a critical factor in the establishment of a free market of religion. Specifically, "The First Amendment's declaration of 'disestablishment'—the United States will have no government-sanctioned official religion—guaranteed that the number of religions would multiply and compete with each other to win over the nation's souls (and wallets). Religions have proliferated in America in part because the First Amendment established what one might call a 'free market of religion.'"[28] As Hendershot argues, the absence of a state (and thus taxpayer-supported) religion has meant that American churches have always had to rely on individuals to provide financial support. Religious leaders must also be religious "entrepreneurs," in order to build congregations and thus funding. Religious communities have a historical infrastructure within capitalist consumer culture, where advertising religion, promoting churches, and manufacturing merchandise that displayed one's faith have been critical elements of religious and spiritual development in the US since its founding. In the contemporary moment of brand culture, this infrastructure, along with religious communities themselves, shifts in yet another way.

Many US religious leaders in the 19th and early 20th centuries had either experience or second careers in the fields of advertising, marketing, and public relations and considered this expertise crucial to the development of congregations and the dissemination of religious messages to the broader secular world.[29] Lears documents the transition in the early 20th century from an ethos centered on a work ethic and a morality of self-denial to one that centered on, among other things, self-fulfillment through consumption: "The crucial moral change was the beginning of a shift from a Protestant ethos of salvation through self-denial toward a therapeutic ethos stressing self-realization in this world; an ethos characterized by an almost obsessive concern with psychic and physical health defined in sweeping terms."[30] The 21st-century, New Age emphasis on self-realization is in many ways a logical extension of this long-standing American ethos, today reimagined as the care and promotion of the self through the logic of branding.

The "obsessive" concerns, or emotional needs, of Americans during the early 20th century were addressed, not surprisingly, by advertisers—but were also the concerns of ministers, pastors, and priests. Advertisers and religious leaders not only addressed similar cultural and emotional needs but also used parallel logics and practices to do so. As Lears points out, though religion has always had a therapeutic function, in the early 20th century in the US, religious leaders redefined the therapeutic meaning of religion for individuals and focused on shifting concepts of the individual of this time, who lived in the moment rather than in the abstractness of theology and religious doctrine.[31] As a way to resonate with this new American individual and the therapeutic ethos that supported him or her, religious practices merged with not only psychology but also corporate business logic. The focus of religion shifted, so that messages to congregations were no longer about abstract (and often unattainable) morality, or an ascetic work ethic, but rather about navigating individual and consumer desires as an important part of being a spiritual or religious self. Being a religious person newly meant taking care of oneself, through work and financial success. This consolidation of religious and business practices allowed for the smooth accessibility of religion as a lifestyle, in that it emphasized the *practice* of religion rather than strict adherence to ritual. Part of the accessibility of religion meant adapting a religious vocabulary for business success and vice versa. Lears cites Bruce Barton, a religious leader and PR man in the early 20th century: "It was no accident, Barton claimed, that credit, the basis of modern business, was derived from credo: I believe." The merging of business and religious vocabulary and logic by religious leaders—"spiritualizing the corporate system"—additionally helped assuage the kind of moral ambiguity that undergirds "selling God."[32]

The transformation of US religious life in the 19th and early 20th centuries provides an important backdrop to not only the branding of religion in the 21st century but also the cultural realms discussed in other parts of this book. The idea that one's spiritual duty is first and foremost to oneself, rather than to the collective good, structures other brand cultures, such as corporate social responsibility. The therapeutic ethos that Lears and others discuss was the context for what Jacque Ranciére calls "the distribution of the sensible," where individuals focused more on self-fulfillment, rather than on the needs of others, as a religious duty to oneself.[33] As Susan Curtis argues in her discussion of this transformation of cultural life and the practice of social gospel (a progressive Protestant social reform movement in the 19th century), "They [social gospelers] articulated their beliefs and aspirations in terms drawn from secular society, terms, indeed, of secular society….Participating in the modern workplace and marketplace provided material comfort, promised psychological security, involved the individual in something larger than himself, and thereby could invest religious meaning in secular acts."[34] Yet, by religious leaders appropriating the techniques and logics of advertising and commerce as part of the promotion of social reform, the involvement of the individual "in something larger than himself" could only be understood in those terms—terms that relentlessly circle back to the individual. The same was true for religious leaders as it was for worshipers. Priests and pastors alike began packaging, marketing, and selling their own particular religious message to their own particular audience of consumers. As Curtis points out, "They believed in the social gospel in much the same way that merchants believed in their products—with zeal for its power to make the user a better person, with conviction that the same results could not be obtained by an off-brand, and with proof of results from the people who had already tried it."[35]

The changes and redefinitions in religious meanings, then, were parallel to and interactive with similar shifts in the larger culture. In the 21st century, religious meaning is reimagined yet again, in ways that also invoke and interact with shifts in the larger culture—namely, advanced capitalism. The neoliberal embrace of the individual entrepreneur in business, for instance, mirrors the acceptance of an entrepreneurial perspective in the contemporary evangelist. The abdication of the state in terms of responsibilities to the social that is characteristic of neoliberal ideology is a move that can also be found in religious institutions, where individuals are required to provide financial support to the church in the name of personal spiritual obligation. The increasingly interconnected relationships between the state and the private corporate sector that define the contemporary landscape are similar to the tendency for religious leaders to serve simultaneously as purveyors of faith and marketers.

The embeddedness of religion in branding allows for a prioritizing of the individual, rather than of issues such as power inequities manifest in racial, gendered, and class divisions. The transformation of religion into a commodity, and then a brand, means that individuals relate to it more and more as consumers, in terms of individual fulfillment and the meeting of individual desires, and less and less as a manifestation of collective meaning. But while particular elements of consumer culture remain similar across historical periods—the endless commodification of nontangibles into goods, the continued maintenance of a therapeutic ethos, the divisions of labor required for consumerism to function efficiently—consumer culture, and the commodity itself, shifts in accordance with broader cultural, political, and economic transformations. Religion, always tied to moral values, is no different: as brand culture reimagines and reframes what is moral, ethical, and culturally valuable, then it is not surprising that religion is also something that is not only commodified as it was throughout the 20th century but increasingly understood only through the language of the brand.

Within advanced capitalism, the care of the self is expressed as a particular kind of "freedom"—the freedom to govern oneself, to make individual and privatized choices, and to release oneself from a dependency on the state. These processes work in a variety of ways in the branding of religion. Branding, after all, is about reaching individual "consumers," and though a religious congregation is somewhat different than an audience of consumers, the practice of branding religion collapses the boundaries between the two. As I discussed in the previous chapter on green branding, where "buying good is doing good" and green business is "good" business, a similar dynamic can be applied to religion, where buying good is *being* good, and religion branding is "God's business." Religion is relegated to the private realm, a matter for the individual citizen. Traditional organizing principles of religion as a domain for decision making, a mode of practice, a site of rewards, and a conduit for salvation, all become individualized, so that religion becomes something one can custom order; individual consumer customization, after all, is central to building brand relationships. Though situating religion within the realm of the private is not necessarily an outgrowth of advanced capitalism, and can be traced to the Enlightenment and its notion of liberal individualism, what Jeremy Carette and Richard King call "the individualization of religion" holds true with even more force in the contemporary moment.[36] In particular, Carette and King see a second component of the privatization of religion as having a heightened significance within advanced capitalism, which builds on the individualization of religion but also departs from it: "It can be characterized as a wholesale *commodification* of religion, that is the selling-off of religious buildings, ideas and claims to authenticity in service of individual/corporate profit and the promotion of a particular worldview and mode of life, namely corporate capitalism."[37]

The double mobilization of the individualizing and commodification of religion authorized by advanced capitalism provides a broader context for the branding of religion. In particular, branding religion loosens the ties between individuals and religious institutions and communities, generating a closer connection with what Mara Einstein calls "an autonomous, self-oriented religion."[38] The seeming contradictions involved in "self-oriented" religion tap into a broader dominant ideology about the individual, where community involvement is recoded as the choices made by each individual consumer. Community involvement in this context focuses on the material gains and opportunities *for individuals* within that community, rather than for the community as a whole. This recoding process emerges powerfully in the form of contemporary Prosperity evangelists and the selling of spirituality as an important personal consumption choice.

God Will Make You Rich: Prosperity Christianity

Prosperity Christianity, or what some call "health and wealth" religion, is largely a North American religious movement, connected to Pentecostal Christianity and Word of Faith teachings, and is often tied to Oral Roberts and other evangelists who became well known in the 1980s and 1990s. However, Prosperity Christianity is also historically related to faith healing; in the early 20th century, evangelicals focused on physical well-being as the therapeutic ethos of culture became normative and activities like the "mind cure," which stressed the power of positive thinking as a cure for disease, became popular. Additionally, Prosperity Christianity is related to the rise of Christian free enterprise in the mid-20th century and the interrelation between professional business and theology. For instance, business schools began to attract religious individuals as both students and administrators by midcentury, and as business schools began to take a more prominent role in higher education,[39] Christian business schools (specifically in the midwestern US) emerged as places in which future evangelists could be trained to merge business skills with religious principles.

In the later half of the 20th century, schools such as the University of Arkansas, the University of Ozarks, Southern Methodist University, and others developed business schools as a response to a variety of factors, including national market concerns, postwar inflation and debt, an increasing national demand for vocational business instruction, and a growing desire for white-collar workers in the US. Christian business schools, however, could provide a conservative and "moral" framework for this kind of education.[40] In her careful history of the global corporation Wal-Mart, Bethany Moreton argues that the figure of the contemporary religious entrepreneur became important to the rise of business programs at schools and universities around the US in the late 1970s. In the economic recession during this period, combined with residual countercultural fears of big business and bureaucratic businessmen, small-business enterprises and business schools cultivated the individual entrepreneur as an important element to Christian free enterprise, which found a particularly rich home in small towns, farms, and local churches. Outside the crowded, competitive urban industrial landscape, the emphasis on religion and American heritage that often characterized rural areas in the 1970s provided a welcoming context for the emergence of Christian free enterprise. These cultural spaces, as Moreton argues, "provided the cultural resources to enable a massive shift of economic possibility."[41]

In the small business schools that cropped up along the Sunbelt in the late 1970s, courses were offered in entrepreneurship, where, as Moreton states, the entrepreneur was cast as a special and rare type, not your typical bureaucratic businessman: "In this guise, the entrepreneur inherited the mantle of Jeffersonian virtue from the independent farmers and the Populist rebellion—a hero for the age of the mass office, a foil to sissified bureaucrats and the distant Shylocks of Wall Street."[42] As Moreton points out, the Waltons, the founders of Wal-Mart, promoted Christian business schools and Christian free enterprise and free trade, which serve a vital function in the economic backdrop of advanced capitalism in the branding of religion.

The commodification of religion had been a practice for centuries, but the use of the commercial marketplace to "sell" religion to reluctant, hard-to-reach, or otherwise inaccessible potential congregations proved successful in making religion "relevant" to an increasingly modern and pro-corporate population. But Christian free enterprise is not simply the use of the marketplace to sell religion. It is the adoption of the logic of free enterprise and branding as a way of understanding, experiencing, and proselytizing Christian religious values. This not only is a necessary condition for the branding of particular religions but also changes the understanding of religion itself.

Indeed, the connection between Christian religious values and a kind of pro-corporate populism is crucial for branding Christianity because it offers the possibility of a wide audience for the brand. As Moreton points out, pro-corporate populism (which argues vehemently against government or state intervention) imbues the political economy with moral legitimacy, infusing it with the conservative values of a "rural white virtue."[43] In the contemporary moment, the merging of Christian values with capitalist entrepreneurship takes the form of megachurches and charismatic evangelist leaders. A focus on "free" enterprise—meaning (in part) an opposition to organized labor, state intervention, and public resources—made Christian enterprise compatible with conservative, anticommunist ideologies and the ideology of whiteness.[44] As Moreton argues, the wedding of conservative corporate ideologies to not simply Christian enterprise but Christian education in the formation of private Christian business schools created a context in which these two discourses were completely compatible, each informing the other: "The southwestern Christian college and the new mass white-collar workplace were just beginning a quietly historic partnership, and the terms of the bargain were clear enough."[45]

In the advanced capitalism of the later 20th century, the terms of the bargain find purchase in Prosperity Christianity.[46] As a set of religious teachings and training, the theology is centered on the notion that God provides material wealth—prosperity—for those individuals he favors. Prosperity Christianity cuts across denominational boundaries and is defined "as the teaching that believers have a right to the blessings of health and wealth and that they can obtain these blessings through positive confessions of faith and the 'sowing of seeds' through the faithful payments of tithes and offerings."[47] Prosperity preaching has found a welcome home in many megachurches across the US in the early 21st century, spaces in which an evangelist preaches to hundreds, if not thousands, of individuals, as well as offering services to even larger audiences through live streams online. While there are certainly many religious detractors from Prosperity Christianity—indeed, *Christianity Today* describes it as "false gospel," "unethical and unChristlike," and "spiritually unhealthy"—it has garnered attention from thousands of followers, its message of gaining material wealth through prayer and commitment to one's own congregation especially powerful since the global recession of 2008.

Recent headlines tell us something about how this reimagined relationship between religion and the economy has become increasingly mainstream: a cover of *Time* magazine, in 2006, asked, "Does God Want You to Be Rich?"; a later cover, after the global economic collapse in the fall of 2008, asked a follow-up question: "Maybe We Should Blame God for the Subprime Mess?"

The *Atlantic Monthly* in 2009 asked a similar question: "Did Christianity Cause the Crash?"[48] Christian blogs have taken up the issue of merging money talk with scripture in sermons (alternately defined as Prosperity Christianity or "Christianity Lite"), with vehement defenders on both sides of the debate. The most popular evangelical in the US in the 21st century, Joel Osteen, whose Prosperity megachurch in Houston boasts more than 40,000 weekly worshipers, writes in his best-selling book *Your Best Life Now,* "Telling yourself you are poor, or broke, or stuck in a dead-end job is a form of sin and invites more negativity into your life."[49] Another popular Prosperity evangelist, T. D. Jakes, emphasizes personal achievement in his role as pastor of Potter's House, a 28,000-member, primarily African American church in Dallas, Texas. As Shayne Lee and Phillip Luke Sinitiere point out, Jakes "argues that his ministries provide African-Americans with the life skills, emotional health, and psychological well-being to be successful." They continue: "[Jakes's] brand of personal empowerment promotes the bourgeois conservatism of the new black church."[50] In yet another example of Prosperity preachers, televangelists Kenneth Copeland and Gloria Copeland, founders of the Kenneth Copeland Ministries and authors of books such as *The Laws of Prosperity* and *Prosperity: The Choice Is Yours,* preach that the more money worshipers give to the church, the more they will receive in their own lives.[51]

The focus of evangelicals on personal empowerment and individuals (and, in this case, individual wealth) has reached a heightened significance in the early 21st century. Prosperity Christianity has become an important non- or postdenomination for many contemporary evangelical preachers, where sermons focus on the righteousness of acquiring individual wealth and material success, a pursuit that becomes its own sort of salvation.

Not only are religious messages packaged like other brands, through infomercials, merchandise, and sophisticated media distribution, but also the content of the message can only be understood within a brand context: materialism, consumption, capitalist exchange, and personal empowerment. As Einstein says about Prosperity preaching, "In order to draw in the masses, preachers must include what will attract the largest number of people—ideas about how their lives will be better, more prosperous, more fulfilling—and exclude those things that will lead viewers to reach for the remote control—mentions of Jesus, requests for contributions, suggestions that they are going to hell."[52] A mention of Jesus is a turnoff for Christians? If Jesus is not an appropriate focus for spiritual leaders, the question then becomes: How does a spiritual leader become a valuable brand in a rapidly changing society? Evangelists now need to self-brand, in the ways discussed in chapter 2, but another element obviously has to do not only with how particular individuals are skilled at making religion "relevant" to a contemporary culture (through communication technologies, social media, and so on) but with what identities are particularly brandable. That is, a *lack* of specificity in religious branding is important in order to reach a broad audience of religious consumers, so that megachurches and other contemporary religious institutions (including many religious websites) are strategically nondenominational or "postdenominational" in their religious messages and practices. Within branded religions such as Prosperity Christianity, vague references to a Christian tradition that are individualized, such as how to make one's life better, are more lucrative than specific and community-oriented content, such as a mention of Jesus.

As I have discussed, contemporary evangelists, including Prosperity preachers, are the latest in a long history, dating back to the 18th century, of successful evangelists in the US. George Whitefield, who came to the US in 1738, was arguably the first successful evangelist; he was also an early marketer of religious ephemera.[53] The most successful early evangelists were skilled orators and entrepreneurs who were particularly savvy at using communication technologies to publicize their messages. Radio was a very useful medium for early 20th-century evangelists (as well as for advertisers and politicians). Religious leaders such as Aimee Semple McPherson, Charles Fuller, and Charles Coughlin became expert at using mass media to spread religious messages. In the 1930s, Coughlin's weekly broadcasts reached more than 30 million listeners.[54] In the 1980s, televangelists like Jerry Falwell, Billy Swaggart, and Jimmy Bakker used television to build huge congregations across the nation.[55] Today, as Lee and Sinitiere point out, evangelicals draw millions of followers by reimagining Christianity, and part of this reimagining has been enabled by the normalization of the entrepreneur: "Through the power of their appeal, rather than the authority of ecclesiastical positioning, [contemporary evangelists] assemble multi-million-dollar ministries and worldwide renown. With weak or no denominational ties, they are 'free agents' who make their mark on contemporary American society."[56] One way contemporary evangelicals "make their mark" is through the efficient use of new communication technologies to distribute their messages, from live streaming online videos of their services, to selling books and DVDs on iTunes, to Facebook pages. Self-branding, for some contemporary evangelists, has become an effective way to promote both themselves and the religious teachings they provide. Since, as I have argued elsewhere, self-branding is becoming a more normative practice in contemporary US culture as a way to craft personal identity, it makes sense for some evangelists to consider themselves "free agents" in a neoliberal marketplace. In other words, it is not simply more sophisticated media technologies, or a shifting capitalist system, or new understandings of individual subjectivities that authorize the emergence of the new evangelists in the late 20th and early 21st centuries. It is all of these elements, along with a more general cultural ethos of promotion, which suggests that branding is an aspect of new media logic that is altering even seemingly unconnected domains (such as religion).

The mass white-collar workplace Moreton details as emerging in the mid-20th-century US is precisely the demographic on which 21st-century advanced capitalism depends, both as a source of labor (itinerant labor, antiunion) and as the locus of racialized fears about immigrant labor (outsourcing, denial of immigration rights). Historically, the church has been an advocate of some state intervention and support—social gospelers, for instance, worked with New Deal policies in the early 20th century. Additionally, various Christian denominations have been community oriented rather than individually oriented. But rather than challenge neoliberal economic practices of "free enterprises" and work toward reestablishing state and federal public policies and practices, Christian "free" enterprise and individual entrepreneurship provide solutions to increased alienation (an alienation that ostensibly is caused partly by a multiracial and multicultural workforce and widening income gaps). The church becomes a site of refuge:

> In the vacuum that was left by the eradication of the safety net [public provisions], churches and other faith-based organizations became the provider of last resort. Their family values rendered care a private privilege awarded in defense of marriage, not a mutual social duty of citizens to one another. The irony was that both the corporations and the churches were already public-private partnerships by definition, built with public subsidy and dependent on state nurturance.[57]

Advanced capitalist doctrine is expert in circumnavigating this kind of irony, where the emergence of the private, individual entrepreneur is validated by the state and public-private partnerships. In the context of the religious, individual entrepreneur, this irony manifests not only in the public-private partnerships of the church but also in the practice of spiritual leaders of simultaneously disavowing of capitalism and embracing of its logic. For instance, an immensely popular evangelist, Rick Warren, with an impressive megachurch of his own (the Saddleback Church in Orange County, California, currently the eighth-largest church in the US, averaging 22,000 weekly attendees) strongly disagrees with emphasizing a relationship between God and personal financial success. As he says, "This idea that God wants everybody to be wealthy? There is a word for that: baloney. It's creating a false idol. You don't measure your self-worth by your net worth."[58] Warren's comments are another example of how religious leaders purport to use the strategy of capitalism in the name of faith, without capitulating to capitalism's system of value. This double mobilization maintains authenticity for such leaders; Warren's statement that Prosperity teaching is "baloney" is another way to articulate it as inauthentic. Yet Warren has also been described being "as much Bill Gates as he is Billy Graham." *Forbes* magazine "called Warren a 'spiritual entrepreneur'" and stated that if Warren's ministry were a business, it "would be compared with Dell, Google, or Starbucks."[59] Of course, Warren's ministry *is* a business, so it makes perfect sense to situate it alongside Google or Starbucks. His book *The Purpose Driven Life* is a *New York Times* best seller and offers a personal guide for individuals to figure out their purpose in life (and despite the first line of the book, which answers this question with "It's not about you," it clearly *is* about you, and buying the book, and following his "Purpose Driven" philosophy). Warren gave the benediction at President Obama's inauguration in 2008, and *Time* magazine named him one of "15 World Leaders Who Mattered Most in 2004" and in 2005 one of the "100 Most Influential People in the World." Also, in 2005 *U.S. News & World Report* named him one of "America's 25 Best Leaders."[60] So while Warren may preach against Prosperity Christianity, he is nonetheless part of a broader pattern of branding Christianity.[61]

Warren and other contemporary evangelists like him, even when not expressing Prosperity Christianity explicitly, demonstrate the various ways in which religion is increasingly understood through the language of the brand. As Linda Kintz argues in her work *Between Jesus and the Market,* the fundamentalism of Christian ideology works in concert with the fundamentalism of the market, so that "prosperity" preaching provides a space in which the contradictions of "free" enterprise are resolved.[62] That is to say, the practice of branding religion does not merely indicate that religious doctrine is simply communicated and experienced in an economic context. The branding of religion in contemporary capitalism also means that neoliberal ideologies of the individual, the "free" market, and a lessening of state intervention of any kind are increasingly part of religious ideologies. For example, the Prosperity leader Benny Hinn preaches about the specific ways in which God "wants" people

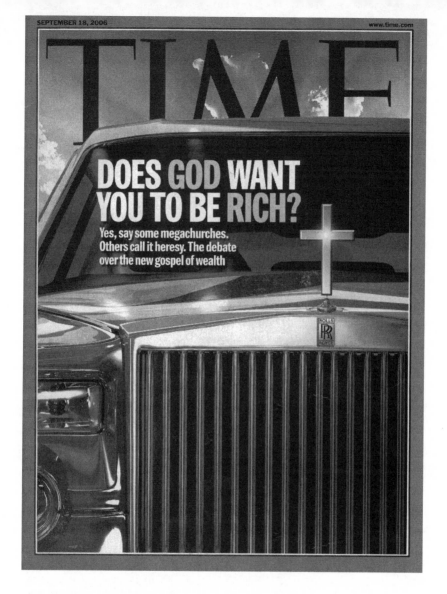

DOES GOD WANT YOU TO BE RICH?

Yes, say some megachurches.
Others call it heresy. The debate
over the new gospel of wealth

Time magazine cover on Prosperity Christianity, September 18, 2006.

to become wealthy. In one of his articles on his website, "Your Supernatural Wealth Transfer Is Coming," Hinn cites Psalm 35:27: "Yea, let them say continually, Let the Lord be magnified, which hath pleasure in the prosperity of his servant." Hinn interprets this as "It is God's will that you prosper!" In this article, Hinn lists six "wealth transfers" that have happened throughout history, offering narratives of biblical figures such as Abraham and Isaac as benefiting materially from God's will. The seventh person on Hinn's list in line for

A parody of the "For Dummies" franchise covering Prosperity Gospel.

a "wealth transfer" is, not surprisingly, "you" ("Next in line for a great wealth transfer is you!"). The key to becoming rich, Hinn tells his congregation, is to pray and spread the word of the gospel.[63] Alongside tabs on his website like "spiritual life" and "healing," Hinn features "financial freedom," where he gives advice on money management, tithing, and God's prosperity.

Hinn, like Osteen and other Prosperity preachers, is committed to an ideology of free-market capitalism and has found ways to imbricate this ideology into religious practice. Indeed, as Jonathan Walton points out, too little attention has been paid by religious scholars to evangelists as proselytizers of a particular Christian identity, "an identity defined, for the most part, by theological, cultural and political neoconservatism."[64] While neoconservatism cannot be collapsed with neoliberal culture, they share similar tenets in terms of a prioritizing of individualism, a privileging of the free market, a distrust in the state—and the way all of these discourses form a nationalist sensibility. As Walton continues, "For the vast majority of televangelists, commitments to hyper-American patriotism, free-market capitalism, and patriarchal conceptions of the ordering of society are regularly transmitted through mass-mediated images and 'Christian' discourse."[65]

If branding in its contemporary form emerges from a kind of fundamentalism of the free market, then this connects to (though does not always neatly map onto) a particular fundamentalism within religion. "Fundamentalism" here indicates not merely a strict adherence to religious doctrine as the truth but also a powerful belief in the set of neoliberal principles that structure contemporary cultural, political, and economic life. The fundamentalism of the free market, in turn, implies not only a strict adherence to capitalist doctrine as the truth (though it is about this kind of observance) but also a loyalty to capitalist logic as structuring principles for everyday life.

As Kintz argues, part of this fundamentalism has been the use of women as spokespeople for a kind of Christianity. Women have helped move fundamentalist religious concerns, once thought to be on the extreme margins, to the mainstream by collapsing these concerns into affective feelings about family, home, and domesticity: "That collapse has also paradoxically helped establish a symbolic framework that returns manliness to the center of culture."[66] A brief glance at US politics in the first decade of the 21st century demonstrates this, as former Alaskan governor Sarah Palin has efficiently built a self-brand as a religious American woman. In all her roles, as running mate to Republican presidential candidate John McCain, a political pundit for conservative news network Fox News, a spokesperson of the Tea Party, and a reality television star, Palin has clearly proselytized that the moral principles of the right wing in US politics and those of a masculinized religious sentiment can be merged—and merged most effectively in a feminine, preferably maternal, body.[67] The collapse of conservative ideologies into affective, indeed nostalgic, sentiments, especially those of a neoliberal definition of morality, is achieved through the use of conservative women as spokespeople for the nation. This collapse is also the crux of religious brand culture, which retools capitalist strategies and logics into cultural norms.

Branding the Dot: New Age Capitalism and Eastern Spirituality

With some exceptions (T. D. Jakes the most visible one), the audience for Prosperity Christianity consists of a white demographic. Inasmuch as whiteness always requires its opposition for cultural definition, the branding of religion taps into other racialized constituencies as well. The branding of spirituality relies on cultural constructions of race and ethnicity as a mobilizing element in the commodity process. As Stuart Hall and others have argued, the commodifying process frequently includes the commodification of racial vernacular traditions.[68] In this section, I examine what Kimberly Lau calls "new age capitalism" as a way to discuss how the cultural concept of the East—particularly India—is commodified and branded as a spiritual practice in contemporary US culture.[69] Certainly, the branding of Indian spiritual traditions relies on what Edward Said famously called "Orientalism," which he argues is a Western hegemonic ideology, a European invention that authorizes interrelated definitions of the East as mystical and exotic and European/West as a central mechanism of power. For this mechanism of power to function efficiently, Western practices have to assiduously maintain and continue the circulation of Orientalist practices within Western forms of culture. One way this works in contemporary US culture is through the branding of spirituality. However, the branding of spirituality is a process that exceeds Orientalism, as it is animated and enabled by advanced capitalist culture. It is a response, in particular ways, to the bullying powers of capitalism, even as those practices encourage Eastern spirituality to emerge as a brand. This branding of Eastern spirituality I term "New Age spirituality," which takes branding religion in a different direction from Prosperity Christianity and is mobilized by an impulse of choice and self-fulfillment.

Although advanced capitalist culture recodes and reimagines the concept, individual self-improvement has long been a central tenet of religious practice. Bettering oneself, learning from one's mistakes, atoning for individual sins, becoming as close to God(s) as possible are all common themes in religious teaching. While this focus on the individual self reveals a contradiction in the social or collective reach of religion, I am more interested in how this focus has been incorporated into late capitalism, so that self-improvement, a crucial component of the neoliberal individual, becomes a part of the religious marketplace as much as it is part of religious ideology. As Lears reminds us, the therapeutic discourse of selfhood is, in many ways, a hallmark of modernity, what Eva Illouz calls a "qualitatively new language of the self."[70] As such, therapeutic discourse "enables us to throw in sharp relief the question of the emergence of new cultural codes and meanings and to inquire into the conditions that make possible their diffusion and impact throughout society."[71] Therapeutic discourse circulates in many different forms that are constitutive of these "new cultural codes and meanings," ranging from the self-help industries to child-rearing practices to reality television, especially of the makeover genre.[72] And therapeutic discourse is, of course, a crucial element in religious and spiritual practice, from the preachings of evangelicals in megachurches to the increasingly popular practice of yoga. Therapy, in the contemporary moment, connects with a focus on the individual and what Foucault calls the "care of the self" and, as such, is part of the overall context for the branding of religion.

Yet, therapeutic discourse does not have the same valence across different religious contexts. In the context of Prosperity Christianity, material wealth is positioned as the conduit to self-worth; it is through accumulation of capital that one "takes care of the self." In contrast, for what Lau calls "new age capitalism," therapeutic discourse provides a respite from material culture and the pressures of capital—even as the practices of new age capitalism, such as yoga and Eastern religious philosophy, are branded and make sense precisely within the logics of advanced capitalism.[73] Indeed, the therapeutic products and services often associated with new age capitalism—yoga, macrobiotic eating, feng shui, spiritual journeys to the East—are luxury items for most people, so that in a familiar paradoxical scenario, one must have substantial material means in order to "escape" from material culture. This is perhaps most obviously borne out through the spiritual performances of celebrities; in one of many examples, as Nitin Govil has argued, "India has functioned as a location for spiritual transcendence and personal transformation for the Hollywood glitterati."[74] In another example, the popular 2006 book and subsequent 2010 film *Eat, Pray, Love* traces the spiritual journey of a woman as she travels to Italy, India, and Indonesia, to find inner happiness and serenity. Only those with considerable financial means, it goes without saying, have the luxury to take a yearlong journey across the globe as a means of escaping the burdens of urban life. In predictable fashion, *Eat, Pray, Love* has expanded to a clothing, jewelry, and furniture line. The designer of the *Eat, Pray, Love* clothing collection, Sue Wong, said about her inspiration: "Because of the immediate connection I felt to the story, as well as its emphasis on the culture, philosophy, and, in particular, alluring mystique of the East, I was able to create a collection that was striking, exotic, and timeless, and organic to the journey in the book and forthcoming film."[75]

While laments about the decline of mainstream religion in contemporary culture are voiced in popular discourse, there is at the same time an inverse (and to many of these lamenters, an equally disturbing) trend: a boom in "spirituality." Spirituality is, of course, connected to religion but is more personal and individual, less organized and formal. The branding of spirituality takes many forms in contemporary US culture, including the burgeoning yoga industry and the mainstream commodification of "new age" products and resources. The context for what quickly became the enduring "mystique" of Asian cultures was set early in the 19th century, though it was in the 20th century that spirituality, racial hierarchies, and self-help ideologies were brought into bold relief, as Jane Iwamura, Vijay Prashad, Lau, and others have demonstrated. The 19th-century metaphor of the East, one "that represented the spiritual in general, whereas the West represented the material," continues to have both cultural and economic capital, and indeed this binary of spiritual/material is crucial for the normalizing of "new age capitalism."[76] The distinction between the spiritual and the material, reductive as it is, is a vital element in the contemporary branding of both religion and spirituality. A neoliberal religious divide positions, on one side, US Christian evangelism, and its adherence to a dominant US ideology of individual and material entitlement and conservative politics, which made the blurring of the boundaries of the secular and the sacred a logical fit for branding, especially for the "wealth and health" message from Prosperity Christianity. On the other side of this divide, the branding of New Age spirituality, rather than focus so directly on materiality (in terms of wealth, ownership, or actual institutions such as the megachurch), shifts its attention to the spiritual, and thus to a more diffused set of discourses that go into branding. Of course, the direction of this focus is not arbitrary; for practitioners of New Age spirituality, their particular "practice" is often influenced by class identity. Those who are already prosperous, and thus do not "need" Prosperity gospel, turn to spirituality.

Like Christian evangelism, New Age spirituality is non- or postdenominational. Built as it is on a racist ideology of Orientalism and Asian "mystique," the specificity of the "spiritual" is clearly peripheral to its self-help promises. Indeed, as Prashad points out, a vague *concept* of India served during the 19th century and early 20th century as a kind of Whitman-inspired metaphor of the soul itself, appealing to "that sublime spirit that was lost in the throes of capitalism."[77] As I have discussed in this chapter, the contradiction, or perhaps more accurately, irony, of the ways in which the "sublime spirit" missing from capitalism is marketed and branded within capitalist logic is again another characteristic of a capitalist shell game. The search for spiritualism as an antidote to the alienation that accompanies capitalism's material quest is understood and experienced not as ironic by practitioners but rather as making a kind of sense through the veneration of the market.

New age capitalism found its market most powerfully in the US in the 1960s, with the Beat generation (although as Iwamura, Prashad, and others point out, the introduction of yoga and Eastern religious practices in the US can be seen as early as the 19th century). Along with bohemian culture, the hippy movement, and a general antimaterialist ideology that characterized much of US youth culture in the 1960s, Buddhism, the Hare Krishna movement, and "gurus" such as Maharishi Mahesh Yogi (who founded the Transcendental Meditation movement) inspired the eventual mainstreaming of (nondifferentiated) Eastern philosophies and practices into everyday life. As Prashad points out:

> The United States welcomed these gurus as a tonic against the disaffection produced first by abundance (during the boom cycle from 1945–67) and then by economic instability (after the start of stagflation from 1967 onward). The social discontent with economic surfeit was triggered by the long-term crisis generated by a collapse of the demand side (rising oil prices) and of the supply side (deterioration of productivity rates and labor unrest).[78]

Thus, New Age spirituality became embedded in some parts of US life as a response to the market, imbricated in its logics and practices. As such, a concept of "Indian spirituality" dissociated from its national, historical, and economic context became a sought-after state of being and mind for *individuals*, not a collective experience. The individuals who became enamored with Eastern religions and philosophies during the 1960s and 1970s related to these religions and philosophies not only as material forms to be consumed but also as a specific remedy to US capitalism. Communities such as the hippies and New Age practitioners identified the industrial capitalism of the US as morally bankrupt and the opposite of spiritual fulfillment. India represented the antidote to the capitalist and materialist syndromes of the West not because it offered an alternative political economy or commercial policy but because it was seen as severed from America's economy.[79]

US capitalism and New Age Orientalism are entangled discourses and practices, both focusing on the individual self, not the social or the collective world. Youth culture of the 1960s took hold of notions of personal spiritual fulfillment, achieved through practices such as yoga, homage to gurus, and New Age philosophies, which ignored the complexity of social problems by offering "banal solutions in exotic garb."[80] The inherent racism that frames much of the US adoption of Eastern religious practices is not raised as an issue or a question; instead, the "Orient" is fetishized and commodified. I would add that while the adoption of spiritual ideologies as a kind of exoticism does work to ignore social problems, the embrace of Eastern spiritualism also functions (and even more so in the 21st century) as a kind of *symptom* of neoliberal capitalism, which works assiduously to ensure that broader social problems are *never* on the agenda (and thus are not necessarily consciously ignored), and instead privileges individual issues. So the "banal solutions in exotic garb" are not actually solutions, as problems are not raised as issues in the first place.

Religious scholar Jane Iwamura points out, "Popular media allowed a popular engagement with Asian religious traditions, and relied upon and reinforced certain racialized notions of Asianness and Asian religiosity."[81] Popular representations, such as the Oriental monk Iwamura discusses, or styles and fashions, such as mendhi, henna, and the *bottu*, become transformed in some contexts as elements of "faith brands"—though not necessarily for the people for whom they have religious meaning. The branding of religious symbols and styles relies on what Meenakshi Gigi Durham calls "ethnic chic"[82] and is located within a history of East-West relations shaped by and embedded within histories of imperialism, colonialism, and exoticization. Here, I am not so interested in Asian-influenced style trends as they are commodified and become part of a fashion circuit of capitalist exchange. Rather, I am interested in how these style trends and their connection to broader practices such as yoga are branded as spiritual or religious. While these branded forms of spirituality certainly have an undergirding logic of normative "Orientalism," they are not understood by their practitioners merely as fashion statements.

What is needed for Eastern spirituality to be branded, rather than merely commodified, in advanced capitalism? For instance, how do we make sense of the user rating system of social news sites like Reddit, where users receive "karma" for their contributions?[83] I have argued throughout this book that a broad cultural dynamic is needed in order for a brand culture to emerge. This dynamic includes more than the strictly economic components of capitalism, such as a product, a distribution system, and consumers. A promotional culture, a therapeutic ethos, public relations mechanisms, and technologies of communication are also needed to support and build a brand culture, as are cultural narratives, ideologies that privilege the individual over the social and work to secure the prominence of the individual entrepreneur. As Iwamura points out, much of the general knowledge in the US of the spiritual East emerges from the historical tangle of immigration patterns, mass media, and channels of consumption. Documenting what she calls "virtual orientalism," Iwamura utilizes Said's argument about the Western construction of the East as it is expressed through different media forms. Asian religions and practices of spirituality are themselves branded through channels of consumption and media representation.

Perhaps one of the most visible Eastern spiritual enterprises today is the self-brand of Deepak Chopra, whom Prashad describes as a "New Age orientalist."[84] Prashad situates Chopra within a variety of orientalist discourses, from medicine to individualism; here, I focus on the ways in which Chopra is part of spiritual branded culture. Chopra, who has written more than fifty books on spiritual health and personal transcendence, is widely recognized in the US as one of the most important figures within the cultural realm of New Age spirituality. He has founded the Chopra Foundation, whose mission is to "scientifically and experientially explore non-dual consciousness as the ground of existence . . . and to apply this understanding in the enhancement of health, business, leadership, and conflict resolution."[85] Chopra has a YouTube channel (Deepak Chopra Global), a program on Sirius radio (Deepak Chopra's Wellness Radio), and a host of other media sites and organizations—and even iPhone apps.

As Prashad points out, despite Chopra's claims to create global communities of spiritual well-being, his work is intensely focused on the individual and away from the social, thus refusing to confront material and social divisions, such as those of race and gender, as institutionalized practices based in power relations. Prashad argues, "Chopra walks away from such real social divisions and offers a set of neutral divisions called 'essences' that tell us about something inherent in our beings. . . . The conditions and circumstances that fetter real, living, embodied individuals are cast aside, and our imaginary, bourgeois selves are asked to be indulgent, pleasant, and nonconfrontational."[86] Like Christian Prosperity preachers, the Chopra philosophy depends on brand logic for its validation, though in Chopra's case this path is organized around Orientalism and the exoticism of the East. Relying on vague terms such as "essence," the public presence of Chopra helps build the brand of Eastern spirituality. It forms part of a broader set of practices and institutions that are organized around brand logic, focusing on the individual and capitalist exchange.

This brand logic moves from Chopra, the epitome of the individual entrepreneur in the New Age field, to the epitome of a New Age entrepreneurial practice: yoga. In the last three decades, yoga in the US has transformed from a relatively small practice, with clear Hindu roots, meant to promote a state of stability, calm, introspection, and reflexivity, to a full-fledged trendy business available only to those with the financial and cultural means to support it. There is no better example of the branding of spirituality today. As Carette and King argue, the wide adoption of yoga by practitioners as a particularly lucrative business in the West renovates "yoga from a set of renunciatory practices for attaining liberation from the cycle of rebirths either into a psychologised 'spirituality of the self' on the one hand or into a

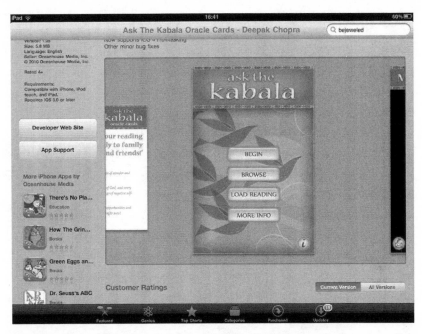

The iPhone app: Deepak Chopra's Ask the Kabala Oracle Cards.

secularized system of therapy, physical exercise and/or mood-enhancement on the other."[87]

Indeed, the magazine *Yoga Journal,* founded in 1975, a publication in the US with a readership of nearly a million per month, estimates the annual market for the yoga industry in the US as approximately $6 billion in 2008—an 87 percent increase since 2004. The magazine further estimates that in 2008, almost 16 million Americans were practicing yoga in one form or another.[88] Yoga is a practice given an authority or cultural weight by its adoption by celebrities, health practitioners, and alternative lifestyle experts, and is clearly a successful way to brand a particular kind of spirituality. Indeed, so many different forms of yoga are practiced in the US in the current moment that it is difficult to see how the origin of the practice as a "radical critique of the conventional ego-driven and particularized self that sees itself as the all-important focus on our lives—as the centre of our universes"[89] is retained. For instance, the authors of "The Rise and Rise of Yoga," Anirudh Bhattacharyya and Dipankar de Sarkar, point out: "A quick round up of some of America's takes on yoga can leave you metaphorically standing on your head. There's Circus Yoga, Nude Yoga, Pre- and Post-Natal Yoga, Ball Yoga (with a ball as an accessory) and even Yoga for dogs (or Doga). Not to forget Acro Yoga (acrobatics!) and Hip-Hop Yoga."[90]

Doga: Yoga for dogs.

As the authors argue, the widespread transformation of yoga from a spiritual practice to a lucrative industry has meant, ironically, that the spirituality that is at the origin of yoga, connected with Hinduism or with various forms of Indian spirituality, has been severed from the practice itself. Indeed, it is hard to see how "circus yoga" and its efforts to blend the "skills of the circus" remain connected to the notion that yoga is meant to center individuals spiritually. Yet the tie to Hinduism and Indian religions more broadly, however vague it might be, is as important as celebrity endorsements for the economic success of yoga; it is Hinduism that constitutes, for Americans at least, an important, and authentic, "home of spirituality."

This historical and philosophical authenticity is, as Carette and King remind us, and in a process that by now will sound very familiar, recoded in terms of the individual and Western norms of entrepreneurship: "In this way

Sexy yoga, a manifestation of the yoga industry

yoga loses much of what is genuinely counter-cultural, transformative and challenging to western cultural norms. It becomes secularized, de-tradition-alized and oriented towards the individual."[91] This process is a kind of double movement, where the decoupling of Hinduism from the practice of yoga makes it something that can be sold as a particular sort of branded commodity to a wide audience of consumers (who are often not Hindu), while retaining the spiritual mystique of Hinduism. The branding of yoga repurposes Indian religion as "authentic," in which the practitioner, not the actual practice, is "authentic."

The decoupling of the specifics of Hinduism from yoga is not without cri-tique; in 2010 a group of Indian Americans started a campaign called "Take Back Yoga." The campaign asks that people who practice yoga be aware of its traditions within the Hindu faith (though it does not ask yoga practitioners to become Hindu). As Aseem Shukla, the cofounder of "Take Back Yoga," has said, "In a way, our issue is that yoga has thrived, but Hinduism has lost con-trol of the brand."[92] Debates around the spiritual and religious histories and legacies of yoga become centered on ownership: who owns yoga?[93] Indeed, Shukla has posed this question in specific capitalist terms and has claimed that yoga has become a victim of "overt intellectual property theft."[94] The answer to his question of "Who owns yoga?" is inseparable from who con-trols the brand of yoga. The idea of owning a spiritual practice depends on a discourse of authenticity, and, indeed, "Take Back Yoga" is organized pre-cisely around authenticity. US commercial business practices have, accord-ing to this campaign, tainted the authenticity of yoga. Such critique speaks to the ambivalence of branding, where because it circulates in culture, it can be misconstrued; but Shukla's protests also speak to the power of branding, where even opposition to the branding of yoga is articulated through the lan-guage of the brand.

Through branding, the cultural meanings of spiritual practices such as yoga are reimagined not merely economically but also in terms of the rela-tionship individuals have with this practice. Branding Eastern spirituality means that for some individuals, brand cultures can be built around sym-bols, practices, and ideologies. But whose assumptions, fears, and hopes become the affective stuff, the authentic base, of building a spiritual brand culture? Again, who owns the brand? As Prashad argues, the wide cultural adoption of South Asian symbols and practices into white hegemonic US culture does not in turn indicate a lessening of racist practices toward South Asians, or more "tolerance" toward communities of color. The branding of Eastern spirituality is not about South Asians as a set of communities, a het-erogeneous group of peoples, but about a group of individual consumers who have pledged loyalty and affinity to a brand culture. This loyalty and affinity are based on a brand of authenticity, in this case the authenticity of Eastern spirituality, mysticism, and "essence." As the history of the visual and media representation of Asian spirituality demonstrates, the dynamic of commercial culture and Eastern spirituality has been imbricated in dis-courses of whiteness.[95]

Branded spirituality, in other words, is less closely tied to religious institu-tions, histories, and communal practice and more connected to individual affiliation and circuits of consumer culture. Asian spirituality is positioned, through media representation and individual practice alike, through celebrities showing off their henna tattoos or through yoga as a means for all of us to find ourselves, as an aid for dominant white Americans to gain spiritual insight and an individual sense of morality.[96] As Iwamura forcefully argues, "The particular way in which Americans write themselves into the story is not a benign, non-ideological act, but rather constructs a modernized cultural patriarchy in which Anglo-Americans re-imagine themselves as the protectors, innovators, and guardians of Asian religions and culture and wrest the authority to define these traditions from others."[97] Participating in brand cultures is partly about situating oneself as a central character in the narrative of the brand—of "writing" oneself into the story. When it comes to spiritual practice, writing ourselves into the story both strengthens the power of New Age spirituality and diminishes the power of historical spiritual cultures. The "story" of branded religion, as I have discussed it here through the examples of Prosperity Christianity and New Age spirituality, is represented as a neoliberal religious divide, representing both residual and emergent directions in brand culture.

"Jesus Is My Homeboy": Neoliberal Secularism and Constructions of Religious Value

The boundaries of religious communities are continually redrawn, in relation to other cultural factors, such as shifting conceptions of the individual, political and economic changes, ideological shifts in what constitutes "Americanness," and so on. Branded religions also rely on a specific audience in order to become a visible brand. As with many other branding endeavors, American youth have been the target for religious branding, for a number of reasons. As I discussed in chapter 2 regarding girls and young women, the general youth demographic (broadly defined as between the ages of twelve and twenty-four) uses more social media than older generations, has influence across a broad range of industries, and because of its media savvy and hard-to-reach status, is the target of nontraditional marketing for branding companies.[98] Specifically in terms of religion, in part because of the constantly shifting terrain upon which religious institutions and practices rest, religious institutions have lost much of their authority with youth in the 21st century; as a 2010 Pew study on youth and religion reveals, Americans aged eighteen to twenty-nine are considerably less religious than older Americans, and fewer belong to a specific faith. Indeed, 25 percent of the Millennial generation (defined as those born after 1980, and young adults by 2000) are unaffiliated with any particular faith. The Pew study also claims that young adults attend religious services less often than older Americans today, and fewer young people say that religion is a very important factor in their lives.[99] This decrease in the importance of religion is aided by highly publicized sexual scandals involving religious leaders from a variety of faiths that reverberate through the culture.

Yet branded religions, by contrast, have been embraced by youth culture. There is a concerted effort on the part of branded religions to be relevant to young people; the use of social media, rhetorical strategies of irony and parody, and an emphasis on the interrelations between popular culture and religion have been important for branded religions to reach a young demographic, far more convincing than a didactic religious message that promises punishment for lack of faith. For instance, an evangelical group founded in the first decade of the 21st century, Off the Map, has the professed mission of "helping Christians be normal."[100] The group's founder, Jim Henderson, was a preacher for twenty-five years and purportedly became disenchanted with many of his peers' obsession to "collect believers." Members of Off the Map view themselves as "critics" of churches, and the group offers services for "nonbelievers" to see which church might be right for them. The religious emphasis is nondenominational (though there are frequent references to Jesus), and the group's website resembles a *Consumer Reports* profile more than a religious space. Indeed, the group received some notoriety when Henderson had the winning bid on eBay for Hemant Mehta, an atheist who was "selling his soul" in order to be saved (the winning bid was $504).[101]

The group also has created another site, Church Rater, where users attend churches and then rate the services, much like other evaluative websites that are part of the social fabric of brand culture such as Hot or Not, Rate My Professor, and Rate My Face. These rating services also resonate with user aggregator sites such as the website Yelp, which offers user reviews and recommendations for restaurants, stores, business, *and* churches, rating churches with one to five stars and including comments such as this one, about a San Francisco church:

> Not your parents' church, definitely not your grandparents' church, and possibly perhaps not even your elder siblings' church. Yet, this church reaches out to everyone, and when I say "reaches," I mean really extend a hand out to folks as they are. It's true that if this was a restaurant review, I'd give them 3 Stars, tops. (With the exception of last weekend's Easter dinner with the crab pasta, 5 Stars!!!) However, how many churches can you think of where you can give them a restaurant review?[102]

Vaguely referencing traditional functions of churches—"this church reaches out to everyone"—as well as acknowledging the connection between rating churches and restaurants, practices such as this are demonstrative of the imbrication of religious culture with market logic, reinforcing the perceived democracy of the free market of religion. There are also ways to encourage youth culture to embrace branded religions by the use of familiar popular cultural artifacts and tropes as conduits for religious messages. Feeling the need to confess one's sins? There's an app for that: Confession: A Roman Catholic App. The app was designed by Patrick Leinen, who said he was inspired by the pope to use new media for good purposes: "Our desire is to invite Catholics to engage in their faith through digital technology.... taking to heart Pope Benedict XVI's message from last year's World Communications Address, our goal with this project is to offer a digital application that is truly 'new media at the service of the Word.'"[103]

Off the Map and Confession: A Roman Catholic App are examples of some of the residual and emergent themes of the current moment of religious branding. Without diminishing the intentions of the founders of Off the Map, especially their critique of the way megachurches fetishize numbers in terms of actual people and in dollars, the organization's website feels like "one-stop shopping" for religion: from the nondenominational position of the group, to the blogs evaluating various spiritual issues, to the Church Rater services that rates churches (and religions) as products, and, finally, to religious products sold through the site. The nondenominational character of the website positions it squarely within an assumed democratic free market, where individual consumer choices are prioritized. While the organization stresses community as an important part of spirituality, the focus is on the individual; for instance, Henderson, the founder of Off the Map, sells his book on the website Evangelism without Additives, advertising it with the tagline: "What if sharing your faith meant just being yourself?" The organization, in other words, underscores the notion that one can be an individual entrepreneur within a branded religious culture.

The "one-stop-shopping" character of Off the Map also resonates with an American youth population. In other ways, religious beliefs and practices remain important in the lives of youth—though the traditional church or synagogue may no longer be the venue for these practices. As the concept of the individual shifts within advanced capitalism, the individual has realized a shifted sort of personal authority and empowerment, aided by dominant ideologies.[104] Lynn Schofield Clark, in her work on US teens and religion, points out that "teens, like their parents and other adults today, do not seem to be very interested in learning about ultimate truths from authoritative sources like the Bible or religious traditions. They consider *themselves* to be the ultimate authority on what it might mean for them to be religious or spiritual."[105] In other words, the notion that religious institutions and organized religion have declined in importance in the lives of many young Americans does not in turn indicate that values, morals, and beliefs that might be termed religious have disappeared, as the mainstreaming of the religious, conservative right in US culture shows us, in the last several years. On the contrary, as Diane Winston has shown in her work on religion and television, religious messages and ideologies turn up in popular television frequently, often without an overt signal that the programs are "religious."[106] If young people are the "ultimate authority of what it means to be religious or spiritual," it then makes sense that the culture they both create and live within provides them with a kind of customized set of religious messages and ideologies.

Despite Putnam's faith in more formal institutions of civic society as the primary sources for community, it seems that while people of all ages in contemporary US society may be frustrated, disillusioned, or simply not interested in the formal authority of the church or synagogue, there is an additional or concurrent explanation: the contemporary world is awash in a more diffused but equally abundant notion of religion or spirituality.[107] Current practices of spirituality have a particular appeal to contemporary citizens because of both their practicality and their accessibility in consumer culture. This justification of faith practices through the elaboration of their practical purposes is often articulated as a religious "lifestyle choice" in which the individual is authoritative and makes her or his own choices, and one that has a supportive commercial framework not only to make this lifestyle not only tangible but also to "promote" it. The commercial framework of religion enables the construction of it as a lifestyle; the accoutrements of consumer culture make a religious lifestyle not only accessible but also very easy to practice and opt into for individuals.

Spiritual values and practices are incorporated in the contemporary moment as lifestyle, rather than religious, choices by embedding them within popular culture—especially popular culture targeted to white US youth culture. Movies produced in the early 21st century, such as *Saved!*, *A Walk to Remember*, and *Easy A*, targeted toward the ever-powerful tween and teen audience, feature teens who embrace their religion as a kind of lifestyle choice, so that the films' narratives position religious affiliation as yet another clique, another brand in a competitive high school landscape (as Charlotte, the main character in *Easy A*, exclaims, "If there's one thing that trumps religion, it's capitalism"). Perhaps ironically, the "lifestyle" concept is amplified in the way the central narratives of these films *mock* religious affiliation as a lifestyle choice. *Saved!* and *Easy A* poke fun at religious teen groups in a similar way as other teen genre films poke fun at sorority girls, mean girls, or nerds. The mocking of religious teens constructs these groups as normative, just another group sitting in the high school cafeteria.

Recent heightened visibility in teen celebrity culture of purity rings and purity balls, where rings engraved with the words "Purity" or "True Love Waits," signifying chastity, is also part of this Christian consumer and popular culture.[108] Christian toys, such as the "Life of Faith" historical dolls (which were produced after the US religious right demonized the historical line American Girl Dolls because the company donated money to Girls, Inc., a nonprofit organization that promotes "progressive" values such as tolerance and reproductive rights), action figures, and games, are sold at both Christian retail conventions and traditional retail stores such as Wal-Mart. In 2006, Americans spent more than $7 billion on Christian products, and roughly half of all Christian goods are bought at retail chain stores such as Wal-Mart, Barnes & Noble bookstore, and Amazon.com.[109] Between 2002 and 2005, sales of Christian products increased by 28 percent, and according to a 2005 survey, more people consume Christian popular culture, such as radio, television, and music, than attend organized religious institutions such as churches.[110]

There has always been a material religious culture, of course; as Colleen McDannell writes, "Artifacts become particularly important in the lives of average Christians because objects can be exchanged, gifted, reinterpreted, and manipulated. People need objects to help establish and maintain relationships with supernatural characters, family, and friends."[111] Yet, religious brand cultures are not simply about the commodification of religion into discrete products and services. Rather, branding religion signals a deeper structure to the organizing of religious institutions and congregations, where economic exchange not only is a way to get a religious message heard but also forms the basis for understanding religion and spirituality.[112]

Part of this branding process requires a commercial identity, of course. The teen retail store C28 (for Colossians 2:8; "Not of this world") features a banner across its website: "Not just a brand, it's a lifestyle." The mission of the store, which sells apparel for Christian teens, is "to glorify God by sharing the life changing gospel message of grace, truth and love found only in Jesus Christ through prayer, evengelism [sic] and God's written word on apparel."[113] The vision of the store is "to run a profitable and growing business that provides the finances required to preach the gospel!" C28, like other religious retail stores, is an example of the ways in which religion branding authorizes the use of strategies of capitalism, as long as there is an accompanying public disavowal of the ethos of capitalism. To reach these ends, C28 sells items of clothing to young men and women that have religious messages emblazoned across them, capitalizing on a growing industry of Christian T-shirts for a young, hip consumer base.

As Daniel Radosh writes about this burgeoning industry, T-shirts "are the uniform in which evangelicals under thirty suit up for battle, and the companies that make them are constantly scrambling to come up with slogans and designs that appeal to today's youth, generally to embarrassing effect: 'God is my DJ'; 'Jesus has skills'; 'I'm like totally saved.'"[114] Some T-shirts sold at C28 are more overt in their ideological message: a black T-shirt for girls states in stark white letters, "Abortion Is Murder"; another bold red T-shirt features the silhouette of Ronald Reagan, with the quote "I've noticed that everybody who is for abortion has already been born." Others capitalize on the importance of music in the life of teens, so that religious T-shirts resemble concert shirts: "Jesus Tour" (first stop, Galilee); or "Jesus Is Jealous for Me . . . He Loves Like a Hurricane." Still others tap into a contemporary hipster style, using nostalgia and irony as a way to brand religion: one T-shirt features the iconic image of Rosie the Riveter from a World War II poster that proclaims "We Can Do It!," which became a kind of visual anthem for female empowerment both during and after the war. In the C28 version, however, the words are changed from "We Can Do It!" to "I Can Do All Things through Christ," not only changing the broader political message of the original image but also, and importantly, changing the "We" to "I," thus changing the entire tenor of the iconic statement from one of collectivity to one of individualism.

Other products sold at C28 are hard to distinguish as religious at all, tapping into contemporary styles and motifs—until one notices the brand logo on a T-shirt that says "NOTW," for "Not of This World" (referencing the biblical text that proclaims that Jesus does not walk on this Earth). The website resembles most other retail sites, such as those for the Gap or Urban Outfitters, by depicting images of merchandise complete with sizes, colors, and instructions to "add it to my shopping cart." T-shirts are featured alongside "layering tanks" and toe rings that say "Walk with Jesus." Additionally, the C28 website advertises religious events alongside ministries and requests users who want to be "saved" to email the company. Indeed, the company claims that more than "16,173 have come to faith with Jesus while at C28 stores" (with no explanation of the methodology they used in coming up with this number).

"I Like Jesus" T-shirt

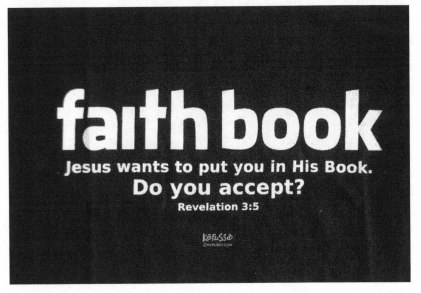

"Faithbook." T-shirt

"Holy Spirit" T-shirt

Christian music for teens is another burgeoning industry. Christianity has long had a staple of rock bands offering more or less explicitly religious messages, but in recent years the umbrella category of contemporary Christian music (CCM) has expanded beyond the rock genre to encompass punk, reggae, folk, pop, and rap. In 2006, Americans spent more than $720 million on CCM, and sales have increased 80 percent since 1995.[115] Part of the reason for this increase in sales is not that more people have become religious but that the boundaries between Christian music and mainstream pop music are more and more difficult to discern. In the 1970s and 1980s, Christian rock was produced as a "safe" alternative to the apparent evils of mainstream rock, solidifying CCM as a discrete genre. During the 1990s and early 2000s,

"Sacrificed for Me" T-shirt.

however—the era in which brand cultures begin to become normative—this boundary was slowly eroded (signaled, in one of many examples, by the Christian band Sixpence None the Richer's mainstream 1997 hit, "Kiss Me"). As Heather Hendershot has pointed out, more and more Christian brands are seeking to break through to a mainstream audience, desiring less a niche market of clearly identified Christians than a more diffused community branded around a vague message of faith.[116]

Other Christian products similarly blur these boundaries in ways that maintain a compartmentalized religious theme, while borrowing visual packaging from mainstream culture. The Christian publishing company Revolve! produces "Biblezines" for young girls, magazines that feature text from the Bible, but in a visual format that so closely resembles fashion magazines such as *Teen Vogue* or *Teen Cosmo* it is difficult to tell the difference.

Difficult, that is, until one gets to the actual text: one magazine, *Psalms and Proverbs*, contains a section on relationships, with the words of Job 21:26–22:24. A sidebar offers these words of advice: "Do date nice guys. Don't go too far on a date." Another sidebar, titled "Blab," is styled after advice columns, with questions and answers. One question is: "My mom doesn't want me learning about condoms and sex in school. But we never talk about it at home either. How am I supposed to learn anything?" Among other things, the answer suggests discussing this issue with one's pastor or preacher, as well as a vague (and ironically maternal) admonition: "Christians are supposed to keep their bodies pure. That doesn't mean their minds should remain ignorant." It is not simply, then, the visual packaging of Biblezines that resembles commercial fashion magazines but the actual structure of the magazines, with their staples of "Dos and Don'ts" features and advice columns, which mirror teen magazines.

While these and other examples are part of a broader commodification of religion, they are also part of the way in which religion is branded in contemporary culture. The plethora of religious products available in the contemporary marketplace and the ways in which these products are packaged and distributed in formats and distribution channels shared by other commodities testify to the normalization of religious branding. It is perhaps the ultimate proof of the power of the brand that religious products are no longer a discrete, niche industry but are incorporated into mainstream consumer culture.

Spiritual Capitalism

As is clear within the examples of Prosperity Christianity and New Age spirituality, in thinking through the permeable boundaries between secular and religious worlds in the contemporary US, it is necessary to connect the ways people understand and experience religion with broader historical shifts within culture, politics, and economics. Recall that part of what prompted Putnam's discussion of the deterioration of civil society was the declining attendance at religious institutions. But it is not that people simply stopped going to church because of a sudden lack of faith. In contemporary US culture, a constellation of ideological factors have doubtless contributed to this decline, including a global spiritual marketplace, dominant ideologies of "personal choice" and individualism, and a reimagined understanding of the US Constitution's freedom of religion. The "unregulated market" for religion in the US is encouraged by the country's most basic rules about the free exercise and establishment of religion, as well as about the definition of religious

Biblezines for girls: Revolve! The Complete New Testament.

institutions as tax-exempt corporations (though both of these are also *regulating* discourses, even if the result of such regulation is to ensure equal competition among religions).

In many cases, the traditional moral framework of religions has, in the 21st century, been retooled and reimagined as a definition of morality particular to advanced capitalism, one that is understood through the logic of the market. The contemporary market does not pose a challenge, or a disruption, to religious and spiritual practices but rather makes possible the realization and communication of these practices. Recall Raymond Williams's "structures of feeling," which he described as lived experiences of the quality of life in a particular time and place, experiences that are "as firm and definite as 'structure' suggests, yet . . . [operate] in the most delicate and least tangible part of our activities."[117] The current branding of religion represents a structure of feeling, where the structure of economics, business, and marketing enables the production of particular practices and artifacts within religion and spirituality, those "least tangible parts" of our everyday activities.

One of religion's uses has been to make the unpredictable world feel predictable and safe. The importance of culture in attempting to build predictability into an unpredictable system such as entrepreneurial capitalism and a global economy is undeniable and is demonstrated powerfully through the branding of religious practices, where faith, belief, and affect are newly understood as particular kinds of products. The role religion has historically played as an authoritative moral voice in society has not changed wholesale, then, but has shifted shape, as the definition of morality itself has shifted shape within neoliberal culture, so that morality is understood as prioritizing the interior, how individuals care for the self, rather than external factors, such as collective good. The question of who benefits from the branding of religion is part of this reimagined sense of morality: in branded forms of religion and spirituality such as Prosperity Christianity and New Age spirituality, the conservative religious right, for example, benefits far more clearly than racialized and exoticized constituencies. Together, these entangled communities and discourses build religious brand culture.

Thus, the brands of religion and spirituality constitute cultural spaces in the 21st century for the promotion of particular values—those that are tethered to consumerism and advanced capitalism. Individual entrepreneurship within religion, authorized by its normalization in other cultural realms (such as the crafting of self-identities, creative production, and political brands) is increasingly understood as the only way to build congregations (and thus funding). Unlike some of the other cultural formations that have been branded as a result of neoliberal global capitalism that I examine in this book, religion has had the infrastructure to be branded for hundreds of years, yet the branding of religion takes hold when brand culture more generally starts to become normative. Religious cultures are organized in contemporary culture around brand logic—the use of social media, the understanding of congregations as audience demographics, the adoption of marketing strategies by evangelical preachers, the connection between conservative political ideologies and religious ones, the infrastructure of educational institutions that promote "Christian free enterprise," the use of an exoticized, mystical "East" as a way to harness economics to spirituality—a brand logic that increasingly makes sense not only to religious leaders but also to congregations.

Making religion "relevant" in a global media context is the challenge for current evangelicals, and relevancy means, among other things, making a normative connection between religious practices and brand culture. While there are religious detractors who argue that branding cheapens the message of God and crassly commercializes faith and belief, the contemporary understanding of branding as a story, a narrative in which authentic relationships are built between corporations and individuals, animates a startlingly broad swath of contemporary religion. As religious marketing consultant Phil Cooke (his team "gets hired when a church or ministry has lost their voice")[118] argues in his book *Branding Faith,* at a media-saturated moment, when a variety of voices are positioned as authoritative, Christianity needs "to dramatically change the way we publicly *express* [Christian] belief. A critical key to accomplishing that goal is *branding.*"[119] Cooke positions religion like other advertising messages, as one of many within the constant clutter of media messages people in the US are exposed to on a daily basis. Part of that positioning has meant a constant movement between and within the boundaries of the secular and religious worlds, and it is precisely this porousness of boundaries that allows branding to become normative. In other words, the fact that there is not simply a bounded commercial world in which branding strategies and practices reside but rather a moving boundary, a constantly shifting terrain, allows evangelicals with "weak or no denominational ties" to become religious and business leaders, with powerful personal brands. The notion that individuals, including religious leaders, are "free agents," and that religion is a particular kind of marketplace, is important for convincing a religious public that the best way to make religion relevant is to brand it, to construct brand cultures around churches in ways similar to the brand cultures around companies such as Apple or Starbucks.

The cultivation of media savvy is a recent innovation in the ongoing effort to give religion a mass appeal. From 19th-century print and radio technologies to the niche cable television market of the 1970s and 1980s, where televangelists could have their "own" channels, evangelists have long explored new media environments. In the 21st century, this innovation extends to live streaming video online and posts on YouTube, the ultimate expression of

one's "own" channel. In a digital media context with an ethos of individualism and entrepreneurialism that favors consumer-generated content, and
where individuals can have their own channel on YouTube, it is not just the
message of the gospel that is customized but also the way users receive it. As
branding becomes normative for all "products," including the self, it makes
sense within this logic for branding to be the mechanism by which religion
seeks to make itself relevant to the current population.

CONCLUSION

THE POLITICS OF AMBIVALENCE

One of the reasons I became so interested in brand culture is because of a personal investment. A few years ago, my then eight-year-old daughter and her friend posted a silly video of themselves on YouTube. My initial shock and dismay at having an image of my daughter displayed on a global video site soon transmuted into another sort of shock. Each day for several weeks, my daughter came home from school and immediately checked on "how many hits" she had. After watching my daughter's newfound compulsion, I began thinking deeper about the connections between visibility, consumer participation (such as making and then posting a video of oneself), and brands (such as YouTube).

While my work has often focused on the media economy of visibility, this need for personal visibility felt different, and it inspired me to delve deeper into amateur videos posted on YouTube. Certainly YouTube is a media site that fosters creative production, but it also cannot be separated from a general media economy of visibility and recognition. The gendered politics of this economy, where, as I argued in chapter 2, the stakes for girls and young women to "put themselves out there" are differently organized than for men, especially troubled me in this personal context.

It also became clear that the media economy of visibility is intimately tied to the discourses of "everyone is creative" and "everyone is an entrepreneur" that are crucial to the formation of brand cultures. The professional lifecasters I discuss in this book, such as iJustine, occupy a completely different part of the online video economy than young girls singing into their hairbrushes, joyously dancing in their bedrooms. Yet the two kinds of videos *look the same*—both are posted on YouTube, both have a similarly formatted URL, both have comments evaluating the performances. They *feel* as if they are part of the same system. And it is this structure of feeling that needs to be considered when examining the wide and varied ambivalences and assemblages of brand cultures. There are thousands of videos of young girls dancing, and only a few spaces for career iJustines. But both are mobilized and authorized by a discourse of "everyone is creative."

The world of branding is both more obvious and more complex than I initially thought. Brand cultures are more than cultural practices and artifacts. They are made, and remade, by both brand intermediaries and consumers. For instance, one of the first interviews I conducted while researching this book was with Rob Stone, cofounder of the New York–based marketing firm Cornerstone, which focuses on hip, urban, "under-the-radar" marketing. Eager to hear what industry professionals had to say about how to sell new trends, I approached this interview with what I considered a healthy dose of cynicism about the contemporary political economy. Yet, Stone's account of how he felt branding should work was unexpected. He related an interesting history of "engagement" marketing: he began his career in the traditional music industry during the 1990s, when the industry was booming, and, as he said, "everyone was making money." Stone and his partner, Jon Cohen, were successful in giving individual bands a marketing signature and decided to expand their efforts into brands. From the beginning, Cornerstone branded under-the-radar music—indie bands, emerging hip-hop artists. In a prescient move, the marketing firm focused on the Internet, which in the 1990s was not yet recognized as a productive place for branding. By utilizing digital media, Cornerstone found a way to put brands in spaces not yet discovered by its competitors. It also relied on more traditional media and conventional strategies, such as creating CD compilations featuring new bands and sending the CDs to DJs, who played them in underground clubs in urban cities such as New York and Los Angeles. Using both conventional and nonconventional marketing strategies, Cornerstone was developing not only its own brand but also an effective brand strategy and logic.

Of course, we can read this narrative as a sophisticated spin on ever-encroaching capitalist markets, and indeed, Stone was unapologetic about his commitment to the development of more complex and engaged marketing strategies. He felt strongly about what these strategies should look like, arguing that the basis for contemporary branding is transparency and authenticity, that marketers should "never try to trick the consumer."[1] The key to branding in the contemporary moment, he said, involved several intersecting practices: keep branding scalable, real, and three-dimensional. Branders needed to utilize multimedia platforms as a way to activate "real" people as a market, instead of relying on industry-produced statistics or imagined audiences. Branding, he said, was about deep integration, one that has circular logic: the integration of brands into culture, tapping into and extending culture that brands are already creating. So, brand intermediaries that sponsor free concerts for up-and-coming bands, or compile CDs to give to DJs to play at clubs, create a brand culture, one that is also simultaneously made and remade by consumers who go to the concert or listen to the music.[2] Given that historically marketing and advertising have been understood primarily as economic mechanisms, this insistence on the importance of culture was—to my cynical eyes—a radical move.

Indeed, I was taken aback by the sheer variety of practices with which Cornerstone was involved: promotion of independent artists, renewal of urban neighborhoods, free concerts for kids. I was also intrigued by the philosophy of the firm. Stone argued that successful (measured both financially and culturally) brands are built organically, that branders are *curators* of content. My cynicism around consumer culture and marketers stemmed from my assumption that commercial culture is about *selling* lived experience, not actually *being* lived experience. To this, Stone responded that in the contemporary moment one could have authentic lived experience and sell it at the same time, but nontraditional methods are needed.

As I came away from this interview, the ambivalence, rather than the economic determinism, of brand cultures stuck with me. Some brand managers, I would soon learn, are passionate about what they see as the possibility of politics within consumer capitalism. Stone and other brand managers like him see themselves as performing an alternative service from capitalist business as usual. They do not see themselves as anticapitalist; rather, their positions are more utopian. In other words, the brand managers I spoke with were invested in working within the system of capitalism, not overthrowing it. In this sense they understood cultural practices that take shape within shifted forms of capitalism—such as political activism or artistic creativity—as a utopian project.

Now, after several years of talking about and researching this book, two questions emerge most often: where I might locate possibility within brand culture, and whether alternative brands are possible. As I discuss throughout *Authentic™*, brands by definition strive to cultivate relationships with consumers, relationships that have at their core "authentic" sentiments of affect, emotion, and trust. Brand cultures attempt to cultivate a faith in consumers as to what brands might accomplish, a faith that despite convictions that everything is for sale, brand culture might enhance possibilities for individual identities, cultural practices, everyday politics. As for the possibility of alternative brands, the answer to this is not the now-common corporate practice of attaching hip, progressive symbols, icons, and even politics to mainstream brands, such as Target selling T-shirts featuring the iconic image of Che Guevara, or even the clothing company American Apparel selling shirts emblazoned with "Free L.A." as an effort to bring public attention to immigrant rights in Los Angeles. As Stone reminded me, brand logic and strategies are often used in ways that do not simply further a neoliberal project of individualism and prioritizing corporate profit.

To take one example of this, Adam Werbach, whom I discussed in chapter 4, resigned from the Sierra Club to work for a new sustainability department at Wal-Mart. There is certainly a great deal to criticize about Wal-Mart in terms of its labor practices, gender and race politics, and politics of exclusion, not to mention its dedication to Christian "free enterprise," as I discuss in chapter 5. The fact that these critiques are valid does not, however, invalidate the way in which the corporation has built a significant culture around green branding. Green branding in general has sparked debate and critique about environmental awareness and thus has an ambivalent impact outside, and in addition to, the economic and cultural capital accumulated by companies that have "gone green."

Thinking about possibility within brand cultures might also mean taking Banksy seriously in, say, his collaboration with *The Simpsons,* which I discuss in chapter 3. While certainly his presence on the popular television show helped build his own brand, it also called attention to Fox's labor practices (as well as those of other corporations) with exploited labor and support of sweatshops. Did Banksy's presence on *The Simpsons* change these labor practices? Perhaps not; as I have argued, the articulation of critique, or of subversion, is often co-opted and displaced within brand cultures. But its *function*—calling attention to inequities in global labor practices—remains subversive of power.

It is too sweeping and, frankly, moralistic to merely dismiss these affective feelings of authenticity as either corporate ruses or simply symptoms of neoliberal capitalist culture. That is, as became clear to me when talking to marketers, while it is tempting to situate branding strategies as determined to "capture" an audience, it is selling culture short if we think it is so easily, and simply, destroyed. Much of contemporary capitalism *is* about capturing minds and dollars, but there are always loose threads, and culture is shaped by this kind of incongruity. We are not going to turn back the clock on consumer capitalism—indeed, most people in the US would not want to. But does that mean we are in a forced march toward corporate co-optation? Or can we imagine a trajectory that is not linear, that twists and turns, that does not follow the predetermined path of a branding cycle, a cycle that necessarily ends up wholly in the service of advanced capitalism? As I have demonstrated throughout this book, brand culture is neither a historical inevitability nor uncontested. On the contrary, brand cultures emerge from the deeply interrelated discourses and practices of capitalism, history, culture, technology, and individual identity formation. Because brands form culture, they are—like culture itself—often unstable and precarious.

Consumer capitalism is a nuanced, multilayered context for identity formation—as such, it is an explicitly *cultural* space. The brand intermediaries, such as Rob Stone, are part of this culture—and so are consumers. Recalling Raymond Williams, culture is "ordinary," built by people, and by living both alongside and within the relations of production.[3] Brand managers often set the terms for brand cultures, but because brand culture is deeply cultural, it relies on the labor of consumers—"ordinary" people, creative producers, artists, laborers—as well as brand managers. David Hesmondhalgh reminds us that while attention to "immaterial labor" is important when thinking through the multiple strategies and engagements of contemporary capitalism and consumers, it is just as important to think through the concept of "labor" itself and to remember that all labor does not exploit in the same ways. I discuss "immaterial" or free labor throughout this book, but some practices of "free labor" might also include rewards for such work, such as contributing to projects that are for social good, or "in the form of finding solutions to problems and gaining new skills which could [be applied] later in other contexts."[4] It is true that participating in brand cultures often furthers the building of the brand, and thus adds to the coffers of the corporate owner of the brand. But it is also true that consumers may benefit—as in working toward a common goal or forming a networked public—in and through the building of brand cultures.

Consider again the Dove Real Beauty Campaign discussed in chapter 1. This campaign furthered the Dove brand but also facilitated the emergence of a networked public or a community, formed around a common interest of

"healthy self-esteem." The relationship between the consumers who participate in the Dove campaign and the Dove brand is structured by ambivalence;
individual consumers are part of building a kind of collective politics while
these same collective politics are authorized by the brand itself. Consumers
feel safe, secure, and relevant in brand cultures. This does not necessarily
imply "an assignation with inauthenticity."[5] Rather, we should think about
why safety, security, and relevance are experienced so profoundly within the
spaces of brand culture and think about those spaces as a place to address
questions such as: Why does it make sense for Dove to create ads that directly
critique the beauty industry? How is participating in this brand community
"living" ambivalence? Is this a productive interaction with ambivalence? Perhaps. Even while I was analyzing the Dove video "Onslaught" for the way in
which it instantiates the brand ever more firmly for the consumer, the video's
tagline—"Talk to your daughter before the beauty industry does"—resonated with my own convictions about the value of critique. More than that,
the video sparked a larger cultural conversation in social media: Greenpeace
made a parody video ("Onslaught(er)") detailing the devastation of the rain
forests that occurs in the manufacture of Dove products; other parodies of
the video were produced that critique and comment on the campaign; the
blogosphere exploded with commentary about the Real Beauty campaign;
and countless undergraduates, no doubt, wrote papers on the video for gender and media classes.

Healthy self-esteem for girls is a "brandable" commodity—which does
not negate the gender politics that are challenged through and within the
Dove campaign. Rather, the ambivalence of the Dove Campaign for Real
Beauty is one example of a reimagining or repositioning of older forms of
community. This requires our attention not because it means that all people
are manipulated as products within brand culture but more because of what
this reimagining does in terms of excluding and discounting other possibilities. The Dove campaign mobilized a broad cultural conversation about the
contradictions within the beauty industry and directed our attention to how
these contradictions can have serious consequences. Yet it did not confront
some of the structural issues that shape the market for girls' self-esteem, such
as a heightened cultural significance on visibility and the physical body, or
the privileging of personal fulfillment as a means to establish community
with others.

Dove, Wal-Mart, and Banksy accumulate cultural capital from their
branding efforts, which then assists in the building of brand cultures around
the companies and artist. But because brand cultures are *cultures,* there is
a flexibility of movement within their spaces, an unpredictability to their

articulation, a potential for destabilization. For *The Simpsons* to move in the direction of critiquing its host network's labor practice, or for Dove to call attention to the ways the beauty industry capitalizes on girls' and women's insecurities, or for Wal-Mart to dedicate funds to green efforts not only potentially precludes direct financial profit but also involves risk. These kinds of risks are not normative for all corporations (either because they literally cannot afford to, or because ideologically it is not in their best interests to venture too far from a more instrumental market logic of advertising, marketing, and profit accumulation). Yet, ambivalence is found within the spaces where risks are taken.

Though it is clear that not all corporations will take risks, the discourse of "freedom" within advanced capitalism romanticizes risk itself and thus obscures the varied sorts of productions that emerge from its context. The mantra of advanced capitalist freedom that I have detailed throughout this book—everyone is creative, everyone is entrepreneurial, everyone is an activist—is a crucial dynamic in the contemporary era of brand cultures. Yet the term "everyone" works as an actor on an ostensibly equal playing field. As I argued with the example of iJustine, the discourse of "everyone is creative" actually means *not* everyone but only those who are provided with specific opportunities, whether these opportunities are tied to identities, such as racialized or gendered identities, or material conditions, such as socioeconomic class or access to technology. The politics, practices, and identities that are not easily or even possibly branded represent what might be called the surplus value that emerges from contemporary brand culture.

To address the question of surplus value as it is present in brand cultures, it is helpful to return to Marx's definition. Marx theorized surplus value as the accumulation of profit by corporations off the backs of laborers who saw none of the profit, and who were themselves considered surplus value. In advanced capitalism, we need to think more carefully about the surplus of individuals, of consumers, who craft relationships with the ambivalence of brands, and who might be out of reach of the discourse of "everyone is creative." Current brand culture involves the labor of consumers but also, and perhaps especially, the labor of consumers as producers. I mean this not in the way of a celebration of the "prosumer," or as a statement of newfound consumer empowerment. Rather, I mean that we need to carefully attend to the ways in which the production and consumption of culture within the logic of branding involve not only those practices that are easily branded but also those who build cultures that are not immediately amenable to branding.

Brand cultures, I have argued, are structured by ambivalence. The question, though, is to figure out how affect and emotion are manifest in these everyday politics, and how ambivalence is discernible in cultural practices. Connecting ambivalence to actual praxis is a difficult thing and has no guarantees. For one thing, most elements of culture are *not* seen as ambivalent. Ambivalence, its lack of certainty, its inconsistency, the way it both harbors and is defined by doubt, is generally understood as a problem, something to avoid. Yet, it is important to take seriously the cultural value of emotion and affect and the *potential* of ambivalence, its generative power, for it is within these spaces that hope and anxiety, pleasure and desire, fear and insecurity are nurtured and maintained. Brand marketers realize the potential of ambivalence and capitalize on it. But their strategies do not in turn mean that affect and ambivalence are simply, or only, spaces of corporate manipulation. Rather, affect and ambivalence can be utilized in different ways.

The ambivalence of brand cultures, then, is about incongruity—not all brand cultures mean the same thing, either culturally or individually. If, as I have maintained, consumer capitalism demands that we live our lives within brand spaces and subjectivities, we need to think carefully about what this kind of life looks like and, conversely, what potential spaces and actions threaten to disrupt the expected flow of consumption. To theorize ambivalence as a structuring element of brand cultures means not that *all* cultural practices are spaces of possibility but rather that some carry more potential than others, that some cultural practices are easier to brand than others. Those practices that can be integrated within brand relationships, such as girls' self-esteem, environmental politics, or street art, are not evacuated of political possibility, but that possibility itself takes shape within a branded space. When a brand, a genre, or a product circulates in culture, its meaning is ambivalent. In other words, the fact that a brand circulates in culture is not a guarantee of its meaning; rather, the circulating brand is constantly under the threat of breakdown and destabilization. Within brand culture, this threat forms a crucial contradiction: brands are designed for stability, and their logic is based on regularity and singularity. Yet they are ultimately precarious, and are subject to cultural misunderstanding. To theorize brand cultures as subject to misunderstanding and misrecognition is to deliberately hold on to the generative potential of brand cultures.

Lauren Berlant, in her book *The Female Complaint,* develops the idea of "intimate publics," shared spaces that are structured by expectations that the consumers within a given intimate public share a worldview and an emotional connection that is bound together by a common historical experience. Brand cultures are much like "intimate publics," in that they form communities of consumers who are bound together by affect and emotion, and by a sense of authentic experience and history. Like intimate publics, brand cultures are formed within a circular logic: individual consumers who are members of a brand culture have a shared history, and that history is then produced and reproduced not only in the narrative of the brand but also in its tangible objects (such as a video of oneself, or street art). This history is then maintained and expanded as people participate and create in brand culture. As Berlant describes an intimate public, through "expressing the sensational, embodied experience of living as a certain kind of being in the world, it promises also to provide a better experience of social belonging—partly through participation in the relevant commodity culture, and partly because of its revelations about how people can live."[6] Brand cultures exceed the products they represent and, through this excess, offer community to individuals that assures affective connection with others as well as with themselves. Individuals often feel "held" by the intimacy of a brand culture: participating in brand cultures feels like participating in an ethical or moral frame, and they offer the "ongoing potential for relief from the hard, cold world."[7] This affective sentiment, the feeling of authenticity, often does the cultural work of an inducement, attracting and retaining consumers as loyal members of a brand culture. Individual consumers trust the affective knowledge offered by brand cultures, even as they are aware that brand marketers carefully cultivate this trust, even when this knowledge is recognized by consumers as "irrational" or "emotional."

Indeed, this kind of internal contradiction is key to ambivalence; this kind of ambivalence is an *expectation* of brand culture—it defines brand cultures as much as singularity and regularity. The way in which brands nurture a politics of ambivalence is vital; the spaces that consumers open up by contesting regularity and singularity are those that utilize the dynamics of neoliberal capitalism in unpredictable and unexpected ways. Berlant argues that within popular culture, ambivalence "is seen as a failure of a relation, the opposite of happiness, rather than as an inevitable condition of intimate attachment and a pleasure in its own right."[8] Like Berlant, I see ambivalence as potentially innovative, not a foreclosure but as a possible opening. The meaning that individuals create through consumption often extends beyond a general immediate economic goal, so that the relationship between consumers and producers is often not as predictable as marketers would like—or as they may profess.

The idea that ambivalence is generally understood as a "failure of a relation" continues to have sway in ongoing cultural debates about artists, creative industries, politicians, and others "selling out" in culture. The creative labor by consumers and brand intermediaries necessary to build brand cultures should be understood as a coexistence and intersection between creative activity and exploitation. For instance, in February 2011, the *Wall Street Journal* published "Branding WikiLeaks," about a new branding endeavor. In the story, Jeanne Whelan detailed the efforts to brand the information website WikiLeaks and its founder, Julian Assange, a few months after the site released highly classified government documents to a global public. The German merchandising company Spreadsheet AG (which has previously been involved in marketing the Spice Girls and other pop groups) "is at the center of a burgeoning branding empire based largely on Mr. Assange's status as a nascent outlaw icon."[9] While the article states that proceeds from the WikiLeaks merchandise go toward maintaining the website and paying Mr. Assange's legal fees (he was at the time fighting extradition to Sweden based on sexual assault charges), it also discusses the business potential of the WikiLeaks brand. Spreadsheet AG is quoted as saying that the WikiLeaks brand has "better than average" sales potential because "WikiLeaks is an emotional proposition: People love it or hate it. For those that love it and wish to show support for WikiLeaks by wearing a T-shirt, it is a good proposition." Other branding experts challenge this by invoking the discourse of "selling out." As one marketer cited in the article states, "Turning that into a global brand...sounds a lot more like cashing in with the general establishment rather than being subversive."[10] The specter of "selling out," or in this case "cashing in," and its subsequent undermining of authenticity haunts all brand endeavors, as the notion that authenticity cannot easily exist within the space of corporate profit continues to have public and cultural currency.

To traverse boundaries of different economies, market and nonmarket, profit-oriented or reciprocal, means not to jump from one "side" of a neoliberal divide to the other, one a space of authenticity, the other one of complicity, as the discourse of "selling out" implies. The WikiLeaks website challenges the history of "official" information and the public's right to access this information; the leaked documents have already disrupted routines of national security around the globe. Regardless of where it goes from here, WikiLeaks *is* subversive. And the branding of this subversion is, as the marketer cited earlier points out, "an emotional proposition." WikiLeaks is "brandable" because it inspires affect and emotion from individuals, needed to create a relationship between the branding company and consumers. The traversing of boundaries involved in branding WikiLeaks is not about whether the branding process transforms or taints WikiLeaks, but is an articulation of a politics of ambivalence, which enables the site to be potentially subversive even as it is branded as a consumer product.

The politics of ambivalence within brand cultures are found in this kind of excess of meaning—who, and what, is left out of brand messages, and who or what exceeds brand logic?[11] Does the subversiveness of the WikiLeaks site surpass the transformation of it into a brand? This is an indication of what Berlant notes as a "confidence in the critical intelligence of affect, emotion, and good intention," which in turn produces a kind of individual agency that is often imaginative and ambivalent rather than limited and determined.[12] Authenticity and conventionality are intimate bedfellows, not contradictions.

My questions in this book, and my focus on the politics of ambivalence, have been directed at thinking of brand cultures as specific utopian spaces. Berlant argues that utopianism "is in the air, but one of the main utopias is normativity itself, here a felt condition of general belonging and an aspirational site of rest and recognition in and by a social world."[13] Brand culture is a foundation for a kind of utopic normativity. What that means is not that we should uncritically accept the felt condition of general belonging that emerges from normative brand culture but that we need to carefully consider the power dynamics that create normativity in the first place. Individuals may indeed be "empowered" through their participation within brand cultures, but if this empowerment is directed toward normativity because they desire the "utopic" feeling of belonging, what is its value? That is, the normativity of brand cultures more often than not reinscribes people back within neoliberal capitalist discourse rather than empower them to challenge or disrupt capitalism.

Brands are slippery, mobile, which makes them both difficult to accurately predict and explain and also powerful as cultural products. But rather than moralize about the luxury of risk taking, it makes more sense to historicize this dynamic and situate it within an entangled set of discourses, haphazardly arranged, never sitting still, opening up spaces of ambivalence. Brand cultures are different, with varied possibilities and constraints. In that spirit, brand cultures carry within themselves the generative potential of ambivalence.

NOTES

NOTES TO INTRODUCTION

1. Maurice Blanchot, *The Writing of the Disaster*, trans. Ann Smock (Lincoln: University of Nebraska Press, 1986), 60.

2. The film received critical acclaim, winning the Prix Kodak at the Cannes Film Festival in 2009 and the award for Best Animated Short Film at the Eighty-Second Academy Awards in 2010.

3. Quote from "H5: Logorama," *designboom*, accessed February 8, 2010, http://www.designboom.com/weblog/cat/8/view/7079/h5-logorama.html.

4. The research in this book involved talking to marketers, advertisers, and brand managers and investigating new forms of brand strategies tailored to the early 2000s in the US. Over the past four years, I have interviewed people specifically involved in "engagement marketing" to youth cultures, a form of marketing that extends beyond conventional advertising into new technologies (such as YouTube videos and Facebook pages), different genres (such as creating CD compilations for radio stations and short DVDs on popular cultural events), and one that relies heavily on consumer-generated content. My interviews were not limited to engagement marketers, however. I also interviewed brand marketers who were recruited to brand cities and discussed with them the various practices involved in creating urban environments around the logic of branding (such as "theming" cities as particular kinds of places—who knew that Phoenix is a "desert oasis"?). I directed a research group with a focus on branding over three years, where we had a variety of brand marketers come to talk to the group about what branding looks like in the contemporary moment. I also conducted a mini-ethnography, in which I "worked" at a major advertising firm in Los Angeles for two weeks and interviewed marketers and branders from leadership to entry-level employees. And, over the course of the past four years, I participated in dozens of seminars, meetings, and focus groups at the Annenberg School at the University of Southern California with branders and marketers regarding new practices of marketing in 21st-century culture.

5. Liz Moor, *The Rise of Brands* (Oxford: Berg, 2007).

6. Ibid.; Celia Lury, *Brands: The Logos of the Global Economy* (New York: Routledge, 2004); Naomi Klein, *No Logo: No Space, No Choice, No Jobs* (New York: Picador, 2000).

7. Moor, *Rise of Brands*, 21.

8. Klein, *No Logo*.

9. Viviana Zelizer, *Economic Lives: How Culture Shapes the Economy* (Princeton: Princeton University Press, 2011), 24.

10. Ibid.

11. Lury, *Brands*.

12. Ibid., 24. See also Adam Arvidsson, *Brands: Value and Meaning in a Media Culture* (New York: Routledge, 2006).

13. Tiziana Terranova, "Free Labor: Producing Culture for the Digital Economy," *Social Text* 18, no. 2 (2000): 33–58.

14. Ibid., 38–39.

15. Political action within brand cultures is inconsistent and often unpredictable, and individual acts of political participation in brand cultures do not necessarily result in cultural resistance. As Stephen Duncombe points out, it is tricky to conflate the consumer use of products—even the "right" use of products—with resistance: "There is a big difference between rereading reality and acting to make it anew. To not recognize this distinction is to confuse the everyday action of making meaning with the much rarer tasks of creation and transformation." Stephen Duncombe, *Dream: Re-imagining Progressive Politics in an Age of Fantasy* (New York: New Press), 15. Marketers are quick, of course, to capitalize on resistance through commodifying it, as Duncombe points out.

16. Raymond Williams, *The Long Revolution* (Peterborough, ON: Broadview Press, 1961), 64.

17. Consider culture in the way of Williams, as the conjunction of two understandings: "to mean a whole way of life—the common meanings; to mean the arts and learning—the special processes of discovery and creative effort." See Raymond Williams, "Culture Is Ordinary," in *Conviction*, ed. Norman Mackenzie (London: MacGibbon and Kee, 1958), 5–6. Culture is "ordinary," Williams insisted, the process and production of everyday life, of individual and collective experience. It is also, as Vicki Mayer reminds us, "a sense of place, its physicality and material environment [and] each place has a history, shaped by struggles over resources and authority." See Vicki Mayer, "My Media Studies, Fifty Years Later," *Television & New Media* 10, no. 1 (2009): 103. Williams, advocating a neo-Marxist concept of "cultural materialism," argued that "a culture must be finally interpreted in relation to its underlying system of production." However, Williams disagreed with Marx in his point that "since culture and production are related, the advocacy of a different system of production is in some way a cultural directive, indicating not only a way of life but new arts and learning" (8).

18. Examining the contemporary moment, in other words, means that we need to, as James Scott has eloquently pointed out, understand how neoliberalism authorizes not just corporate institutions and governments but also individuals to "see like a state." James Scott, *Seeing Like a State: How Certain Schemes to Improve the Human Condition Have Failed* (New Haven: Yale University Press, 1999). As Judith Halberstam has pointed out, "For Scott, to 'see like a state' means to accept the order of things and to internalize them; it means that we begin to deploy and

think with the logic of the superiority of orderliness and it means we erase and indeed sacrifice other more local practices of knowledge, practices, moreover, that may be less efficient, may yield less marketable results, but may also, long term, be more sustaining." See Judith Halberstam, "Beyond Broadway and Main: A Response to the Presidential Address," *American Quarterly* 61, no. 1 (2009): 35. But, importantly, the neoliberal context is also a broader set of ideologies that allows for what Jacques Ranciere calls a "distribution of the sensible," where "seeing like a state" within neoliberalism is conceived of precisely in *antistate terms*, where what is considered "sensible" is understanding the state as the enemy of the people and privileging the individual as the central interlocutor in all areas of life, and where those practices that "may be less efficient, may yield less marketable results" are positioned as the opposite of the sensible, indeed, as pure nonsense. Jacques Ranciere, *The Politics of Aesthetics: The Distribution of the Sensible*, trans. Gabriel Lockhill (London: Continuum, 2004).

19. David Harvey, *A Brief History of Neoliberalism* (Oxford: Oxford University Press, 2005), 3.

20. See Karl Marx, "The German Ideology," in *The Marx-Engels Reader,* ed. Robert Tucker (New York: Norton, 1978); Jean-Jacques Rousseau, *Discourse on the Origin of Inequality* (New York: Createspace, 2010); Henry David Thoreau, *Walden,* introduction by Jonathan Levin (1854; New York: Penguin Classics, 2003). Also see Daniel Miller, *Stuff* (London: Polity Press, 2009), and Andrew Potter, *The Authenticity Hoax: How We Get Lost Finding Ourselves* (New York: Harper, 2010) for discussions.

21. As Webb Keane notes about Thoreau's concept of the authentic, "For Thoreau, the distinction between inner and outer provides ontological support for his individualism, which sees in social relations a threat to personal authenticity. For both Thoreau and Marx, despite their obvious political differences, the misapprehension of material things is not merely a mistake—it has grave consequences. It leads us to invert our values, imputing life to the lifeless and thereby losing ourselves." Webb Keane, "Signs Are Not the Garb of Meaning: On the Social Analysis of Material Things," in *Materiality,* edited by Daniel Miller (Durham, NC: Duke University Press, 2006), 184. Andrew Potter similarly notes that for Rousseau, "Commerce is itself an intrinsically alienating form of social interaction because it takes the direct and natural relation of mutual esteem and replaces it with relationships mediated by stuff. Because commercial transactions are motivated entirely by the desire for private gain, human contact becomes thoroughly instrumentalized." Potter, *Authenticity Hoax,* 21.

22. Lury, *Brands*.

23. Klein, *No Logo*.

24. 24. For more on guerrilla marketing, see Michael Serazio's "Your Ad Here: The Cool Sell of Guerrilla Marketing" (PhD diss., University of Pennsylvania, 2010).

25. Klein, *No Logo*; Kalle Lasn, *Culture Jam: How to Reverse America's Suicidal Consumer Binge—And Why We Must* (New York: William Morrow, 1999); Juliet Schor,

Born to Buy: The Commercialized Child and the New Consumer Culture (New York: Scribner, 2004).

26. See Thomas Frank, *The Conquest of Cool: Business Culture, Counterculture, and the Rise of Hip Consumerism* (Chicago: University of Chicago Press, 1998); Joseph Heath and Andrew Potter, *Nation of Rebels: Why Counterculture Became Consumer Culture* (New York: HarperCollins, 2004); Klein, *No Logo.*

27. Serazio, "Your Ad Here," 296.

28. Henry Jenkins, *Convergence Culture: Where Old and New Media Collide* (New York: NYU Press, 2008); Clay Shirky, *Here Comes Everybody: The Power of Organizing without Organizations* (New York: Penguin, 2009); Yochai Benkler, *The Wealth of Networks: How Social Production Transforms Markets and Freedom* (New Haven: Yale University Press, 2006); also see Heath and Potter, *Nation of Rebels,* for a slightly different twist on the consumer-as-agent perspective.

29. Dan Schiller, *How to Think about Information* (Urbana: University of Illinois Press, 2007); Mark Andrejevic, *iSpy: Surveillance and Power in the Interactive Era* (Lawrence: University Press of Kansas, 2007); danah boyd, "Why Youth (Heart) Social Network Sites: The Role of Networked Publics in Teenage Social Life," in *Youth, Identity, and Digital Media,* ed. David Buckingham (Cambridge: MIT Press, 2008), 119–142; Jenkins, *Convergence Culture*; Jarod Lanier, *You Are Not a Gadget: A Manifesto* (New York: Random House, 2010).

30. Following the lead of social anthropologist Daniel Miller, I resist the (traditional Marxist) idea that material brand culture necessarily mystifies and obscures real relationships between people, arguing instead that relationships between people are often made possible by our relationship with branded commodities (or what Miller calls, more generally, "stuff"). Miller says about the relationship between subjects (individuals) and objects (commodities): "Material culture matters because objects create subjects rather than the other way around....the closer our relationships with objects, the closer our relationships with people." Miller, *Materiality,* 7. Miller makes a philosophical argument about material culture; I similarly argue that commodities do not circulate in the same way in different spheres of life, and that these different patterns of circulation mean that individuals establish relationships with commodities in different ways.

NOTES TO CHAPTER 1

1. A viral video is a film clip that gains popularity through the process of Internet sharing, typically through email or blogs or other media-sharing websites. It has different meanings depending on who is using the term: for instance, marketers often strategize to create campaigns as "viral," so that consumers can circulate advertising messages among themselves. Consumers often circulate messages as "viral" to circumvent marketers.

2. Dove Campaign for Real Beauty, Unilever Corporation, accessed October 21, 2009, http://www.dove.us/#/cfrb.

3. Aside from viewers sharing the video, it has received more than 3 million hits on YouTube.

4. Roopali Mukherjee and Sarah Banet-Weiser, eds., *Commodity Activism: Cultural Resistance in Neoliberal Times* (New York: NYU, 2012).

5. Ibid.

6. Joseé Johnston, "The Citizen-Consumer Hybrid: Ideological Tensions and the Case of Whole Foods Market," *Theory and Society* 37 (2008): 246.

7. Ibid. See also Toby Miller, *The Well-Tempered Self: Citizenship, Culture, and the Postmodern Subject* (Baltimore: Johns Hopkins University Press, 1993).

8. Gary Cross, *An All-Consuming Century: Why Commercialism Won in Modern America* (New York: Columbia University Press, 2000); Johnston, "The Citizen-Consumer"; Jo Littler, *Radical Consumption: Shopping for Change in Contemporary Culture* (Berkshire, UK: Open University Press, 2009).

9. "Dove Home," Unilever Corporation, accessed April 6, 2009, http://www.dove.us.

10. "Dove Campaign for Real Beauty."

11. Michelle M. Lazar, "Entitled to Consume: Postfeminist Femininity and a Culture of Post-Critique," *Discourse & Communication* 3, no. 4 (2009): 317–400.

12. Victoria de Grazia and Ellen Furlough, eds. *The Sex of Things: Gender and Consumption in Historical Perspective* (Berkeley: University of California Press, 1996), 275.

13. Lazar, "Entitled to Consume."

14. Susan Bordo, *Unbearable Weight: Feminism, Western Culture and the Body* (Berkeley: University of California Press, 2003); de Grazia and Furlough, *Sex of Things*; Lynn Spigel, *Make Room for TV: Television and the Family Ideal in Postwar America* (Chicago: University of Chicago Press, 1992).

15. de Grazia and Furlough, *Sex of Things*, 4.

16. Anne McClintock, *Imperial Leather: Race, Gender, and Sexuality in the Colonial Contest* (London: Routledge, 1995).

17. Ibid., 209.

18. Thus, cosmetics were sold to US women as accoutrements of not only femininity but also national identity: "Clothes and cosmetics helped immigrant women define themselves as 'American' and enabled them to compete in the dating game. Similarly, African American cosmetics (especially skin whiteners and hair straighteners) were advertised as 'glorifying our womanhood,' giving dignity of sorts to women stereotyped with racial and rural images." See Cross, *An All-Consuming Century*, 41.

19. Kathy Peiss, "Making Up, Making Over: Cosmetics, Consumer Culture, and Women's Identity," in *The Sex of Things: Gender and Consumption in Historical Culture*, ed. Victoria de Grazia and Ellen Furlough (Berkeley: University of California Press, 1996), 331.

20. See Elaine Tyler May, *Homeward Bound: American Families in the Cold War Era* (New York: Basic Books, 1999); Peiss, "Making Up"; Spigel, *Make Room for TV*; and others.

21. See Stephanie Coontz, *The Way We Never Were: American Families and the Nostalgia Trap* (New York: Basic Books, 1992); George Lipsitz, *The Possessive Investment in Whiteness: How White People Profit from Identity Politics* (Philadelphia: Temple University Press, 1998); Robert Weems, *Desegregating the Dollar: African American Consumerism in the Twentieth Century* (New York: NYU Press, 1998); and others.

22. The history of consumer culture in the US is clearly beyond the scope of a single chapter. The shifts from bourgeois consumption to mass consumption that began in the late 18th century through industrial and political revolutions, the influx of immigrant cultures and the subsequent new consumer communities in the US in the 19th century, the impact of consumer capitalism on class, race, and gender formations in the late 19th century represent just some of crucial transitions and transformations in the relationships between individuals and their consumption habits. See Cross, *An All-Consuming Century*; de Grazia and Furlough, *Sex of Things*.

23. Marita Sturken and Lisa Cartwright, *Practices of Looking: An Introduction to Visual Culture* (New York: Oxford University Press, 2001).

24. Lizabeth Cohen, *A Consumer's Republic: The Politics of Mass Consumption in Postwar America* (New York: Vintage Books, 2003).

25. Sturken and Cartwright, *Practices of Looking*, 274.

26. See Alison J. Clarke, *Tupperware: The Promise of Plastic in 1950s America* (Washington, DC: Smithsonian Institution Press, 1999); Cross, *An All-Consuming Century*; May, *Homeward Bound*; Spigel, *Make Room for TV*.

27. William Boddy, *Fifties Television: The Industry and Its Critics* (Urbana: University of Illinois Press, 1992); Lipsitz, *Possessive Investment*; Spigel, *Make Room for TV*.

28. See, for example, Cross, *An All-Consuming Century*.

29. Coontz, *The Way We Never Were*; Lipsitz, *Possessive Investment*; Roland Marchand, *Advertising the American Dream: Making Way for Modernity, 1920–1940* (Berkeley: University of California Press, 1985); Angela McRobbie, *The Aftermath of Feminism: Gender, Culture and Social Change* (Los Angeles: Sage, 2009); and others.

30. Cross, *An All-Consuming Century*.

31. Bobby Wilson, "Race in Commodity Exchange and Consumption: Separate but Equal," *Annals of the Association of American Geographers* 95, no. 3 (2005): 587–606.

32. Weems, *Desegregating the Dollar*.

33. Daniel J. Boorstin, *The Image: A Guide to Pseudo-events in America* (New York: Vintage Books, 1992); Max Horkheimer and Theodor Adorno, *Dialectic of Enlightenment* (New York: Continuum, 1993); Herbert Marcuse, *One-Dimensional Man* (Boston: Beacon Press, 1964); Dwight MacDonald, *Against the American Grain* (New York: Random House, 1962).

34. Peiss, "Making Up."

35. Weems, *Desegregating the Dollar*; Wilson, "Race in Commodity Exchange."

36. Stephanie Capparell, *The Real Pepsi Challenge: The Inspirational Story of Breaking the Color Barrier in American Business* (New York: Wall Street Journal Books, 2007), xiii.

37. Vance Packard, *The Hidden Persuaders* (New York: D. McKay, 1957).

38. See Cross, *An All-Consuming Century*; see also Ralph Nader, *Unsafe at Any Speed: The Designed-In Dangers of the American Automobile* (New York: Grossman, 1965), for a discussion on these texts and movements.

39. Cross, *An All-Consuming Century*.

40. See also the way that resistant discourses of consumption existed in other forms of popular culture, such as popular fictions, from *MAD* magazine to science fiction, which encouraged skepticism about consumerism and branding.

41. Lazar, "Entitled to Consume."

42. Ibid., 507.

43. Fredric Jameson, *Postmodernism, or, the Cultural Logic of Late Capitalism* (London: Verso, 1991).

44. Cross, *An All-Consuming Century*; Thomas Frank, *The Conquest of Cool: Business Culture, Counterculture, and the Rise of Hip Consumerism* (Chicago: University of Chicago Press, 1997); Joseph Heath and Andrew Potter, *Nation of Rebels: Why Counterculture Became Consumer Culture* (New York: HarperCollins, 2004).

45. Fred Turner, *From Counterculture to Cyberculture: Stewart Brand, the Whole Earth Network, and the Rise of Digital Utopianism* (Chicago: University of Chicago Press, 2006).

46. See, among others, Alice Echols, *Daring to Be Bad: Radical Feminism in America, 1967–1975* (Minneapolis: University of Minnesota Press, 1989); Elana Levine, *Wallowing in Sex: The New Sexual Culture of the 1970s* (Durham, NC: Duke University Press, 2007); Hilary Radner, *Swinging Single: Representing Sexuality in the 60s* (Minneapolis: University of Minnesota Press, 1989).

47. Cross, *An All-Consuming Century*, 167 (emphasis in original); also see Heath and Potter, *Nation of Rebels*.

48. Heath and Potter, *Nation of Rebels*, 3.

49. Marlo Thomas, *Free to Be...You and Me* (New York: Ms. Foundation, 1972).

50. Ads accessed on http://www.tvhistory.tv/1960s-Advertising.htm, June 2010.

51. Of course, *Free to Be . . . You and Me* is a different sort of product than Tampax tampons or Dove soap. People are brought into diverse consumer markets in wide-ranging ways, with products appealing to consumers on multiple levels. The specific practices of production, distribution, and consumption have extensive meanings, and surely when "difference" itself *is* the product, there is not one generalized manner in which to describe the circuit of commodity exchange.

52. Herman Gray, *Watching Race: Television and the Struggle for Blackness* (Minneapolis: University of Minnesota Press, 1995).

53. Steve Classen, *Watching Jim Crow: The Struggles over Mississippi TV, 1955–1969* (Durham, NC: Duke University Press, 2004); Gray, *Watching Race*; Katherine Montgomery, *Target: Prime Time: Advocacy Groups and the Struggle over*

Entertainment Television (Oxford: Oxford University Press, 1989); Sasha Torres, *Black, White, and in Color: Television and Black Civil Rights* (Princeton: Princeton University Press, 2003).

54. Stuart Hall, "Encoding/Decoding," in *Culture, Media, Language: Working Papers in Cultural Studies, 1972–79*, ed. Stuart Hall, Dorothy Hobson, Andrew Lowe and Paul Willis (London: Hutchinson, 1980), 128–138.

55. Celia Lury, *Brands: The Logos of the Global Economy* (London: Routledge, 2004).

56. Sarah Banet-Weiser, Cynthia Chris, and Anthony Frietas, eds., *Cable Visions: Television beyond Broadcasting* (New York: NYU Press, 2007), 4.

57. Joseph Turow, *Breaking Up America: Advertisers and the New Media World* (Chicago: University of Chicago Press, 1998). The emergence of segmented markets does not, however, necessarily represent a profound economic and social transformation for all communities. As Robert Weems, Grace Elizabeth Hale, and others argue, within African American culture, there is no clear distinction between an earlier mass era of undifferentiated marketing and a later more targeted interpellation of citizen consumers; arguably, there is a way in which African Americans have always been a niche market in American consumer culture. Weems, *Desegregating the Dollar*; Grace Elizabeth Hale, *Making Whiteness: The Culture of Segregation in the South, 1890–1940* (New York: Vintage, 1999).

58. Sarah Banet-Weiser, *Kids Rule! Nickelodeon and Consumer Citizenship* (Durham, NC: Duke University Press, 2007).

59. See Banet-Weiser, Chris, and Freitas, *Cable Visions*, 8–9. Cable television was just one result of what Turow calls the "breaking up of America." Turow, *Breaking Up America*. While certainly the cable industry may have set out to move toward greater diversity, this diversity was a category within the limits already set up by broadcast channels, which appealed to broader audiences. Robert Weems, for example, focuses on the cultivation of the African American market during the 1960s and 1970s through a variety of commercial venues, including mass-market magazines such as *Ebony*, Hollywood film, an increased interest in white-owned companies in producing African American personal care products, and moves by white-owned insurance companies to cultivate black policyholders. This shift toward focusing on the "difference" of African Americans from whites, rather than sameness, reflected a larger shift in consumer capital toward separate consumer communities rather than mass consumption. As Weems points out, "Ad campaigns in the early 1960s that sought to promote the image of a racially desegregated society were replaced with attempts to exploit blacks' growing sense of racial pride. The development of the 'soul market' exemplified corporate America's attempt to adapt to African American consumers' political and cultural reorientation." See Weems, *Desegregating the Dollar*, 76. The creation of the "soul market" helped to deliver African Americans to consumer markets in vast numbers, even as it also cultivated white consumption by encouraging white consumers to be "hip" in their taste values. The success in cultivating the African American market led to a new emergence of entertainment and communication

technologies that catered to this market. For instance, the 1970s witnessed the emergence of the blaxploitation film genre, which catered more exclusively to an African American market (though it also prompted many African Americans to protest the extreme racial and gender stereotyping that characterized that genre). Black-owned mass magazines such as *Ebony* and *Essence* thrived in the consumer context of the 1970s and 1980s, with other communication organizations, such as Black Entertainment Television (BET), emerging in 1980 as part of what seemed to be a growing understanding of black consumer communities. As Beretta Smith-Shumade comments: "While the name 'Black Entertainment Television' expressed the network's intention, the company's marketing relied on several circulating discourses for support, including the legacy of the black press to expose white injustices upon blacks, the call for black business ownership, the diversity promise of the cable industry, and the view of representation as a sign of equality. Furthermore, Johnson's [the owner of BET] entrepreneurship and vision developed with knowledge of African Americans' craving for representation and their assumption of capitalism's value for black communities." See Beretta E. Smith-Shumade, "Target Market Black: BET and the Branding of African America," in *Cable Visions: Television beyond Broadcasting*, ed. Sarah Banet-Weiser, Cynthia Chris, and Anthony Freitas (New York: NYU Press, 2007), 178.

60. Smith-Shumade, "Target Market Black," 183.

61. Robert Goldman, Deborah Heath, and Sharon L. Smith, "Commodity Feminism," *Critical Studies in Mass Communication* 8 (1991): 333–351.

62. Lazar, "Entitled to Consume," 506.

63. Henry Jenkins, *Convergence Culture: Where Old and New Media Collide* (New York: NYU Press, 2006).

64. Gustavo Cordosa, unpublished paper, Lisbon, Portugal, July 7, 2011; Manuel Castells, *Communication Power* (New York: Oxford University Press, 2009); Jenkins, *Convergence Culture*.

65. Viviana Zelizer, *Economic Lives: How Culture Shapes the Economy* (Princeton: Princeton University Press, 2011), 19.

66. Denise Shiffman, *The Age of Engage: Reinventing Marketing for Today's Connected, Collaborative, and Hyperinteractive Culture* (Ladera Ranch, CA: Hunt Street Press, 2008), 58.

67. Rosalind Gill, *Gender and the Media* (Malden, MA: Polity Press, 2007), 270; Anita Harris, *Future Girl: Young Women in the Twenty-First Century* (New York: Routledge, 2004); McRobbie, *Aftermath*.

68. Writing about "power femininity" in ads, Michele Lazar characterizes this "knowledge as power" trope within contemporary marketing as an element of consumer-based empowerment: "Although the educational discourse is premised upon asymmetrical power relations between knowledgeable and authoritative experts and novices in need of guidance, empowerment in educational settings is derived from the acquisition of knowledge and skills that enable one to become self-reliant and experts in one's own right." See Lazar, "Entitled to Consume," 509.

69. Adam Arvidsson, *Brands: Meaning and Value in Media Culture* (New York: Routledge, 2006).

70. Maurizio Lazzarato, "Immaterial Labor," in *Radical Thought in Italy: A Potential Politics,* ed. Paolo Virno and Michael Hardt (Minneapolis: University of Minnesota Press, 2006), 132–146.

71. Dan Schiller, *How To Think about Information* (Champaign: University of Illinois Press, 2010).

72. Tiziana Terranova, "Free Labor: Producing Culture for the Digital Economy," *Social Text* 18, no. 2 (2000): 38.

73. The idea that some products and their connection to social change are more "authentic" than others is one that continues to have cultural relevance; in a recent article lamenting the purchase of the organic and eco-friendly beauty product line Burt's Bees, the author tells the story of Burt Shavitz, the company's founder, as one in which the "authentic" creator, despite the evil takeover of his product by Clorox, continues to live in the "wilderness inside a turkey coop without running water or electricity." The juxtaposition between the hypercommerciality of Clorox (which, after all, makes products that destroy the environment) and the Thoreau-inspired "free" life of Burt Shavitz demonstrates the continued cultural significance of "authenticity." See Andrea Whitfill, "Burt's Bees, Tom's of Maine, Naked Juice: Your Favorite Brands? Take Another Look—They May Not Be What They Seem," March 17, 2009, accessed March 18, 2009, http://www.alternet.org/health/131910.

74. Castells, *Communication Power,* 421.

75. Mark Andrejevic, "Watching Television without Pity," *Television & New Media* 9, no. 1 (2008): 24–46.

76. David Harvey, *A Brief History of Neoliberalism* (Oxford: Oxford University Press, 2005), 7.

77. George Yúdice, *The Expediency of Culture: Uses of Culture in the Global Era* (Durham, NC: Duke University Press, 2003).

78. Ibid.

79. Jeremy Rifkin, *The Age of Access: The New Culture of Hypercapitalism, Where All of Life Is a Paid-For Experience* (New York: Tarcher Press, 2001), 4–5.

80. Ibid., 5.

81. Ibid.

82. Personal interviews with brand marketers, from December 2008 to July 2010.

83. Terranova, "Free Labor."

84. See, for instance, Clay Shirky, *Here Comes Everybody: The Power of Organizing without Organizations* (New York: Penguin, 2009); Dan Tapscott and Anthony Williams, *Wikinomics: How Mass Collaboration Changes Everything* (New York: Portfolio Trade, 2010); Jeff Howe, *Crowdsourcing: Why the Power of the Crowd Is Driving the Future of Business* (New York: Crown Business, 2009); and others.

85. Arvidsson, *Brands.*

86. As Terranova points out in her discussion of "free" labor on the Internet, "The Internet does not automatically turn every user into an active producer, and every

worker into a creative subject. The process whereby production and consumption are reconfigured within the category of free labor signals the unfolding of a different (rather than completely new) logic of value, whose operations need careful analysis." See Terranova, "Free Labor," 75.

87. Ibid., 36.

NOTES TO CHAPTER 2

1. "Voyeur Web Site JenniCam to Go Dark," CNN.com, December 10, 2003.
2. "April 14, 1996: JenniCam Starts Lifecasting," Hugh Hart, April 14, 2010, *Wired*, http://www.wired.com/thisdayintech/2010/04/0414jennicam-launches/.
3. "22-Year-Old Natalie Dylan Auctions Virginity Online," *Herald Sun*, January 13, 2009, http://www.heraldsun.com.au/aussie-tops-bids-for-virgins-prize/story-fna7dq6e-1111118552115.
4. "Ebay," http://www.ebay-master.co.uk/what_cant_i_sell_on_ebay.php.
5. Natalie Dylan, "Why I'm Selling My Virginity," *Daily Beast*, January 23, 2009, http://www.thedailybeast.com/articles/2009/01/23/why-im-selling-my-virginity.html.
6. Ibid.
7. Lev Grossman, "Tila Tequila," *Time*, December 16, 2006, http://www.time.com/time/magazine/article/0,9171,1570728,00.html.
8. Ibid.
9. Ibid.
10. Again, I am not implying that Tequila was offering sex through her cultivation of her MySpace persona (her reality program was ostensibly dedicated to "looking for love").
11. Michel Foucault, "Technologies of the Self," in *Technologies of the Self: A Seminar with Michel Foucault*, ed. Luther Martin, Huck Gutman, and Patrick Hutton (Amherst: University of Massachusetts Press, 1988), 18.
12. Michel Foucault, *The Birth of Biopolitics: Lectures at the College de France, 1978–1979* (New York: Palgrave Macmillan, 2008).
13. Angela McRobbie, *The Aftermath of Feminism: Gender, Culture and Social Change* (Thousand Oaks, CA: Sage, 2009); Rosalind Gill, "Postfeminist Media Culture: Elements of a Sensibility," *European Journal of Cultural Studies* 10, no. 2 (2007): 147–166; Anita Harris, *Future Girl: Young Women in the Twenty-First Century* (New York: Routledge, 2004); Yvonne Tasker and Diane Negra, eds., *Interrogating Postfeminism: Gender and the Politics of Popular Culture* (Durham, NC: Duke University Press, 2007). These ideals of postfeminism are similar to the political ideologies I discuss in the previous chapter.
14. Harris, *Future Girl*.
15. In this sense, there is a distinction between interactive technology and the participatory user. In my argument, I use the term "interactive subject" to invoke both technology design and the participation of the user.
16. The general age range of girls and young women that I explore in this chapter is between twelve and twenty.

17. David McNally and Karl D. Speak, *Be Your Own Brand: A Breakthrough Formula for Standing Out from the Crowd* (San Francisco: Berrett-Koehler, 2002), 5.

18. Catherine Kaputa, *U R a Brand! How Smart People Brand Themselves for Business Success* (New York: Nicholas Brealey, 2009), xv.

19. McNally and Speak, *Be Your Own Brand*, 4.

20. See Kaputa, *U R a Brand!*, 209, xvi; McNally and Speak, *Be Your Own Brand*. In his work on neoliberalism, Nick Couldry puts a different spin on this: referencing Marx's notion of the alienation of the self through labor, Couldry theorizes how a similar type of alienation could potentially come from the immaterial labor involved in building the self-brand. By replacing the self with the self-brand, one based in market logic, the self that is a potential site of alienation "because it has an inherent capacity to develop its own projects and voice" is eradicated. See Nick Couldry, *Why Voice Matters: Culture and Politics after Neoliberalism* (London: Sage, 2010), 35. This entrepreneurial self is validated by a popular moralist framework that is articulated as a duty to brand ourselves.

21. McNally and Speak, *Be Your Own Brand*.

22. This insecurity of marketers was clear to me throughout my interviews and observations of contemporary advertising and marketing, where I noted how marketers were constantly scrambling not only to keep pace with new media options but also to engage and interact with increasingly savvy consumers.

23. Foucault, "Technologies of the Self."

24. Andrew Potter, *The Authenticity Hoax: How We Get Lost Finding Ourselves* (New York: HarperCollins, 2010), 165.

25. As Wendy Brown points out, moralism within the current era is often about a "reproachful moralizing sensibility" more than a "galvanizing moral vision." The moralist framework that undergirds self-branding signals this kind of righteousness, where the practice of self-branding in a media economy of visibility invokes a moralism that "would appear to be a kind of temporal trace, a remnant of a discourse whose heritage and legitimacy it claims while in fact inverting that discourse's sense and sensibility." See Wendy Brown, *Politics Out of History* (Princeton: Princeton University Press, 2001), 22–23.

26. Angela McRobbie, "Notes on Postfeminism and Popular Culture: Bridget Jones and the New Gender Regime," in *All about the Girl: Culture, Power and Identity,* ed. Anita Harris (New York: Routledge, 2004), 5.

27. Ibid.

28. Rosalind Gill, "Postfeminist Media Culture: Elements of a Sensibility," *European Journal of Cultural Studies* 10, no. 2 (2007): 147–166.

29. Harris, *Future Girl*, 20.

30. Gill, "Postfeminist Media Culture."

31. Harris, *Future Girl*.

32. A 2009 Nielsen online study confirmed what for most middle-class Americans already is a truism: "Kids are going online in droves—at a faster rate than the general Web population—and are spending more entertainment time with digital

media." The report continues by stating that as of May 2009, the two- to eleven-year-old audience had reached 16 million, or 9.5 percent of the active online universe. Nielson study, "How Teens Use Media," June 2009, http://blog.nielsen.com/nielsenwire/reports/nielsen_howteensusemedia_june09.pdf.

33. See Anastasia Goodstein, *Totally Wired: What Teens and Tweens Are Really Doing Online* (New York: St. Martin's Press, 2007); Kathryn C. Montgomery, *Generation Digital: Politics, Commerce, and Childhood in the Age of the Internet* (Cambridge: MIT Press, 2007); John Palfrey and Urs Gasser, *Born Digital: Understanding the First Generation of Digital Natives* (New York: Basic Books, 2008); Don Tapscott, *Grown Up Digital: How the Net Generation Is Changing Your World* (New York: McGraw-Hill, 2008). Much of the discourse surrounding the Internet focuses, from a range of negative and positive vantage points, on its democratizing potential. There are multiple reasons for why the Internet is understood as a democratizing space: to name but a few, its flexible architecture, the relative accessibility of the technology, the capacities for users to become producers, and the construction of the Internet as participatory culture. See danah boyd, "Why Youth (Heart) Social Network Sites: The Role of Networked Publics in Teenage Social Life," in *Youth, Identity, and Digital Media,* ed. David Buckingham (Cambridge: MIT Press, 2008), 119–142; Jean Burgess and Joshua Green, *YouTube: Online Video and Participatory Culture* (Cambridge, UK: Polity Press, 2009); Manuel Castells, *Communication Power* (New York: Oxford University Press, 2009); Henry Jenkins, *Convergence Culture: Where Old and New Media Collide* (New York: NYU Press, 2008). To these more optimistic characterizations of the Internet, challenges have been launched, especially those focusing on the multitude of ways the market has shaped and continues to shape what content is on the Internet, the labor that produces this content, and the conditions of possibility for future content. See Mark Andrejevic, *iSpy: Surveillance and Power in the Interactive Era* (Lawrence: University Press of Kansas, 2007); Jodi Dean, "Communicative Capitalism: Circulation and the Foreclosure of Politics," in *Digital Media and Democracy: Tactics in Hard Times,* ed. Megan Boler (Cambridge: MIT Press, 2008), 101–122; Dan Schiller, *How to Think about Information* (Champaign: University of Illinois Press, 2006); Tiziana Terranova, "Free Labor: Producing Culture for the Digital Economy," *Social Text* 18, no. 2 (2000): 33–58.

34. For example, Amy Shields Dobson, "Femininities as Commodities: Cam Girl Culture," in *Next Wave Cultures: Feminism, Subcultures, Activism,* ed. Anita Harris (New York: Routledge, 2008), 123–148; Mary Celeste Kearney, *Girls Make Media* (New York: Routledge, 2006); Sharon R. Mazzarella, ed., *Girl Wide Web: Girls, the Internet, and the Negotiation of Identity* (New York: Peter Lang, 2005); Susannah Stern, "Expressions of Identity Online: Prominent Features and Gender Differences in Adolescents' World Wide Web Home Pages," *Journal of Broadcasting and Electronic Media* 48, no. 2 (2004): 218–243.

35. Kearney, *Girls Make Media.*

36. Mark Andrejevic, "Watching Television without Pity: The Productivity of Online Fans," *Television & New Media* 9, no. 1 (2008): 32.
37. See Kearney, *Girls Make Media*, 5. Kathryn Montgomery echoes this notion in her work on youth, digital media, and civic engagement, where she argues, "Interactive technologies have created capabilities that alter the media marketing paradigm in significant ways, extending some of the practices that have already been put in place in conventional media but, more important, defining a new set of relationships between young people and corporations." Montgomery, *Generation Digital*, 26.
38. See Jenkins, *Convergence Culture*; danah boyd, "Social Network Sites as Networked Publics," in *A Networked Self: Identity, Community and Culture on Social Network Sites*, ed. Zizi Papacharissi (New York: Routledge, 2010), 39–58; and others.
39. "I kissed a girl," July 25, 2008, YouTube.
40. Burgess and Green, *YouTube*, 2.
41. Ibid., 6.
42. Ibid., 5.
43. Of course, my focus on girls' postfeminist self-branding on YouTube indicates that I am looking at only one kind of production practice out of the multitudes that take place via digital media and only one subgenre of video that is posted on YouTube. There are many different kinds of girls' media production in online spaces, as well as on YouTube itself, so user interactivity and the space of the Internet as one of possibility need to be analyzed in particular, specific terms.
44. Erica Rand, *Barbie's Queer Accessories* (Durham, NC: Duke University Press, 1995); Lynn Spigel, *Welcome to the Dreamhouse: Popular Media and Postwar Suburbs* (Durham, NC: Duke University Press, 2001).
45. For more on the idea of scripts and technological imagination, see Anne Balsamo, *Designing Culture* (Durham, NC: Duke University Press, 2011).
46. Stern, "Expressions of Identity Online."
47. Andrejevic, "Watching Television without Pity"; Schiller, *How to Think about Information*, 2006.
48. Andrejevic, *iSpy*.
49. Jodi Dean, "Communicative Capitalism: Circulation and the Foreclosure of Politics," *Cultural Politics: An International Journal* 1, no. 1 (2005): 51–74.
50. Ibid.
51. Andrejevic, "Watching Television without Pity."
52. "13 year old Barbie Girls," YouTube.
53. McRobbie, *Aftermath*; Dean, "Communicative Capitalism."
54. See McRobbie, *Aftermath*, for more on this new social arrangement.
55. Kaputa, *U R a Brand!*, xvi.
56. McRobbie (borrowing from Deleuze) situates these processes as "luminosities": "Within this cloud of light, young women are taken to be actively engaged in the production of self. They must become harsh judges of themselves. The visual (and

verbal) discourses of public femininity come to occupy an increasingly spectacular space as sites, events, narratives and occasions within the cultural milieu."
McRobbie, *Aftermath,* 13.

57. Naomi Klein, *No Logo: No Space, No Choice, No Jobs* (New York: Picador, 2000).

58. Jeremy Rifkin, *The Age of Access: The New Culture of Hypercapitalism, Where All
of Life Is a Paid-for Experience* (New York: Tarcher Press, 2001); Jenkins, *Convergence Culture.*

59. Arjun Appadurai, *The Social Life of Things: Commodities in Cultural Perspective*
(Cambridge: Cambridge University Press, 1986). On material culture, see also
Daniel Miller, *Stuff* (Cambridge, UK: Polity Press, 2010).

60. Terranova, "Free Labor," 33–58; Maurizzio Lazzarato, "Immaterial Labor," in
Radical Thought in Italy: A Potential Politics, ed. Paolo Virno and Michael Hardt
(Minneapolis: University of Minnesota Press, 1996), 132–146; Andrejevic, *iSpy.*

61. Lazzarato, "Immaterial Labor," 132.

62. Terranova, "Free Labor," 38.

63. Lazzarato, "Immaterial Labor."

64. Alison Hearn, "Meat, Mask, Burden: Probing the Contours of the Branded Self,"
Journal of Consumer Culture 8, no. 2 (2008): 197–217.

65. Kaputa, *U R a Brand!,* xvi.

66. Lazzarato, "Immaterial Labor."

67. See Laurie Ouellette and James Hay, *Better Living through Reality TV: Television and Post-welfare Citizenship* (Malden, MA: Blackwell, 2008), 9. The rise of
reality television, for instance, in the past several decades is a demonstration of
the normalization of the self-brand, where, as Oullette and Hay discuss, reality
television offers a venue for the entangled discourses of citizenship, visuality, self-
representation, and self-branding. Brenda Weber, in her discussion of makeover
reality television (which promises the transformation of the self), situates the
construction of citizenship within what she calls the "Makeover Nation": "In its
emphasis on progress, its desire to provide access to restricted privileges, and
its insistence on a free-market meritocracy, the project of citizenship imagined
across the makeover genre comes deeply saturated with Americanness and this,
in turn, imports neoliberal ideologies, which position the subject as an entrepreneur of the self, who does and, indeed, must engage in care of the body and its
symbolic referents in order to be competitive within a larger global marketplace."
See Brenda Weber, *Makeover TV: Selfhood, Citizenship, and Celebrity* (Durham,
NC: Duke University Press, 2009), 38–39. Reality television, including makeover
shows but also life narratives such as *The Hills* and MTV's *Real World,* are one way
that individuals can access and experience a particular kind of self-narrative—the
self in these programs is situated as both a process and a commodity, and the
labor that is performed (and the makeover shows centrally feature labor on the
self as a defining narrative) is decidedly immaterial. Reality television is clearly
dedicated to self-presentation and the constructed nature of identity, both key in
animating the normalization of the practice of self-branding. Reality television

is also a site in which gender constructions are continually discussed, debated, and made normative. Though certainly men are as engaged in self-branding as women, in this chapter I focus on the self-branding practiced by young girls and women within the context of postfeminism.

68. http://www.ehow.com/how_2059779_be-star-youtube.html.

69. http://www.businessinsider.com/
meet-the-richest-independent-youtube-stars-2010-8.

70. *Vanity Fair*, February 2011.

71. YouTube.com, press release on YouTube Partner Program, April 25, 2011.

72. Ibid.

73. Alex Hawgood, "No Stardom until after Your Homework," *New York Times*, July 17, 2011, 1, Style section.

74. Ibid. Hawgood discusses how very young girls—thirteen to fifteen years old—are achieving success on YouTube through such videos. He details Megan Parken, a fifteen-year-old video blogger with a makeup tutorial site, meganheartsmakeup, who became so successful as a YouTube partner that she dropped out of high school in the ninth grade and is now taking online courses. Her mother is cited as saying, "The financial opportunity is incredible....She has saved enough money to buy her first car and has put away money for college." Hawgood, "No Stardom."

75. Randall Stross, "A Site Warhol Would Relish," *New York Times*, October 14, 2007.

76. Marc Andrejevic, *Reality TV: The Work of Being Watched* (Lanham, MD: Rowman and Littlefield, 2004), 61.

77. Ibid., 195.

78. Ibid., 198.

79. Kaputa, *U R a Brand!*, 68.

80. http://www.youtube.com/user/ijustine#p/search/7/8jEoGWIOuy8.

81. Jessica Guynn, "It's Justin, Live! All Day, All Night! S.F. Startup Puts Camera on Founder's Head for Real-Time Feed, and a Star Is Born." *San Francisco Chronicle*, March 30, 2007.

82. An example of this is Ezarik's most viewed video, "'I Gotta Feeling' Black Eyed Peas SPOOF," which was posted in August 2009; as of December 2009, it had received almost 5 million views. The video has also received more than 17,000 comments and eighty video responses from fellow YouTubers. In the video she sings, "I gotta feeling, that tonight's gonna be a profile pic," to the tune of the popular 2009 Black Eyed Peas song, and dances around in a sexy, low-cut dress.

83. See Eva Illouz, *Oprah Winfrey and the Glamour of Misery: An Essay on Popular Culture* (New York: Columbia University Press, 2003).

84. Harris, *Future Girl*, 128.

85. See Justine Cassell and Meg Cramer, "Hi Tech or High Risk? Moral Panics about Girls Online," in *Digital Youth, Innovation, and the Unexpected: The Macarthur Foundation Series on Digital Media and Learning*, ed. Tara MacPherson (Cambridge: MIT Press, 2008), 53–75.

86. Sandra Lee Bartky, "Foucault, Femininity and the Modernization of Patriarchal Power," in *Feminism and Foucault: Paths of Resistance,* ed. Lee Quinby and Irene Diamond (Boston: Northeastern University Press, 1988), 77; Michel Foucault, *Discipline and Punish: The Birth of the Prison* (New York: Random House, 1975).

87. "Foucault, Femininity and the Modernization of Patriarchal Power," 77.

88. Harris, *Future Girl*, 16.

89. For a very useful discussion of girls' media production, see Mary Celeste Kearney, *Girls Make Media.*

90. McNally and Speak, *Be Your Own Brand.*

91. Alison Hearn, "Variations on the Branded Self: Theme, Invention, Improvisation and Inventory," in *The Media and Social Theory,* ed. David Hesmondhalgh and Jason Toynbee (New York: Routledge, 2008), 207–208.

92. Dobson, "Femininities as Commodities"; Ashley D. Grisso and David Weiss, "What Are gURLS Talking About?" *Girl Wide Web: Girls, the Internet, and the Negotiation of Identity,* ed. Sharon R. Mazzarella (New York: Peter Lang, 2005), 31–50.

93. Susannah Stern, "Virtually Speaking: Girls' Self-Disclosure on the WWW," *Women's Studies in Communication* 25, no. 2 (2002): 224.

94. Sandra Weber and Claudia Mitchell, "Imaging, Keyboarding, and Posting Identities: Young People and New Media Technologies," in *Youth, Identity, and Digital Media,* ed. David Buckingham (Cambridge: MIT Press, 2008), 27.

95. boyd, "Why Youth (Heart) Social Network Sites," 123.

96. Hearn, "Variations on the Branded Self."

97. Kevin Driscoll, personal correspondence.

98. www.compete.com, accessed November 2009.

99. In other words, the postfeminist self-brand is a slippery slope: one primary aspect of postfeminist culture, empowerment through the body, is sustained and validated through what Ariel Levy critiques as "the mainstreaming of pornography," a normalized "raunch culture" symbolized by *Girls Gone Wild,* adult film star Jenna Jameson's *New York Times* best seller *How to Make Love Like a Porn Star,* the normalization of bodies on constant sexual display (fitness clubs offering strip classes, stripper poles in houses and hotels, fashion calling attention to the sexualized body), and replacement of "beauty" with "hotness": "Hotness has become our cultural currency, and a lot of people spend a lot of time and a lot of regular, green currency trying to acquire it. Hotness is not the same thing as beauty, which has been valued throughout history. Hot can mean popular. Hot can mean talked about. But when it pertains to women, hot means two things in particular: fuckable and saleable." See Ariel Levy, *Female Chauvinist Pigs: Women and the Rise of Raunch Culture* (New York: Free Press, 2005), 25. Women's bodies on private and public sexual display (home sex tapes, amateur videos on YouTube and XTube, sexting, booty shorts) used to be called "objectification" in the old days of feminism. But as many have argued, the emphasis is on "old."

100. As McRobbie, Ariel Levy, and others have pointed out, the visibility of women of color and working-class women within a postfeminist context is typically not focused on "hotness" but rather on consumption behaviors and every-day practices that are pathologized, such as early pregnancy, drug use, and unemployment.

101. Depending on one's privacy settings, different people will be able to see different features.

102. Facebook guidelines.

103. http://www.iandavidchapman.com.

104. Kaputa, *U R a Brand!*, xv.

105. Examples include *16 and Pregnant, Teen Mom, Bad Girls Club,* talk shows, reality television like bad girls club, scripted TV like *Skins,* and others.

106. McRobbie, "Notes on Postfeminism and Popular Culture."

107. Judith Grant, *Fundamental Feminisms: Contesting the Core Concepts of Feminist Theory* (New York: Routledge, 1993); Boston Women's Health Book Collective, *Our Bodies, Ourselves,* 40th anniversary edition (New York: Touchstone, 2011); Linda Nicholson, *The Second Wave: A Reader in Feminist Theory* (New York: Routledge, 1997); Mary Celeste Kearney, *Girls Make Media* (New York: Routledge, 2006).

108. Jean Twenge, *The Narcissism Epidemic: Living in the Age of Entitlement* (New York: Free Press, 2010).

109. Of course, there are many DIY media examples of creating a media channel with few resources, but few on the scale of lifecasters.

110. Twenge, *Narcissism Epidemic.*

111. Burgess and Green, *YouTube,* 57 (emphasis in original).

112. Ibid.

NOTES TO CHAPTER 3

1. In this chapter, street art is defined as art in the historical tradition of graffiti, murals, and tagging, that is, painted, stenciled, stickered, or on public spaces—walls, trains, fences, and so on.

2. *Exit through the Gift Shop,* directed by Banksy (2010; Paranoid Pictures), DVD.

3. Ibid.

4. See Melena Ryzik, "Riddle? Yes. Enigma? Sure. Documentary?" *New York Times,* April 13, 2010. Of course, with this reply, Banksy does not answer the question about how corporate culture might in fact devalue his own work.

5. Banksy, *Wall and Piece* (London: Random House, 2005).

6. Ibid.

7. David Ng, "Banksy Identity Auction Removed from eBay—Was It a Hoax?," http://latimesblogs.latimes.com/culturemonster/2011/01/is-the-banksy-identity-auction-on-ebay-for-real.html, January 18, 2011. Like Natalie Dylan's virginity discussed in the previous chapter, apparently there are some things that are not appropriate for auction on eBay.

8. Sarah Banet-Weiser and Marita Sturken, "The Politics of Commerce: Shepard Fairey and the New Cultural Entrepreneurship," in *Blowing Up the Brand*, ed. Melissa Aronczyk and Devon Powers (New York: Peter Lang, 2011), 263–284.

9. Shepard Fairey, "Obey Manifesto," accessed June 2009, http://obeygiant.com/about.

10. Man One, "How Does Street Art Humanize Cities?" (lecture, Zocalo Public Square, Los Angeles, CA, January 13, 2011).

11. Angela McRobbie, "'Everyone Is Creative': Artists as Pioneers of the New Economy?," accessed November 2009, http://www.opendemocracy.net/node/652.

12. Miriam Greenberg, *Branding New York: How a City in Crisis Was Sold to the World* (New York: Routledge, 2008).

13. Karal Ann Marling, *Wall-to-Wall America: Post Office Murals in the Great Depression* (Minneapolis: University of Minnesota Press, 1982); Allen Cohen and Ronald L. Filippelli, *Times of Sorrow and Hope: Documenting Everyday Life in Pennsylvania during the Depression and World War II* (University Park: Pennsylvania State University Press, 2005).

14. Joe Austin, *Taking the Train: How Graffiti Art Became an Urban Crisis in New York City* (New York: Columbia University Press, 2001); Gregory J. Snyder, *Graffiti Lives: Beyond the Tag in New York's Urban Underground* (New York: NYU Press, 2009); Jeff Chang, *Can't Stop, Won't Stop: A History of the Hip-Hop Generation* (New York: Picador Books, 2005).

15. Austin, *Taking the Train*.

16. For just one example, Cadillac has recently partnered with the Museum of Contemporary Art, Los Angeles, and hired street artists, including Shepard Fairey, to create street murals that exemplify the "spirit of Cadillac." The ad campaign, called "Art in the Streets," featured three public murals by Fairey, Retna, and Kenny Scharf on the exterior walls of the new West Hollywood Library in Los Angeles. The campaign states that for Cadillac, "it was also an extraordinary opportunity to bring to life its core ideologies: bold creativity that surpasses all conceivable expectation, recognition of great risks as opportunities, and daring ingenuity that breaks down all barriers." *Vanity Fair*, November 2011, 61.

17. Retna, "How Does Street Art Humanize Cities?" (lecture, Zocalo Public Square, Los Angeles, CA, January 13, 2011).

18. For instance, the Museum of Contemporary Art, Los Angeles (MOCA), featured the first major US museum exhibition in the history of graffiti and street art, *Art in the Streets*, which ran from April 17 to August 8, 2011, before it traveled to the Brooklyn Museum.

19. Walter Benjamin, "The Work of Art in the Age of Mechanical Reproduction," in *Walter Benjamin and Art*, ed. Andrew Benjamin (London: Continuum, 2005).

20. Richard E. Caves, *The Creative Industries: Contracts between Art and Commerce* (Cambridge: Harvard University Press, 2000).

21. Ben Sisario, "Looking to a Sneaker for a Band's Big Break," *New York Times*, October 6, 2010.

22. Cohen quoted in Sisario, ibid.

23. Rob Stone, interview with author. There are other endeavors in the creative industries that utilize a shifted model of corporate sponsorship of independent creative artists and musicians. Hewlitt-Packard, for instance, partnered with Magnum Photos in 2010 to sponsor amateur photographers through the Expression Awards.

24. Nicholas Garnham, "From Cultural to Creative Industries," *International Journal of Cultural Policy* 11, no. 1 (2005): 15–29; McRobbie, "'Everyone Is Creative.'"

25. Richard Florida, *The Rise of the Creative Class: And How It's Transforming Work, Leisure, Community and Everyday Life* (New York: Basic Books, 2002); Jamie Peck, "Struggling with the Creative Class," *International Journal of Urban and Regional Research* 29, no. 4 (2005): 740–770; Elizabeth Currid, *The Warhol Economy: How Fashion, Art, and Music Drive New York City* (Princeton: Princeton University Press, 2008); Greenberg, *Branding New York.* See also Sarah Banet-Weiser, "Convergence on the Street: Rethinking the Authentic/Commercial Divide," *Cultural Studies* 25, nos. 4–5 (2011): 641–658.

26. McRobbie, "'Everyone Is Creative.'"

27. Greenberg, *Branding New York,* 64.

28. Man One, Zocalo Public Square lecture.

29. George Lipsitz, *The Possessive Investment in Whiteness: How White People Profit from Identity Politics* (Philadelphia: Temple University Press, 1998).

30. Chang, *Can't Stop, Won't Stop,* 2006; Austin, *Taking the Train,* 2001.

31. Austin, *Taking the Train,* 39.

32. Chang, *Can't Stop, Won't Stop,* 2006.

33. Craig Castleman, *Getting Up: Subway Graffiti in New York* (Cambridge: MIT Press, 1999); Chang, *Can't Stop, Won't Stop*; Austin, *Taking the Train*; Snyder, *Graffiti Lives.* A recent *New York Times* article discussed the reemergence of Taki at a graffiti retrospective; see http://www.nytimes.com/2011/07/23/arts/design/early-graffiti-artist-taki183-still-lives.html.

34. Castleman, *Getting Up,* 53.

35. Ibid.

36. Nicolas Rose, *Governing the Soul: The Shaping of the Private Self* (London: Routledge, 1990); Austin, *Taking the Train.*

37. Chang, *Can't Stop, Won't Stop,* 73.

38. Ibid., 74.

39. Norman Mailer, *The Faith of Graffiti* (New York: HarperCollins, 2009), 73; Austin, *Taking the Train.*

40. Castleman, *Getting Up*; Austin, *Taking the Train*; Snyder, *Graffiti Lives.*

41. Greenberg, *Branding New York*; Castleman, *Getting Up*; Austin, *Taking the Train.*

42. Austin, *Taking the Train.*

43. Greenberg, *Branding New York.* See also Austin, *Taking the Train.*

44. See http://articles.latimes.com/2011/feb/17/entertainment/la-et-oscar-banksy-20110218, as well as *Exit through the Gift Shop.*

45. Austin, *Taking the Train,* 45.

46. Aaron Rose, "How Does Street Art Humanize Cities?" (lecture, Zocalo Public Square, Los Angeles, CA, January 13, 2011).

47. Man One, Zocalo Public Square lecture.

48. Rose, *Governing the Soul.*

49. Florida, *Rise of the Creative Class.*

50. Certainly, the distinction between the authentic and the commercial is not new—Henderson calls it a "centuries-long standoff." See Lisa Henderson, "Queer Relay," *GLQ: A Journal of Lesbian and Gay Studies* 14, no. 4 (2008): 569. However, the way in which it is authorized and enabled in the contemporary neoliberal economy has shifted somewhat from previous eras.

51. Inderpal Grewal, *Transnational America: Feminisms, Diasporas, Neoliberalisms* (Durham, NC: Duke University Press, 2005), 87 (emphasis added).

52. Branded cities are part of a larger space-branding pattern, such as nation branding. For more on this, see Melissa Aronczyk, *Branding the Nation: Mediating Space, Value and Identity in Global Culture* (New York: Oxford University Press, forthcoming); and others.

53. Greenberg, *Branding New York,* 19.

54. Ibid., 36.

55. Brandspace meeting, Los Angeles, CA, October 30, 2009. See also Andrew Ross, *Bird on Fire: Lessons from the World's Least Sustainable City,* for the branding of Phoenix, AZ. (New York: Oxford University Press, 2011).

56. Greenberg, *Branding New York,* 119.

57. Florida, *Rise of the Creative Class.*

58. Peck, "Struggling with the Creative Class." See also Banet-Weiser and Sturken, "Politics of Commerce."

59. Creative Class Group, http://www.creativeclass.com/services/creative_communities.

60. Peck, "Struggling with the Creative Class."

61. See Andrew Ross, *Nice Work If You Can Get It: Life and Labor in Precarious Times* (New York: NYU Press, 2009).

62. Greenberg, *Branding New York,* 10.

63. Peck, "Struggling with the Creative Class"; McRobbie, "'Everyone Is Creative'"; Garnham, "From Cultural to Creative Industries."

64. "Shepard Fairey: Obey Collaboration with Levi's," http://www.designboom.com/weblog/cat/11/view/8020/shepard-fairey-obey-collaboration-with-levis.html.

65. See Currid, *Warhol Economy.* I am grateful to Stephen Duncombe for his insight on this.

66. David Harvey, *A Brief History of Neoliberalism* (Oxford: Oxford University Press, 2005); Dan Schiller, *How to Think about Information* (Urbana: University of Illinois Press, 2007).

67. James H. Gilmore and B. Joseph Pine, *Authenticity: What Consumers Really Want* (Cambridge: Harvard Business School Publishing, 2007), 3 (emphasis in original).

68. Indeed, as Jamie Peck argues, "Both the script and the nascent practices of urban creativity are peculiarly well suited to entrepreneurialized and neoliberalized urban landscapes. They provide a means to intensify and publicly subsidize urban consumption systems for a circulating class of gentrifiers, whose lack of commitment to place and whose weak community ties are perversely celebrated....this amounts to a process of public validation for favored forms of consumption and for a privileged class of consumers." Peck, "Struggling with the Creative Class," 764.

69. Ritzy P, personal correspondence, February 2009.

70. DJ | LA, personal correspondence, February 2009.

71. "Wooster Collective," woostercollective.com.

72. Abby Goodnough, "Boston Vandalism Charges Stir Debate on Art's Place," *New York Times,* March 11, 2009.

73. Richard Winton, "7 Alleged Members of L.A. Tagging Crew Arrested," *Los Angeles Times,* January 29, 2009.

74. Cedar Lewisohn, *Street Art: The Graffiti Revolution* (New York: Abrams, 2008), 65.

75. See, for example, Katia McGlynn, "Banksy Directs Dark Opening for 'The Simpsons,'" October 11, 2010, http://www.huffingtonpost.com/2010/10/11/banksy-directs-dark-openi_n_757753.html; see also David Itzkoff, "'The Simpsons' Explains Its Button-Pushing Banksy Opening," in Arts Beat, *New York Times,* October 11, 2011.

76. McRobbie, "'Everyone Is Creative,'" 194.

77. Ibid.

78. Peck, "Struggling with the Creative Class."

79. Ross, *Nice Work If You Can Get It.*

80. McRobbie, "'Everyone Is Creative,'" 189.

81. The creative class, it is important to note, is composed not only of professionals who are paid for their creative labor but also of creative amateurs, whose "empowerment" is animated by the flexibility and openness of new technological formats and expanded markets. Advanced capitalist marketing practices have been reimagined in efforts to reach these new creative amateurs, involving strategies of engagement, authenticity, and creativity. This relates to contemporary street art, which shares space in this creative amateur context with the intensified practice of "stealth advertising," guerrilla marketing tactics, and a focus on user-generated content, where consumers participate in the development of a brand through online competitions, creating videos and advertising for television and other media on personal web pages on social networking sites. As I discussed in chapter 2, YouTube culture allows anyone with access to the web, a video camera, and editing software to disseminate their "amateur" videos and self-brands to potentially wide audiences, and thousands spend countless (unpaid) hours doing so. And amateur street artists, such as Thierry Guetta in *Exit through the Gift Shop,* can become their own brand.

82. David Hesmondhalgh, *The Cultural Industries* (London: Sage, 2007).

83. Jeff Beer, "Shepard Fairey Has a Posse," http://creativity-online.com/news/shepard-fairey-has-a-posse/132743.

84. Helen Kennedy, "Shepard Fairey–Designed Obama Portrait on Cover of Rolling Stone Deifies, Questions President," *New York Daily News,* August 6, 2009.

85. Steven Heller, "Interview with Shepard Fairey: Still Obeying after All These Years," http://www.aiga.org/interview-with-shepard-fairey-still-obeying-after-all-these-year/, June 4, 2004. See also Banet-Weiser and Sturken, "Politics of Commerce."

86. Banet-Weiser and Sturken, "Politics of Commerce," 97.

NOTES TO CHAPTER 4

1. http://abolitionistcall.com/free2work-iphone-app.

2. For more on this, see Jason Farbman, "The Baddest Apple in a Rotten Bunch," socialistworker.org, August 17, 2010. Or, consider Apple's own annual report, which states that the company's suppliers are 80 percent in compliance with "involuntary labor." http://images.apple.com/supplierresponsibility/pdf/Apple_SR_2010_Progress_Report.pdf.

3. For an excellent examination of how activists use branding strategies, see Stephen Duncombe's work on Reverend Billy, the Yes Men, and so on: *Dream: Reimagining Progressive Politics in an Age of Fantasy* (New York: New Press, 2007). Also see Alison Hearn, "Brand Me Activist," in *Commodity Activism: Cultural Resistance to Neoliberal Times,* ed. Roopali Mukherjee and Sarah Banet-Weiser (New York: NYU Press, 2012).

4. Adam Silver, "The Rise of the Political Brand," *Design Mind,* http://designmind.frogdesign.com/articles/green/the-rise-political-brand.html.

5. Sally Kohn, "Shared Identity—Not T-Shirts—Makes a Movement," October 12, 2010, http://www.alternet.org/activism/148476/shared_identity_--_not_t-shirts_--_makes_a_movement/?page=2.

6. Malcolm Gladwell, "Small Change: Why the Revolution Will Not Be Tweeted," *New Yorker,* September 27, 2010.

7. Marita Sturken, *Tourists of History: Memory, Kitsch, and Consumerism from Oklahoma City to Ground Zero* (Durham, NC: Duke University Press, 2007), 5.

8. Wendy Brown, *Politics Out of History* (Princeton: Princeton University Press, 2001); Nick Couldry, *Why Voice Matters: Culture and Politics after Neoliberalism* (London: Sage, 2010); Lisa Duggan, *The Twilight of Equality? Neoliberalism, Cultural Politics, and the Attack on Democracy* (Boston: Beacon Press, 2003).

9. Brown, *Politics Out of History,* 3.

10. Ibid.

11. Couldry, *Why Voice Matters.*

12. Consequently, within neoliberalism and its concomitant reductive definition of politics as "the implementing of market functioning," we risk losing "voice" as a value, as Couldry argues. "Voice," as part of liberalism's "organizing terms and legitimacy," is a particular kind of value, one that discriminates "in favour of ways of organizing human life and resources that, through their choices, put the value of voice into practice, by respecting the multiple interlinked processes of voice

and sustaining them, not undermining or denying them." See Couldry, *Why Voice Matters*, 2.

13. Raymond Williams, *The Long Revolution* (Peterborough, ON: Broadview Press, 1961), 64.

14. Raymond Williams, *Marxism and Literature* (Oxford: Oxford University Press, 1978), 133.

15. I am grateful to Dana Polan for pointing me to this reference.

16. Couldry, *Why Voice Matters*, 3.

17. And, indeed, it is arguable whether or not a "100% compostable bag" is a new product, as paper bags are often biodegradable. The notion of a bag being "compostable" is part of its branding.

18. Lawrence Glickman, *Buying Power: A History of Consumer Activism in America* (Chicago: University of Chicago Press, 2009); Gary Cross, *An All-Consuming Century: Why Commercialism Won in Modern America* (New York: Columbia University Press, 2000); Lizabeth Cohen, *A Consumer's Republic: The Politics of Mass Consumption in Postwar America* (New York: Vintage Books, 2003); Matthew Hilton, *Prosperity for All: Consumer Activism in an Era of Globalization* (Ithaca: Cornell University Press, 2009); Robert Weems, *Desegregating the Dollar: African American Consumerism in the Twentieth Century* (New York: NYU Press, 1998).

19. Glickman, *Buying Power*.

20. George Marcus, *The Sentimental Citizen: Emotion in Democratic Politics* (University Park: Pennsylvania State University Press, 2002), 2.

21. Christopher Holmes Smith, "Bling Was a Bubble," *International Journal of Communication* 3 (2009): 274–276.

22. Sturken, *Tourists of History*.

23. Cohen, *A Consumer's Republic*.

24. Liz Moor, *The Rise of Brands* (Oxford: Berg, 2007); Celia Lury, *Brands: The Logos of the Global Economy* (London: Routledge, 2004); Inderpal Grewal, *Transnational America: Feminisms, Diasporas, Neoliberalisms* (Durham, NC: Duke University Press, 2005); Jo Littler, *Radical Consumption: Shopping for Change in Contemporary Culture* (Berkshire, UK: Open University Press, 2009).

25. Couldry, *Why Voice Matters*.

26. Glickman, *Buying Power*, 257.

27. Ibid.

28. Weems, *Desegregating the Dollar*; Bobby Wilson, "Race in Commodity Exchange and Consumption: Separate but Equal," *Annals of the Association of American Geographers* 95, no. 3 (2005): 587–606.

29. Weems, *Desegregating the Dollar*; Cohen, *Consumer Republic*; Hilton, *Prosperity for All*, Glickman, *Buying Power*.

30. Glickman, *Buying Power*, 87.

31. Ibid., 297.

32. Glickman, *Buying Power*; Duggan, *Twilight of Equality?*; Brown, *Politics Out of History*.

33. Glickman, *Buying Power*, 284.

34. David Harvey, *A Brief History of Neoliberalisim* (Oxford: Oxford University Press, 2005), 3.

35. Duggan, *Twilight of Equality*, 5.

36. Ibid.

37. This approach was one in which the previous consumer movement was conflated with the newly demonized political ideology of liberalism; indeed, the role of politicized consumers that historians such as Cohen and Weems described in the early and mid-20th century became something that was understood as detrimental to the newly configured relationship between the market, the state, and citizens. As Glickman puts it, emerging neoliberal logics and ideologies "depicted consumer protection efforts as counterproductive, overbearing, elitist, bloated, and out of touch, and contrasted the government-centered and social vision of CPA [consumer protection agency] proponents with the wisdom and strength of individual, ordinary people operating in an unencumbered free market." Glickman, *Buying Power*, 279.

38. Couldry, *Why Voice Matters*, 12.

39. Ibid., 308.

40. Surely these practices are complicated and have often resulted in the normalization of particular political acts (such as recycling) and do not always serve the interests of a neoliberal-defined individual entrepreneur. For instance, in the contemporary era, much of progressive politics becomes mired in a moral nostalgia over the absence of "real" politics. Rather than moralism, Stephen Duncombe advocates for what he calls "dream politics," or ethical spectacle; using the tactics and strategies of the media, advertising, and marketing—industries that skillfully traffic in fantasy—the left could organize "spectacular" protests for progressive causes: "The potential for a spectacular politics is far greater [than traditional protests] for everyday fantasy is employed effectively by the mass entertainment industry, and everyday spectacles are enthusiastically embraced by a majority of the world's population. The task at hand is to tap into this wide appeal and use it to build a truly popular progressive politics." Duncombe, *Dream*, 24. Duncombe cites a range of examples of ethical spectacle, including Bill Talen, or "Reverend Billy," a performance artist who "preaches" to people about the "revolution of no shopping." As Duncombe points out, the spectacle of preaching to urban audiences about not shopping is an absurdity, and this is precisely part of the point: "part of this is pure provocation, a bit of absurd theatricality to draw our attention to how much we shop and how often we think about shopping: Brecht's V-effect." Duncombe, *Dream*, 165.

41. Samantha King, *Pink Ribbons, Inc.: Breast Cancer and the Politics of Philanthropy* (Minneapolis: University of Minnesota Press, 2006), 73.

42. "We Are All Workers," Levi Strauss and Co., June 24, 2010, http://www.levistrauss.com/news/press-releases/ levis-proclaims-we-are-all-workers-launch-latest-go-forth-marketing-campaign.

43. Sue Halpern, "Mayor of Rust," *New York Times Magazine,* February 11, 2011.

44. NPR, "Levi's Gives Struggling Town Cinderella Treatment," All Things Considered, October 10, 2010.

45. Ibid.

46. Littler, *Radical Consumption*; Eva Illouz, *Oprah Winfrey and the Glamour of Misery: An Essay on Popular Culture* (New York: Columbia University Press, 2003).

47. Milton Friedman, "The Social Responsibility of Business Is to Increase Its Profits," *New York Times Magazine,* September 13, 1970.

48. Ibid.

49. Inger Stole, "Philanthropy as Public Relations: A Critical Reception on Cause Marketing," *International Journal of Communication* 2 (2008): 21.

50. David Vogel, *The Market for Virtue: The Potential and Limits of Corporate Social Responsibility* (Washington, DC: Brookings Institution, 2005).

51. Ibid., 24.

52. As Laurie Ouellette has pointed out, the public embrace in the US of Robert Putnam's "bowling alone" theory (which posits that individuals have lost their way in terms of community, among other things), the popular fear of the atomizing effect of technology (which, of course, has not stalled the constant introduction of new technological products), and the decline in community participation (in such organizations as the Parent-Teacher Association, etc.), among other things, have coalesced in a discourse about the loss of individual morality and the decline in democratic communities. This emotional response of citizens was accompanied by real material losses, in the forms of less government investment in social services and an increasingly abrasive and instrumental business ethos. Laurie Ouellette, "Citizen Brand: ABC Television and the Do Good Turn in US Television," in *Commodity Activism: Cultural Resistance in Neoliberal Times,* ed. Roopali Mukherjee and Sarah Banet-Weiser (New York: NYU Press, 2012).

53. Vogel, *Market for Virtue.*

54. Ouellette, "Citizen Brand," 68–69.

55. Ibid., original citation of Adam Arviddson, 69.

56. Littler, *Radical Consumption.*

57. Stole, "Philanthropy as Public Relations."

58. Indeed, in the 1990s, a political issue such as global warming was frequently trivialized as an unscientific rant generated by leftist activists and conspiracy theorists (to take just one example of this kind of trivialization, in the WTO protests in Seattle in 1999, the media focused simultaneously most intensely and most dismissively on those protesters who wore sea turtle costumes in an effort to bring environmental causes to the table).

59. "Global Fund to Fight AIDS, Tuberculosis and Malaria," http://www.theglobalfund.org/en/; Sarah Banet-Weiser and Charlotte Lapsanksy, "RED Is the New Black: Brand Culture, Consumer Citizenship and Political Possibility," *International Journal of Communication* 2 (2008): 1248–1268.

60. Brown, *Politics Out of History.*

61. Wendy Brown, "Neoliberalism and the End of Liberal Democracy," *Theory & Event* 7, no. 1 (2003).

62. A case in point: Fox network's Glenn Beck hosted a segment in 2007 called "Exposed: The Climate of Fear," where he predictably compared those concerned with the environment with Hitler and fascism.

63. Hearn, "Brand Me Activist," 33.

64. Ibid.

65. Adam Werbach, "The Death of Environmentalism and the Birth of the Commons Movement" (speech at the Commonwealth Club of California, December 2004).

66. Interview with author, January 15, 2010.

67. Amy Gajda, "From Science to Time to Vanity Fair: Sexing Up Sustainability and How It Happened," proceedings from Geological Society of America annual meeting 2006, October 23, 2006. Interestingly, *Vanity Fair* stopped publishing its green issue in 2009, with Condé Nast, the publisher of the magazine, claiming "that environmental issues are so ingrained in the news that a dedicated issue is unnecessary." Jay Yarow, "Vanity Fair Scraps Annual Green Issue, April, 6, 2009, http://www.huffingtonpost.com/2009/04/06/vanity-fair-scraps-annual_n_183357.html.

68. Fred Turner, *From Counterculture to Cyberculture: Stewart Brand, the Whole Earth Network, and the Rise of Digital Utopianism* (Chicago: University of Chicago Press, 2006). The Whole Earth catalog has been called a pre-Internet example of "user-generated content," as it sought input from consumers.

69. Cross, *An All-Consuming Century*; Glickman, *Buying Power*.

70. Littler, *Radical Consumption*, 96.

71. Lury, *Brands*, 5.

72. Adam Werbach, "The Failure of Chevron's New 'We Agree' Ad Campaign," *Atlantic Monthly*, October 2010, http://www.theatlantic.com/business/archive/2010/10/the-failure-of-chevrons-new-we-agree-ad-campaign/64951/.

73. Ibid.

74. Nikolas Rose, *Inventing Ourselves: Psychology, Power and Personhood* (Cambridge: Cambridge University Press, 1998); Michel Foucault, *The Birth of Biopolitics: Lectures at the Collège de France, 1978–1979* (New York: Palgrave Macmillan, 2008).

75. Gay Hawkins, "The Politics of Bottled Water: Assembling Bottled Water as Brand, Waste and Oil," *Journal of Cultural Economy* 2, no. 1 (2009): 183–195.

76. Ibid., 185.

77. Dasani, www.dasani.com; Calistoga, www.calistogawater.com; Aquafina, www.aquafina.com; see also Hawkins, "Politics of Bottled Water."

78. www.epa.gov/safewater/labs/index.html.

79. Barry Glassner, *The Culture of Fear: Why Americans Are Afraid of the Wrong Things* (New York: Basic Books, 2000).

80. http://water.epa.gov/lawsregs/rulesregs/sdwa/.

81. Mike King, "Bottled Water—Global Industry Guide," PR-inside.com, August 7, 2008.

82. Anna Lenzer, "Fiji Water: Spin the Bottle," *Mother Jones*, September/October 2009.

83. Lance Klessig, "Bottled Water Industry," academic.evergreen.edu/g/grossmaz/klessill/; Lenzer, "Fiji Water."

84. Calistoga, calistogawater.com, Perrier, www.perrier.com.

85. Ibid.

86. Tara Lohan, "Are Greedy Water Bottlers Stealing Your City's Drinking Water?," March 22, 2010,http://www.alternet.org/water/146116/are_greedy_water_bottlers_stealing_your_city%27s_drinking_water/.

87. Hawkins, "Politics of Bottled Water."

88. Josée Johnston and Kate Cairns, "Eating for Change," in *Commodity Activism: Cultural Resistance in Neoliberal Times,* ed. Roopali Mukherjee and Sarah Banet-Weiser (New York: NYU Press, 2012).

89. For more on Oliver's *Food Revolution*, see Garrett Broad, "Revolution on Primetime TV—Jamie Oliver Takes on the US Food System," in *Rhetoric of Food: Discourse, Materiality and Power*, ed. J. Frye and M. Bruner (New York: Routledge, 2012).

90. "FarmVille Arrives on the App Store," *Business Wire*, June 24, 2010.

91. Julie Guthman, "Commentary on Teaching Food: Why I Am Fed Up with Michael Pollan et al.," *Agriculture and Human Values* 24, no. 2 (2007): 264. I am grateful to Garrett Broad for this suggestion.

92. Josée Johnston and Shyon Baumann, *Foodies: Democracy and Distinction in the Gourmet Foodscape* (New York: Routledge, 2010).

93. http://greenzonegarden.wordpress.com/2008/07/20/gardens-on-the-homefront-wwis-war-gardens/.

94. Laura Saldivar-Tanaka and Marianne E. Krasny, "Culturing Community Development, Neighborhood Open Space, and Civic Agriculture: The Case of Latino Community Gardens in New York City," *Agriculture and Human Values* 21, no. 4 (2004): 399–412.

95. Laura J. Lawson, *City Bountiful: A Century of Community Gardening in America* (Berkeley: University of California Press, 2005).

96. See, for instance, the recent film *Homage to Catalonia II,* by Manuel Castells, Joanna Conill, and Alex Ruiz, produced by IN3 under Creative Commons license.

97. Megan Bedard, "Rent an Urban Gardener: Local Produce in Your Own Back Yard," August 23, 2010, http://www.takepart.com/news/2010/07/23/rent-a-gardener-urban-farming-at-your-doorstep.

98. A recent filmic representation of this urbanite gardener, the enterprising, neoliberal masculine subject, is Mark Ruffalo's character in the 2010 film *The Kids Are All Right.*

99. Guthman, "Commentary on Teaching Food."

100. Ibid.

101. George Lipsitz, *The Possessive Investment in Whiteness: How White People Profit from Identity Politics* (Philadelphia: Temple University Press, 1998).

102. Vogel, *Market for Virtue.*
103. Littler, *Radical Consumption.*

NOTES TO CHAPTER 5

1. Liz Goodwin, "In New TV Ads, Mormons Pitch Message to Middle America," *Yahoo News,* August 11, 2010, http://news.yahoo.com/blogs/upshot/tv-ads-mormons-pitch-message.html.

2. Ibid. The idea that Mormons are "not weird" is intended to counteract the position of Mormons that is indicated not only by the financial support by the LDS for California's Proposition 8, the anti–gay marriage act, but also by the successful recent television programs HBO's *Big Love*, which features a polygamous Mormon family, and the reality television show *Sister Wife*, which features a man and his three wives and families.

3. Andrew Wernick, *Promotional Culture: Advertising, Ideology and Symbolic Expression* (London: Sage, 1991), 182.

4. Stuart Hall, *Representation: Cultural Representations and Signifying Practices* (London: Sage, 2007).

5. Vincent J. Miller, *Consuming Religion: Christian Faith and Practice in a Consumer Culture* (New York: Continuum, 2005), 2.

6. Karl Marx, *Marx and Engels on Religion* (Moscow: Progress Publishers, 1976).

7. Viviana Zelizer, *Economic Lives: How Culture Shapes the Economy* (Princeton: Princeton University Press, 2011).

8. I am grateful to Jane Iwamura for thinking through this with me.

9. Arguably, the connection between institutionalized religion and economics in the US started with the Puritans, who taught it was appropriate, and even right, for godly people to succeed economically.

10. John Michael Giggie and Diane H. Winston, *Faith in the Market: Religion and the Rise of Urban Commercial Culture* (New Brunswick, NJ: Rutgers University Press, 2002).

11. Eva Illouz, *Saving the Modern Soul: Therapy, Emotions, and the Culture of Self-Help* (Berkeley: University of California Press, 2008).

12. Mara Einstein, *Brands of Faith: Marketing Religion in a Commercial Age* (New York: Routledge, 2008), 12.

13. Consider just one example of this recontextualization: the debates in the US in the early 21st century about teaching creationism in schools, where arguments about the separation of church and state that formed much of the logic of the US Constitution are often reframed as special interest issues, positioned far to the left on the political spectrum. This is evidenced by proposals to teach intelligent design or to formally institute creationism as part of US public school curricula. http://voices.washingtonpost.com/answer-sheet/science/study-most-high-school-biology.html; also see Michael B. Berkman and Eric Plutzer, "Defeating Creationism in the Courtroom, but Not in the Classroom," *Science* 331, no. 6016 (2011): 404–405.

14. Hanna Rosin, "Did Christianity Cause the Crash?," *Atlantic Monthly*, December 2009, http://www.theatlantic.com/magazine/archive/2009/12/did-christianity-cause-the-crash/7764/.

15. Robert Putnam, *Bowling Alone: The Collapse and Revival of American Community* (New York: Simon and Schuster, 2000).

16. Dan Harris, "Young Americans Losing Their Religion," ABC News, May 6, 2009.

17. Bethany Moreton, *To Serve God and Wal-Mart: The Making of Christian Free Enterprise* (Cambridge: Harvard University Press, 2009).

18. Jeremy Carrette and Richard King, *Selling Spirituality: The Silent Takeover of Religion* (New York: Routledge, 2005).

19. Adam Arvidsson, *Brands: Meaning and Value in Media Culture* (London: Routledge, 2006).

20. Einstein, *Brands of Faith*; Carrette and King, *Selling Spirituality*; Kimberly J. Lau, *New Age Capitalism: Making Money East of Eden* (Philadelphia: University of Pennsylvania Press, 2000).

21. T. J. Jackson Lears, "From Salvation to Self-Realization: Advertising and the Therapeutic Roots of the Consumer Culture, 1880–1930," in *The Culture of Consumption: Critical Essays in American Culture, 1880–1980,* ed. Richard Wightman Fox and T. J. Jackson Lears (New York: Pantheon Books, 1983), 1–38.

22. Giggie and Winston, *Faith in the Market.*

23. Ibid.

24. Because of the rapid emergence of industries within cities during this period, there was a particularly rich environment for the relationship between faith and the market to flourish. This may not have been true for more rural areas.

25. Miller, *Consuming Religion*; Laurence Moore, *Selling God: American Religion in the Marketplace of Culture* (New York: Oxford University Press, 1995).

26. Giggie and Winston, *Faith in the Market*, 2.

27. Moore, *Selling God,* 1995; Heather Hendershot, *Shaking the World for Jesus: Media and Conservative Evangelical Culture* (Chicago: University of Chicago Press, 2004); Giggie and Winston, *Faith in the Market.*

28. Hendershot, *Shaking the World for Jesus*, 29.

29. Lears, "From Salvation to Self-Realization"; see also Susan Curtis, *A Consuming Faith: Social Gospel and Modern American Culture* (Columbia: University of Missouri Press, 2001).

30. Lears, "From Salvation to Self-Realization," 8.

31. Lears focuses on Bruce Barton, and the idea that the preacher wanted to challenge his childhood religious education as "weightless Christianity." Barton sought to "revitalize his religious faith by suffusing it with therapeutic ideals of personal growth and abundant life." Importantly, Barton was an influential populizer of a therapeutic version of Christianity, a founder of an advertising firm, and a journalist, which made him successful but ambivalent: Barton's work "entwined and expressed the major preoccupations of consumer culture"; he "yearned for transcendent meaning even as his profession corroded it." Through "melding

therapeutic religiosity to the ideology of consumption, Barton retailored Protestant Christianity to fit the sleek new corporate system." Ibid., 10.

32. Moore, *Selling God,* 1995.

33. Jacque Ranciére, *The Politics of Aesthetics: The Distribution of the Sensible* (New York: Continuum, 2000).

34. Curtis, *A Consuming Faith,* 10.

35. Ibid., 11.

36. As Carette and King state, "In different ways and variegated forms, religion has been formally separated from the business of statecraft in contemporary Northern European societies (though with different inflections and degrees of smoothness)." See J. Carette and Richard King, *Selling Spirituality: The Silent Takeover of Religion* (New York: Routledge, 2005), 14.

37. Ibid., 15.

38. Einstein, *Branding Faith.*

39. Few industries have had as rapid a rate of growth as graduate management education in business schools in the US. After 1960, business degrees granted grew for twenty years at an average annual rate of 12 percent; in 1981, the total number of graduate business degrees was more than those for law and medicine combined. http://www.chicagobooth.edu/faculty/selectedpapers/sp59.pdf. See also Christopher Newfield on the rise of business schools, *Ivy and Industry: Business and the Making of the University, 1880–1980* (Durham, NC: Duke University Press, 2003).

40. Moreton, *To Serve God and Wal-Mart.*

41. Ibid., 9.

42. Ibid., 156.

43. Ibid., 46.

44. Ibid., 169; George Lipsitz, *The Possessive Investment in Whiteness: How White People Profit from Identity Politics* (Philadelphia: Temple University Press, 1998).

45. Moreton, *To Serve God and Wal-Mart,* 171.

46. David Edwin Harrell, *All Things Are Possible: The Healing and Charismatic Revivals in Modern America* (Bloomington: Indiana University Press, 1975).

47. "A Statement on Prosperity Teaching," *Christianity Today,* December 8, 2009, http://www.christianitytoday.com/ct/article_print.html?id=86009.

48. *Time,* September 10, 2006; *Time,* October 3, 2008; *Atlantic Monthly,* December 2009. Similar questions were asked in the late 19th century and early 20th century as industrial capitalism engendered a furious drive for consumption. However, those questions were asked more generally, as the difference between citizens and consumers became more difficult to discern. In the early 21st century, these questions are asked of a particular religious affiliation, Prosperity theology.

49. See Rosin, "Did Christianity Cause the Crash?," 5.

50. Shayne Lee and Phillip Luke Sinitiere, *Holy Mavericks: Evangelical Innovators and the Spiritual Marketplace* (New York: NYU Press, 2009), 59. As Lee and Sinitiere argue, T. D. Jakes has recently criticized Prosperity theology, saying that faith is not just "a matter of dollars and cents."

51. Kenneth Copeland Ministries. The Kenneth Copeland Ministries were investigated by the US Senate in 2007 for misuse of church funds. Additionally, 2008 Republican presidential candidate Mike Huckabee made numerous appearances on the Copeland television show and pledged support to the ministries.

52. Einstein, *Brands of Faith*, 121.

53. Mark A. Noll, *The Rise of Evangelicalism: The Age of Edwards, Whitefield, and the Wesleys* (Downer's Grove, IL: InterVarsity Press, 2010).

54. See Tona Hangen, *Redeeming the Dial: Radio, Religion and Popular Culture in America* (Chapel Hill: University of North Carolina Press, 2002). Coughlin was also anti-Semitic and has been called both "the radio priest" and the "father of hate radio." See Hangen, *Redeeming the Dial*; Hendershot, *Shaking the World for Jesus*.

55. Lee and Sinitiere, *Holy Mavericks*; Einstein, *Brands of Faith*; see also Stuart Hoover, *Religion in the Media Age* (New York: Routledge, 2006).

56. Lee and Sinitiere, *Holy Mavericks*, 2.

57. Moreton, *To Serve God and Wal-Mart*, 269.

58. http://www.sermoncentral.com/articleb.asp?article=Top-100-Largest-Churches; Warren cited in David Van Biema and Jeff Chu, "Does God Want You to Be Rich?," *Time*, September 10, 2006, http://www.time.com/time/magazine/article/0,9171,1533448,00.html.

59. Karlgaard, "Digital Rules," *Forbes*, February 16, 2004, quoted in Einstein, *Brands of Faith*.

60. www.rickwarren.com.

61. In another example of how religious practices "resolve" the ironies of capitalism, Henry Jenkins, Sam Ford, and Joshua Green offer the example of Christian musical groups and their presence at varied congregations (like a concert tour). There is an expected "love offering" for these performances: "As particular musical acts grew their fame, it became unofficially known that some seemed to gravitate toward the churches who had more 'love' to give. Others became more open about requiring an up-front fee, to varying reactions among church communities." The profits gained from Christian music are even more complicated in the contemporary digital era and the context of file-sharing debates. These debates exemplify the ironies of religious branding more generally: many Christian music fans and artists feel that Christian music should be shared freely, without moving through conventional economic channels of the music industry. As Jenkins et al. write, this contingent feels that "people taking Bibles freely should be the goal, rather than making large profit margins through 'God's gift to humanity': His Word. In short, if the Christian's charge is proselytizing, then content spreading 'the Word' should circulate for free as broadly as possible." Other Christian groups, however, such as the Christian Music Trade Association, offer a moral argument against file sharing, "claiming that it is a sin to 'steal' any type of music." The debates over file sharing and copyright that frame all contemporary production of music structure Christian music as well, capturing the contradiction

within religious brand cultures of disavowing capitalism while simultaneously embracing it. Henry Jenkins, Sam Ford, and Joshua Green, *Spreadable Media: Creating Value in a Network Culture* (New York: NYU, 2012), 216.

62. Linda Kintz, *Between Jesus and the Market: The Emotions That Matter in Right-Wing America* (Durham, NC: Duke University Press, 1997).

63. http://www.bennyhinn.org/default.cfm.

64. Jonathan L. Walton, *Watch This! The Ethics and Aesthetics of Black Televangelism* (New York: NYU Press, 2009), xii.

65. Ibid.

66. Kintz, *Between Jesus and the Market*, 2.

67. Palin's privileging a particular maternal body is demonstrated through the way she makes her own family visible in the media, her self-identification as a "Mama Bear," and her oft-cited remark about her love for "hockey moms:" "You know what they say the difference between a hockey mom and a pit bull is? Lipstick."

68. Stuart Hall, "What Is the 'Black' in Black Popular Culture?," in *Stuart Hall: Critical Dialogues in Cultural Studies*, ed. David Morley and Kuan-Hsing Chen George (London: Routledge, 1996); Lipsitz, *Possessive Investment*.

69. Lau, *New Age Capitalism*.

70. Illouz, *Saving the Modern Soul*, 5.

71. Ibid.

72. Brenda Weber, *Makeover TV: Selfhood, Citizenship, and Celebrity* (Durham, NC: Duke University Press, 2009); Katherine Sender, *Business Not Politics: The Making of the Gay Market* (New York: Columbia University Press, 2004).

73. Lau, *New Age Capitalism*.

74. Nitin Govil, "Conversion Narratives," *Media Fields Journal* 2 (2011), www.mediafieldsjournal.org/conversion-narratives/.

75. "Eat, Pray, Merch: You Can Buy Happiness, After All," Disgrasian.com, July 8, 2010, http://disgrasian.com/2010/07/eat-pray-merch-you-can-buy-happiness-after-all/.

76. Jane Iwamura, *Virtual Orientalism: Asian Religions and American Popular Culture* (Oxford: Oxford University Press, 2011); Vijay Prashad, *The Karma of Brown Folk* (Minneapolis: University of Minnesota Press, 2000); Lau, *New Age Capitalism*.

77. Prashad, *Karma of Brown Folk*, 19.

78. Ibid., 50.

79. Ibid., 52.

80. And musically represented in John Lennon's 1970 hit "Instant Karma." Prashad, *Karma of Brown Folk*.

81. Iwamura, *Virtual Orientalism*, 5.

82. Meenakshi Gigi Durham, "Ethnic Chic and the Displacement of South Asian Female Sexuality in the U.S. Media," in *Media/Cultural Studies: Critical Approaches*, ed. Rhonda Hammer (New York: Peter Lang, 2009), 501–515.

83. Jenkins, Ford, and Green, *Spreadable Media*.

84. Prashad, *Karma of Brown Folk*, 56.

85. "The Chopra Foundation," http://deepakchopra.com/chopra-foundation/mission/.

86. Prashad, *Karma of Brown Folk*, 59.

87. Carette and King, *Selling Spirituality*, 114.

88. Anirudh Bhattacharyya and Dipankar de Sarkar, "The Rise and Rise of Yoga," *Hindustan Times*, May 22, 2010.

89. Carette and King, *Selling Spirituality*, 116.

90. Bhattacharyya and Sarkar, "Rise and Rise of Yoga."

91. Carette and King, *Selling Spirituality*, 117.

92. Paul Vitello, "Hindus Stir Up Debate over Yoga's Soul," *New York Times*, November 27, 2010, http://www.nytimes.com/2010/11/28/nyregion/28yoga.html.

93. Ibid.

94. "On Faith" blog, *Washington Post*, April 18, 2010, http://onfaith.washingtonpost.com/onfaith/panelists/aseem_shukla/2010/04/nearly_twenty_million_people_in.html.

95. As Iwamura and others have pointed out, the relationship of Asian spirituality, media representation, and whiteness was quite literal in the first half of the twentieth century, as it was primarily white actors who played Asian characters.

96. As argued by, among others, Iwamura, *Virtual Orientalism;* Prashad, *Karma of Brown Folk;* and Lau, *New Age Capitalism..*

97. Iwamura, *Virtual Orientalism*, 21.

98. "Religion among the Millennials," a study by the Pew Forum on Religion and Public Life, 2010, http://pewforum.org/Age/Religion-Among-the-Millennials.aspx.

99. Ibid.

100. I am grateful to Melani McAllister for pointing me to this reference.

101. Off the Map website, www.offthemap.com.

102. http://www.yelp.com/biz/mission-bay-community-church-san-francisco#hrid:sjYIzMINgivS2dezs35P5w.

103. Patrick Leinen, littleaps.com.

104. Robert Bellah calls this "Sheilaism," so named after a woman he interviewed who, when asked about her religion, named it after herself: "Sheilaism." For Bellah, this was characteristic of religious affiliations in later 20th-century US culture, where Sheilaists are those who feel that religion is essentially a private matter and that there is no particular constraint placed on them by the historic church, or even by the Bible and tradition. See Robert Bellah et al., *Habits of the Heart: Individualism and Commitment in American Life* (Berkeley: University of California Press, 1985).

105. Lynn Schofield Clark, *From Angels to Aliens: Teenagers, the Media, and the Supernatural* (Oxford: Oxford University Press, 2003), 9.

106. Diane Winston, ed., *Small Screen, Big Picture: Television and Lived Religion* (Waco, TX: Baylor University Press, 2009).

107. Gary Laderman, *Sacred Matters: Celebrity Worship, Sexual Ecstasies, the Living Dead and Other Signs of Religious Life in the United States* (New York: New Press, 2009).

108. The pop trio the Jonas Brothers were a key accelerant in the heightened visibility of purity rings. As a 2008 article in *Details* magazine, "The Total Awesomeness of Being the Jonas Brothers," points out, "Kevin, Joe, and Nick Jonas—the teen-pop trio who stand, at this very moment, on the brink of hugeness—wear the metal bands on their fingers to symbolize, as Joe puts it, 'promises to ourselves and to God that we'll stay pure till marriage.'" See "The Jonas Brothers Wear Purity Rings," http://justjared.buzznet.com/2008/02/22/jonas-brothers-purity-rings/#ixzz1CXslgSlC.

109. Daniel Radosh, *Rapture Ready! Adventures in the Parallel Universe of Christian Pop Culture* (New York: Scribner, 2008), 9–10.

110. "One in Three Adults Is Unchurched," Barna Group, March 28, 2005, http://www.barna.org/barna-update/article/5-barna-update/182-one-in-three-adults-is-unchurched.

111. Colleen McDannell, *Material Christianity: Religion and Popular Culture in America* (New Haven: Yale University Press, 1995), 272.

112. For an interesting example of this, see Kevin O'Neill, "Delinquent Realities," *American Quarterly* 63, no. 2 (2011): 337–365. O'Neill examines the Guatemalan reality show *Desafío 10*, in which former gang members are "rehabilitated" through dual processes of consumption and "good Christian living."

113. C28 Christian Stores, http://www.c28.com/message.asp.

114. Radosh, *Rapture Ready!*, 12.

115. Ibid.

116. Hendershot, *Shaking the World for Jesus*.

117. Raymond Williams, *The Long Revolution* (Peterborough, ON: Broadview Press, 1961), 64.

118. Phil Cooke, *Branding Faith: Why Some Churches and Nonprofits Impact Culture and Others Don't* (Ventura, CA: Gospel Light, 2008), 13.

119. Ibid., 11 (emphasis in original).

NOTES TO CONCLUSION

1. Personal interview with author, December 2008.

2. Or, in another example, I spoke with a representative of the sneakers brand Converse, who reiterated Stone's conviction that authenticity within branding is not so much a cultivated tangible object as something that emerges from an affective relationship, one that is part of an organic development of culture. Converse is the largest shoe company in the world (it sells 55 million pairs of shoes each year), and thus felt as if it could take risks with certain iterations of its brand—customization, amateur videos posted on YouTube, creating a music studio to support up-and-coming musicians in a struggling music industry. The surplus value that emerges from this particular brand effort is not the increasingly integrated relationship between a brand and consumers but rather the music album that develops from the studio.

3. Raymond Williams, "Culture Is Ordinary," in *Resources of Hope: Culture, Democracy, Socialism* (London: Verso Press, 1989).

4. David Hesmondhalgh, "User Generated Content, Free Labour and the Culture Industries," *Ephemera: Theory and Practice in Organization* 10, nos. 3/4 (2010): 267–284.

5. Lauren Berlant, *The Female Complaint: The Unfinished Business of Sentimentality in American Culture* (Durham, NC: Duke University Press, 2008), 3.

6. Ibid., viii.

7. Ibid., 6–7.

8. Ibid., 2.

9. Jeanne Whelan, "Branding WikiLeaks," *Wall Street Journal*, February 23, 2011.

10. Ibid.

11. This is a different sort of surplus than is theorized by Lazzarato and other Marxists in the discussion of the "social factory." Maurizio Lazzarato, "Immaterial Labor," in *Radical Thought in Italy: A Potential Politics,* ed. Paul Virno and Michael Hardt (Minneapolis: University of Minnesota Press, 2006), 132–146.

12. Berlant, *Female Complaint*, 4.

13. Ibid., 5.

INDEX

Advertising, 7, 11–12; and Banksy, 95–96; and Dove, 16, 19, 30–31; and femininity, 22–23, 32–33, 36–37, 66; and the green industry, 132; history of, 26–29, 32–33; and politics, 140, 153; and religion, 166, 174–75, 198, 207; and social media, 45–46, 84, 143, 223n4, 226n1, 234n22; and street art, 98–105, 113–16. *See also* Authenticity; Brand culture; Brands/Branding; Commodity; Consumption

Alienation, 169–70, 182, 189, 234n20

Ambivalence: and Banksy, 93, 111, 117; and brand culture, 5–6, 14, 37, 43–44, 59, 110, 211–221, 148–49; and commodity activism, 17, 47, 111; and Dove, 43–44, 48, 215–217; and self-branding, 69–70, 93; and street art, 106, 111, 113–15, 120, 123–24; and yoga, 194; and YouTube, 63

Andrejevic, Mark, 43–44, 62–63, 67, 76. *See also* Communication technologies

An Inconvenient Truth, 149, 151, 159

Arvidsson, Adam, 42, 47, 171

Asian "mystique," 189, 194

Assange, Julian, 220. *See also* WikiLeaks

Authenticity: and brands, 3, 5, 8, 13–14, 125–26, 213–16, 219–21; and consumption, 29–30, 36–38; definition of, 10–11; and the individual, 10–11, 59–60; and politics, 129, 143, 147, 164; and religion, 167, 173, 183, 194–95; and the self-brand, 80–81; and street art, 92, 96, 99, 104, 106, 109, 111–20; and yoga, 194. *See also* Brand culture;

Brands/Branding; Creative economy; Creativity; Graffiti; Nostalgia; Self-brand

Bakker, Jimmy, 181

Barton, Bruce, 175. *See also* Lears, T. J. Jackson

Banksy, 91–96, 99, 104, 110–117, 120, 123, 214–216

Bartky, Sandra Lee, 78–79

Berlant, Lauren, 218–221

BET, 36, 230n59

Beyoncé, 65–66

Biblezines, 170, 203, 209

Bottled water, 127, 154–158

Brand culture, 4–5, 9, 166; and authenticity, 10–11; and religion, 2014. *See also* Authenticity; Brands/Branding; Commodification; Commodity; Neoliberalism

Brands/branding: and activism, 18, 47, 127, 140–44; affect, 7, 9; and antibranding, 96; authenticity, 3, 5, 8, 138; and the city, 110–11; definition of, 3; and "faith," 191; a history of, 6; and the individual, 10; intermediaries, 212–215, 219; lifestyle brands, 100; and logos, 11; and politics, 126, 128–131, 146; and power, 12; and religion, 168–72, 176–77, 187–191, 201–4; and the self, 3; and spirituality, 4–5, 167–68, 170–73, 186–95, 201, 204–9; and street art, 98–106; and WikiLeaks, 220–21

"Broken windows" theory, 104

Brown, Wendy, 130–31, 149, 234n25

ABOUT THE AUTHOR

Sarah Banet-Weiser is Professor in the Annenberg School for Communication and Journalism and the Department of American Studies and Ethnicity at the University of Southern California. She is the author of *The Most Beautiful Girl in the World: Beauty Pageants and National Identity* (1999) and *Kids Rule! Nickelodeon and Consumer Citizenship* (2007), and the coeditor of *Cable Visions: Television beyond Broadcasting* (2007) and *Commodity Activism: Cultural Resistance in Neoliberal Times* (2012).